Why Would Anyone Do That?

CRITICAL ISSUES IN SPORT AND SOCIETY

Michael Messner and Douglas Hartmann, Series Editors

Critical Issues in Sport and Society features scholarly books that help expand our understanding of the new and myriad ways in which sport is intertwined with social life in the contemporary world. Using the tools of various scholarly disciplines, including sociology, anthropology, history, media studies, and others, books in this series investigate the growing impact of sport and sports-related activities on various aspects of social life as well as key developments and changes in the sporting world and emerging sporting practices. Series authors produce groundbreaking research that brings empirical and applied work together with cultural critique and historical perspectives written in an engaging, accessible format.

Jules Boykoff, *Activism and the Olympics: Dissent at the Games in Vancouver and London*

Jennifer Guiliano, *Indian Spectacle: College Mascots and the Anxiety of Modern America*

Kathryn Henne, *Testing for Athlete Citizenship: The Regulation of Doping and Sex in Sport*

Michael A. Messner and Michela Musto, eds., *Child's Play: Sport in Kids' Worlds*

Jeffrey Montez de Oca, *Discipline and Indulgence: College Football, Media, and the American Way of Life during the Cold War*

Stephen C. Poulson, *Why Would Anyone Do That?: Lifestyle Sport in the Twenty-First Century*

Why Would Anyone Do That?

Lifestyle Sport in the Twenty-First Century

STEPHEN C. POULSON

Rutgers University Press

New Brunswick, New Jersey, and London

Library of Congress Cataloging-in-Publication Data

Names: Poulson, Stephen C., 1966– author.
Title: Why would anyone do that? : lifestyle sport in the twenty-first century / Stephen C. Poulson.
Description: New Brunswick, New Jersey : Rutgers University Press, [2016] | Includes bibliographical references and index.
Identifiers: LCCN 2015028617| ISBN 9780813564449 (hardcover : alk. paper) | ISBN 9780813564432 (pbk. : alk. paper) | ISBN 9780813564456 (e-book (web pdf)) | ISBN 9780813575728 (e-book (epub))
Subjects: LCSH: Extreme sports—Social aspects. | Sports—Sociological aspects. | Risk-taking (Psychology)

Classification: LCC GV749.7 .P68 2016 | DDC 796.04/6—dc23
LC record available at http://lccn.loc.gov/2015028617

A British Cataloging-in-Publication record for this book is available from the British Library.

Visit our website: http://rutgerspress.rutgers.edu

Manufactured in the United States of America

For my father, Don Poulson

Contents

Preface and Acknowledgments

Why Would Anyone Do That? may seem a cryptic, unwieldy, and perhaps unhelpful title with respect to informing readers what they will encounter if they read this book. But it captures the central question of this study: Why do people decide to run (or swim, or bike)—often into exhaustion—and then tell each other that it was "fun," or "an adventure," or an important "challenge" integral to their sense of self?

Marcy Schnitzer is responsible for the title. During a regular meeting of friends for dinner at a local Mexican restaurant, she asked me this question when she found out that I had, while a Ph.D. student at Virginia Tech, joined the Triathlon Club. I had some tentative answers as to why I thought *other people* might want to do a triathlon, but Marcy was actually asking why someone she regarded as normal—and this would be me—would waste his time in such a nonsensical enterprise. At the time, I did not have a good answer.

It might help if you know something about this group generally, and Marcy in particular. Her primary job was at Virginia Tech's Service Learning Center, the campus center that matches students with community service opportunities. At the time my wife, Christine, was working as a mediator and often found herself interacting with Marcy, who also served on the boards of various nonprofit organizations. A few members of our group were talented local artisans and artists unconnected to the university; had they been permitted, they would have happily chain-smoked their way through dinner. Our usual conversations were funny and profane inquiries into some absurdity associated with modern life, and sometime the local politics, which were dominated by the enterprise that is Virginia Tech. These were people who cared about issues and events that might be considered far more important than sport. Indeed, I cannot recall previously talking about any type of sport with this group. So Marcy was flummoxed. She simply could not reconcile the person she knew with someone who would do a triathlon. I have a recollection—particularly after her husband, Frank, showed interest in the topic—that she snorted and laughed and said this was obviously some sort of "man thing."

Many years later, when I was talking about this book with a colleague at James Madison University, Kerry Dobransky, I indicated that the title probably reflected my own ambivalence toward sport, even though I was once a reasonably good athlete. He asked, naturally enough, if I had figured out why I had done these sports, to which I responded that I needed to think harder about that question. The first draft of the manuscript was already out for review at Rutgers University Press, where Peter Mickulas was responsible for masterfully shepherding it through various stages of publication. Kerry knew this, so he laughed and suggested that, having written a book about why people do lifestyle sport, I might want to keep my lack of introspection to myself. Still, Kerry was always optimistic about the text, for which I thank him.

Fletcher Linder, an anthropologist who has studied bodybuilders, sometimes acted as my guide as I navigated the field of cultural studies as associated with the study of sport. I had previously read, largely for my own amusement, a few studies in the field, but this was not an area I had formally studied. Sometimes my interpretation of the sport literature was out of step with ongoing discourses. As I became aware of this I worried: academic texts need to be anchored to current discussions in the field. I asked Fletcher for help. Some time after his initial reading of the manuscript, on which he offered many helpful comments and suggestions, he said that the text might "confound" some readers in the field of cultural studies. But he also convinced me to put aside my concerns and suggested that, rather than make any radical revisions, I simply "stay the course." My text was different than others in the field, but he assumed that readers would understand the spirit in which it was written.

I think that one reason this book is a little idiosyncratic is that it was assembled, and then revisited, over the course of fifteen years. Indeed, it may sometimes read as bricolage, even as work put together by different people, probably because my relationship with sport, particularly as I aged and started a family, changed so much during the writing period. In fact, I had not thought much about this text for many years until another colleague, Chris Colocousis, became indirectly responsible for its resurrection. At the time, Chris had recently been hired by JMU as an environmental sociologist. After arriving in Harrisonburg, Virginia, he quickly set about figuring out large swaths of the National Forest and National Park that surround the university. He started out hiking and eventually bought a mountain bike, then another one. We would sometimes talk about the places he was discovering. Some of them were areas with which I had been intimate a couple of decades earlier. One day, he approached me and said that he had stumbled onto a YouTube video concerning a cycling race to the top of Reddish Knob—the highest local mountain with a paved road to the top—and that I should check it out.

So we decamped to watch the coverage, a local news report about twenty-five years old. At the end of the report the race results rolled onto the screen and to my surprise—but not his—there was my name. I had forgotten about this small race during my JMU undergraduate days, but had admitted to Chris that I once spent a considerable amount of time on my bicycle. When I returned to my office I decided to take a fresh look at this manuscript. Because Chris is such an enthusiastic mountain biker, it was inevitable that we would encounter each other as I reconnected with the Harrisonburg cycling community and worked toward completing this project. Indeed, we spent nearly a week together in the summer of 2014, ostensibly racing in the Tour de Burg, although survival was actually our primary goal. Given how well Chris knows this cycling community, and as participant in this event, he was a particularly helpful reviewer concerning the chapter that details this race.

My wife, Christine, like her friend, Marcy Schnitzer, has never understood why anyone would want to ride a bicycle, or run through the woods, or swim in the ocean, at anything other than a leisurely pace. Once, early in our relationship, I took Chris for a sixty-to-seventy-mile bicycle ride with some old friends, local triathletes who were still competing. Throughout, I was incredulous at her cycling ability. This was a fast ride, with experienced cyclists, and although she was a new rider she managed to hammer along with the group. I joke that this is when I decided we should get married. The reality, however, is that afterward she told me that I was never, under any circumstances, to take her on a ride like that again. She regards this and similar experiences—being miles into the wilderness with little food and water, a bloody wreck during a descent off Reddish Knob, being stuck in the mountains in bad weather with inappropriate gear—as events she grudgingly put up with when we were younger because, in most other ways, I was a perfectly reasonable person.

Importantly, we nearly always enjoy the time spent together on our bicycles, with traveling for weeks at a time through Spain probably our favorite ride. At present, a hike of a few miles with our kids is about as adventurous as we can be. But every once in a while, more often when the weather is nice, I pull out my bike and ask her if I might take off for a few hours. This inevitably forces a change in schedules, a juggling of child care, but Chris most often indulges me.

I do my best to return the favor, but for enduring these inconveniences and others related to my career as a sociologist, I am immensely grateful. I simply could not have written this book without her help.

One weekend shortly after this text was reviewed at Rutgers University Press, I managed to get out for a ride on my bicycle. We had recently built a small cottage just outside of the George Washington National Forest, a mile off the Blue Ridge Parkway in Nelson County, Virginia, about thirty-five miles from our home in Staunton. About sixteen miles of this ride is along the crest of the Blue Ridge Mountains beginning at Rockfish Gap, Virginia. The road then heads south past Wintergreen Resort and into the heart of what was once a strong Appalachian community. Our cottage is near the former community of Love, Virginia—now not much more than a few houses clustered together at the crest of Love Gap. Our five-acre lot is where the community school in "Chicken Hollow" once stood, but there are now very few signs that people once lived along this narrow road surrounded by high mountains. At night this place is dark and the stars literally extend from horizon to horizon. Bears routinely follow the nearby stream. Hawks fly above the house.

Much of my family has lived close to this area for quite some time, so this has long been familiar territory for me, but I still regard it as a spectacular bicycle ride. And I am routinely astounded that a place like the narrow hollow where our cottage sits is only a couple of hours by bicycle from my front door in Staunton. On this particular day, as I am inclined to do when I ride my bike, I was contemplating various family and work events that I had not had time to think about during the week. Because I had just signed a book contract I was also mulling over this text. I had just read through the reviewer comments, which offered plenty of good advice. (I thank these reviewers for their thoughtfulness in this respect.) One of them challenged me to extend myself a bit out of my comfort zone and stand less apart from the action, inviting the reader into the events I described in more detail. On this particular day, as I pedaled along, among the thoughts that flashed briefly through my head was that I should figure out, and probably describe, some reasons why I had once spent so much time in the adventure sport business.

At mile marker six on the Blue Ridge Parkway I looked up and saw Humpback Rock. The hike to this landmark is popular—the parking lot is often full—because it is relatively easy and ends on an extraordinary slab of granite. The top can feel, in climbing parlance, "exposed." This means that the wide ledges are surrounded by enough space to make the world seem very big and this particular perch very small. This is not a wildly exposed slab of rock, a diving board–width crag jutting from the earth. Even so, people not accustomed to the exposure instinctively crouch towards their feet until they acclimate and realize that they are standing on a pretty wide piece of real estate. Parents invariably tell their kids to be careful. Indeed, given the increasingly cordoned-off nature of risk in modern life it is probably surprising for many visitors to discover there are no handrails or warning signs to inform people of the obvious: it is a good idea to keep away from the edge. All of this, of course, is what makes the hike so much fun.

On this particular day, I realized that the last time I had done the hike was a half-year previous when my brothers were in town for my father's funeral. During that time one of my brothers had floated the idea that the family should take some of my father's ashes, hike to the top of Humpback Rock, and scatter them. This was a tough time. My father had been sick for more than a decade with Parkinson's but had, in some ways thankfully, exited the world very quickly, only a few weeks after being diagnosed with leukemia. This memory caused some pain. I missed my father, but as I pedaled along I now considered this act to be extraordinary. My family is not inclined toward marking hard life events with some symbolic dénouement. We had never previously scattered the ashes of the dead. So it was remarkable that, in this particular case, everyone had quickly agreed to this plan. As I pedaled along, not really thinking about my manuscript anymore, I thought to myself: Why had we all decided to hike to the top of that rock and scatter my Dad's ashes? What had driven us to do such a thing?

This book is dedicated to my father, Don Poulson, who was a remarkable man in many respects, but was far from being a sportsman or outdoorsman. In fact, my father—so bold in many of the decisions he made—was cautious and tentative when we were outside. In part this was because he was impossibly fair-skinned: too much time spent in the sun was perilous for him. He never really owned outdoor sporting equipment. In fact, time spent outside sometimes flummoxed him, such as the one time the family tried to camp overnight, an effort we quickly abandoned when it began to rain.

But my father grew up in nearby Waynesboro, Virginia, and had certainly rambled through these woods as a boy. I have gone up and down the trail to Humpback Rock many times with my family. So, as I pedaled along toward the cottage I had this modest insight: We scattered my father's ashes at Humpback Rock because that was the site of the first family adventure in my brothers' and my memory. I knew the exact day, the exact hike that my brothers associated with my father. It is a day I often associate with my childhood.

I remember the hike because it was—and in my mind it remains—an epic adventure. I had recently turned eight years old. At the time, my father was in a very tough spot. He had shuttered his construction company during the recession of 1974 and had suddenly become responsible for childcare while my mother, an emergency room nurse, worked to keep the family afloat. On a cold February morning, my father, on a whim—or to keep me and my two younger brothers occupied—had driven us into the mountains close to his boyhood home and we had climbed to Humpback Rock. My youngest brother, Bill, was almost four years old and my other brother, John, was six.

The sky was grey and overcast. It was very cold. No other cars were parked in the lot when we started. Most people would not have contemplated taking three small children into the woods on this particular day, even though this is a simple hike. It is basically one mile straight up—the elevation gain is just over 700 feet—and then one mile down. It takes an adult about forty-five minutes to amble to the top and half that time to get down. Later, when I was older, I used to run down the trail, just barely in control as my legs churned beneath me. But the steep ascent is a challenge for children: it is common to see them on their parent's shoulders. It is somewhat remarkable that my youngest brother actually walked the entire distance that day.

Part of the reason why my brothers and I remember this hike is because of the weather we encountered. There was occasional snow, followed by icy rain and a couple of brief hailstorms. The wind increased throughout the hike; it sometimes shook the tops of trees and blew hard against us as we bent toward the top. We often scrambled for cover, cowering underneath the rock croppings, bundled against the cold. Perhaps realizing that this was going to be a special day, my father took pictures throughout. My mother has a few snapshots in which we stand bundled against the rocks staring into the grey sky. And then there are the pictures of us at the top, all around us the grey clouds of what was clearly an inhospitable day. In the album where these pictures are posted my father has neatly written the following:

> Mom was working on this day in Feb. (a Sunday) 1974. The boys & I drove to Humpback Rock Trail on the Blue Ridge Parkway—big icicles were hanging off the shaded rocks along the road. We were the only ones on the trail that day. We all walked straight to the rocks, including Bill, who never missed a step. In coming down, a thunderstorm came in and we sheltered under a big rock until it passed. A great day I will never forget.

So as I pedaled along that day forty years later I suddenly realized why my brothers and I had marked my father's passing by climbing to the top of Humpback Rock.

This is not the only landscape, or the only adventure, that I associate with my father. He is known among his peers in Waynesboro for another remarkable accomplishment that occurred in the outdoors. This event might even account for some of the trepidation he often felt when he was outside. At age sixteen, while clambering around Crabtree Falls with his friends, my father became one of the few people to fall over two of the Falls' cascades and live

FIGURE 1 Stephen and John Poulson at Humpback Rock (Feb. 1974). Photograph by the author's father Don C. Poulson.

to talk about it. "I was in pretty good shape at the time," he used to tell me. Since the official fatality report was established in 1982, twenty-nine people have died at Crabtree Falls. A male Virginia Tech student fell from the top cascade in 2010. Four years later, a first-year student at Liberty University named Faith Helbig slipped while wading into the falls and died. Most recently, twenty-year-old El Salvador native Franklin Miguel Madrana Guevara fell on June 15, 2015 while on an outing with a church group. These events occurred despite the presence of signs that emphatically warn people not to climb into water around the falls. One of these states that twenty-three people have died, a number that has been taped over and updated in black marker as the death toll has increased.

Remarkably, some people still feel compelled to wander off the trail and into the pools of water above the cascades. When the water is low the danger is probably small, but as the tabulation of the dead indicates, it can be a more perilous act than people may assume. Indeed, the pools of water at the bottom of the cascades look enticing. It is not necessarily intuitive that scrambling onto the rocks by these pools of water might kill you. I have occasionally watched people do just this. Sometimes would-be photographers with cameras dangling around their necks work themselves along some rocks toward the edge of the falls, clearly unaware that if they lose their footing there is a good chance they will be badly hurt. Mostly, after a few slippery steps, they realize it is a bad idea—or remember the warning signs—and scramble unsteadily back to the trail. On hikes when I have seen people do this and the water is running fast, I most often stop and watch their progress just long enough to be confident they will return from this small adventure unscathed. I usually have some vague idea that someone should be ready to run down the trail and call for a stretcher if it is needed. Perhaps it is notable that I have never told anyone to stop and rethink their actions, even though I am concerned, maybe even a little upset, that I have been put in the position of potentially witnessing an accident. A colleague of mine once observed similar behavior at a different set of falls, but the woman he saw was also carrying her small dog. As we talked about this, he ruefully commented, "I would have felt really bad for the dog."

So why do I refrain from telling these people to stop? I suppose I realize that they will likely consider me meddlesome, perhaps even tell me that I am overly cautious and should mind my own business. But I also believe that I have reconciled myself to the fact that people who wander off this trail have made a choice, and it should be respected. I have occasionally made some spectacularly bad decisions of my own, and accumulated more than a few bruises and scars as a result, so there is probably some manner of shared humanity that compels me to watch and hope that someone else's day does not end badly.

When my father fell down Crabtree Falls in the 1950s, he was sixteen years old and following his friends. The fall knocked him unconscious and broke both his arms. He spent his senior year of high school immobilized, unable to clutch a pencil in either hand, play any sports, or otherwise enjoy himself. My grandmother, recounting this story, would shake her head and say that my father was the most pitiful sight she had ever seen.

Crabtree Falls is an extraordinary place, a 1,200-foot waterfall that, like the hike to Humpback Rock goes up—about 1.8 miles—and then descends steeply. It is a little more than ten mountainous miles away from the family cottage to which I was cycling. Despite the fact that this piece of real estate almost killed his grandfather, it is my son's favorite hike. My daughter, now eight, can scramble to the top and back down too. One of their favorite things to do—after we have labored for an hour and a half to the top—is to lock arms and then run as fast as possible to the bottom. My son often screams in both terror and ecstasy for the entire twenty-minute descent. Recently, I showed both him and his sister some parkour and free-running videos on YouTube. Now we practice our own version of these sports, sometimes jumping off rocks and into the air as we scramble down the side of the mountain. My daughter

FIGURE 2 Sidney Poulson at Humpback Rock (June 3, 2014). Photograph by the author.

routinely mortifies me by deciding to scramble up trees during these trips. My son is loose-limbed and gangly and more inclined toward reading than running, but he loves this particular dash. I suppose these acts could be considered dangerous. They have resulted in some scraped knees and a few tears.

Probably due to sentimentality, I decided as I pedaled past Humpback Rock that these types of experiences were one reason why I once participated in lifestyle sport. But—fair warning—the other reasons chronicled in this text are presented in a far less nostalgic manner. Still, I imagine that many people are sometimes chasing days like my childhood hike with my father and brothers. As I sit here and measure that day against the experiences I have had since, it remains one of the greatest adventures of my life. I probably have some idea, when I am running through the woods or scrambling over rocks with my son and daughter, that they might someday feel the same way about these places.

Why Would Anyone Do That?

Introduction

• •

Why Would Anyone Ride
a Mountain Bike in the
Middle of the Night?

When I first decided to do this study more than a decade ago, I was living in Blacksburg, Virginia, and close to finishing my second year as a Ph.D. student in sociology at Virginia Tech. I was preparing papers for conferences, writing articles for publication, and taking a full load of graduate classes while also teaching undergraduate sociology courses. I was tired all of the time. But the fatigue was more mental than physical. It was the kind that people experience during the course of doing their jobs, taking care of their family, or trying to make ends meet. I was not dissatisfied or otherwise unhappy, but for the first time in my life I sometimes had a hard time sleeping at night even though I felt exhausted. Physically, despite having once been a good athlete, I sometimes felt middling to awful.

During this time I recalled wistfully that I had never had problems sleeping when I was training for a triathlon, a sport I had participated in from ages nineteen to twenty-six, before largely retiring from competition in 1992. Although I had never completely stopped riding my bicycle and going for the occasional run, these were now infrequent outings designed to get me out of my office and away from my books for an hour or so. The shed outside my house held an assortment of dismembered bicycles, racing wheels, helmets, and other equipment that I had hauled through various moves. I occasionally stumbled across this gear while retrieving a garden rake or getting the lawn mower. Although it had once been state-of-the-art, most of it was now obsolete, and I recall thinking that the time had come to get rid of this clutter.

Some of the equipment was related to a business I had sold. For, following that last season of racing, I had decided to establish an adventure travel company, The Pineapple Pedalers, which I operated from the spring of 1993 through the fall of 1998. That enterprise provided adventure travel vacations—mostly mountain biking and road cycling trips—in the Blue Ridge and Alleghany mountains of Virginia and West Virginia. In short, for much of my early adulthood—from ages nineteen to thirty-three—I was intimately involved with both multisport and adventure sporting endeavors, first as an athlete and later as the owner of an adventure travel company. Like many former athletes, I occasionally reflected on my sporting past with some nostalgia.

I credited (and sometimes blamed) the husband of a fellow graduate student, Charles Scott McDonald, for my decision to reenter triathlon and adventure sport.[1] He convinced me to race with him in the 24 Hours at Snowshoe competition in West Virginia. Scott was an avid mountain biker but not a typical one. When we met he had recently lost his right arm, amputated at the shoulder following an accident in which—while jumping from car to car with a friend—he was run over and dragged by a slow-moving train. Scott had found his way into the sport haphazardly after making a bet in a bar with a couple of two-armed mountain biker friends that he could finish a race these men were competing in the following week. He finished (in last place) and then decided to continue riding his bike. Scott did not initially care much for mountain biking, but he was determined to get better at the sport.

Scott had raced in the 24 Hours at Canaan event the previous summer. This is a team mountain bike relay event wherein the distance traveled—the number of laps completed—during a twenty-four-hour period determines the winners. Most people compete with four- and five-member teams, although a few race solo. The course can be difficult. In fact, Scott informed me that he had knocked himself silly during his nighttime ride the previous year and had to be shaken awake by another racer. Even so, he was proud that he had managed to groggily complete a few more laps before the race ended.

I found it remarkable that Scott had competed in 24 Hours at Canaan. Several of my friends, all accomplished racers, had participated in this event and said that it was difficult. I enjoyed mountain biking, but had never been a particularly fast rider, and despite invitations to join twenty-four-hour teams in the past I had studiously avoided this particular lunacy. But the day I met Scott we quickly discovered a shared love for the sport. I told him that, while I was a middling mountain biker, I had once been a reasonably accomplished triathlete. I also told him about a longtime friend, Chris, who had recently retired as a professional mountain bike racer.

Scott filed this information away and about a month later asked me to join his team for the twenty-four-hour race. I was still reluctant, but ultimately signed on because, as I explained to my wife, "You cannot say 'no' to a one-armed mountain biker." By this time Scott had already coaxed another Virginia Tech graduate student, Hanna, into joining the team. She was a good athlete but had never ridden a mountain bike. Soon, I had cajoled Chris, the former professional racer, out of retirement to join the team, along with another childhood friend.

Despite some initial trepidation, I found myself becoming enthusiastic about the prospect of riding a mountain bike through the mountains of West Virginia at odd hours throughout the day and night. In part, I was excited because I would have to begin training for the event. I also had to buy a mountain bike, as my old one was long disassembled and scattered around the shed in boxes. It was now too obsolete to put back together. Mostly, I knew I would enjoy a physical challenge after a few years' sedentary lifestyle. So, despite the fact that I did not really have the time or the money to participate in this expensive sporting endeavor, I was soon committed. I also decided that if I was going to reenter the field as an athlete, I should combine it with work: that I should produce a critical inquiry that explored the growth of what was being increasingly billed as "lifestyle sport."

Orientation to the Study of Lifestyle Sport

This text is a critical inquiry into the creation of new sporting cultures. It sometimes employs postmodern perspectives, which assume that when an enterprise is captured by the market—that is, when sport becomes a commodity—the market largely determines the meaning people assign to it. The commodification of sport, even new types that may have begun as a reaction against corporate and professional sport, inevitably establishes an associated discipline. The market plays a role in determining who takes part, and also how and why the sport is played. It can even help provide the meaning that athletes assign to their participation. Even movements against the commodification of sport—arguments that "pure" sporting traditions are being corrupted by modern life—are ultimately reactions against the intrusion of market values into areas that some would prefer to be more community-minded. Indeed, many athletes prefer their sporting traditions to be a more "authentic" human experience in which the corrupting influence of the market is cordoned off from the spirit of friendly competition.

Critical inquiries generally use multiple methods common in both the social sciences and humanities to describe the historical context in which a particular social phenomenon takes place. In this respect, critical approaches are particularly applicable to explaining the recent creation of what many have described as "lifestyle sports."[2] In this text, I primarily investigate triathlon and mountain biking, which I believe are representative activities. Both were informally practiced in the late 1970s and early 1980s, and it is startling how these haphazard endeavors were quickly transformed from oddball pursuits undertaken by a handful of "characters" into multimillion-dollar industries.

This study also explores sporting discipline, which has become increasingly associated with the work of Michel Foucault. In particular, it investigates how modern institutions associated with sport act on "docile bodies" and quickly establish norms of discipline through the establishment of a "means of correct training."[3] This discipline is maintained by a constant surveillance of individual action.[4] Anyone who has been drilled on the subtleties of footwork under a basketball hoop, running efficient pass routes in football, how to best strike a ball in soccer, or the best stance and swing to use when striking a ball with a bat intuitively understands the concept of the means of correct training and bodily discipline. This text explores the acts of bodily discipline and how institutions conduct surveillance on lifestyle-sport athletes to ensure conformity.

The move from "play" to "sport" has sometimes been associated with the increasing commodification of the athletic experience.[5] Often, it is in the interest of a company to define a sporting experience. For example, defining a cycling discipline is usually related to selling the specific equipment needed to have this experience. Sometimes the very names of the commodities associated with lifestyle sport change people's relationship to a physical act in which they once routinely engaged. As a kid, I merrily rode my one-speed banana-seat bike through the back woods of the subdivision where I lived. I was often accompanied by a small pack of friends who delighted in building ramps and creating obstacles in these very same woods. This looks like mountain-biking to me, but, as a practical matter, I did not officially "mountain bike" until the 1980s, when I could purchase the newly introduced "mountain bike." In this regard my experience was defined less by what I had done in the past and more by the name of the commodity—the "mountain bike"—I purchased. In effect, most people would not feel they were mountain biking until it became possible to purchase the mountain bike as a commodity.

One criticism of some sociological approaches is that they tend to deny people human agency with respect to their ability to change a social condition. Some scholars have begun to address this concern by crafting avenues of resistance that can occur when people confront negative aspects associated with commodification.[6] A few chapters of this text explore aspects of individual resistance associated with participation in adventure sport. Some athletes, for example, regard outdoor recreation—often the mastery of difficult acts in largely noncompetitive endeavors—as a means of creating a more authentic sporting culture. Some also attempt to subvert aspects of lifestyle sport's associated consumer culture.

Methods

The methods used in this inquiry are varied, but qualitative in nature. Some information was gathered through interviews conducted when I reentered lifestyle sport competitions as an athlete in 2000–2001, and then again during the summer of 2013. Some chapters are best characterized as participant observation study and ethnography. In others, I investigate sporting norms as they have been established in the media and within the advertising content of companies that sell lifestyle sport equipment. I also explore the editorial content in adventure sport magazines. While these methods are varied, each was employed in an attempt to make sense of both the growth and increasing appeal of lifestyle sport in modern times.

Participant Observation and Ethnographical Traditions and the Study of Sport

Much of this text is clearly informed by my experiences as a former athlete and one-time owner of an adventure travel company in the Shenandoah Valley of Virginia. During periods of this study, I also systematically observed the practice of sports at races, during training sessions, and during interviews with athletes, and personally when I reentered competitive sport as a triathlete and mountain-biker during the summers of 2000 and 2013.

There is a rich tradition of participant observation studies in my chosen field, sociology, and particularly the sociology of sport.[7] Generally, an ethnographic approach is one in which a researcher enters a culture or subculture and acts as a member of that community in order to understand it. Many ethnographic studies of sport require a considerable amount of physical discipline. To be admitted to a sporting subculture, the researchers must discipline their bodies accordingly. This commitment to training is usually complete enough that they form an affinity with the people they have endeavored to study. Not surprisingly, a considerable number of people like myself—people who became professional sociologists but who were once athletes—decide to circle back and take a look at a sporting culture they were once a part of using the tools of sociology.[8]

Ethnography and participant observation studies are generally defined as when a researcher is (1) a full member in the group or setting, (2) visible as such a member in published texts, and (3) committed to developing theoretical understandings of broader social phenomena.[9] I was once a "complete member" of the subculture I later studied.[10] As a result, some of the people I encountered during this study were former acquaintances and friends. Other people I initially met as interview subjects became and remained my friends even after we migrated from active participation in sport. This intimacy is not uncommon in ethnography. In fact, most sociological studies I found associated with adventure racing, triathlon, and extreme sport were written by former or currently practicing athletes. Many of these ethnographic studies—particularly those of triathlon and adventure sport—tend toward a positive and ennobling account of their subjects, often citing scholars in the tradition of Norbert Elias and Eric Dunning.[11]

Most often, ethnography does not adopt a critical approach in terms of its orientation. Rather, the goal is to describe a community as holistically as possible, largely from the point of view of the participants themselves. While the researcher is present in the text, there is usually an attempt to describe the action within the context of the meaning that its participants have created. At the same time, a researcher should be reflexive concerning his or her own participation within the community, particularly as this affects the dynamics of the groups being observed.

This ethnographic approach has some drawbacks—along with strengths—particularly as it has been applied to sport.[12] Obviously, individual temperament affects a researcher's accounts. In this respect, my experience is unique and probably not generalizable to most athletes. Second, many ethnographic studies, given the demands of gaining entry into the field, are disinclined to critically evaluate a particular subculture. Members of a culture—people who have invested effort into gaining entrance and acceptance into a group—may have a harder time stepping out of the culture when they attempt to make critical evaluation.[13] I admit that this was sometimes true in my case. Indeed, because my "objects of study" are also my friends, that undoubtedly affected how I presented the material in some chapters.[14] At the same time, what I find valuable about the discipline of sociology, including some of the best studies associated with the sociology of sport, is that it compels me to engage in critical reflection.[15] Throughout this text my orientation sometimes shifts from a straightforward analytic ethnography—periods when I describe action largely as the athletes interpret it—toward a more critical analysis that investigates some negative aspects associated with lifestyle sport.

Importantly, many fine ethnographic studies are not inclined toward a critical evaluation of sport. In many of these studies the goal is to describe—usually through thick description—what people feel, what informs their motives, and how "shared meaning" is created within a community. Given that many people who study sport are former athletes, some clearly thrilled by performances that represent the highest level of skill within a sporting culture, many fine studies have been written from a perspective that regards sport as mostly virtuous and ennobling.[16] Obviously, the strength of these studies is that the reader gets an account of a social phenomenon from a participant rather than a bystander. We get the local knowledge vital to understanding "why someone would do that." Indeed, the strength of the approach is that it generates an intimate view of how participants create meaning through their actions. This is particularly useful when the action looks quixotic and nonsensical.

There is also a tradition in sociology of gaining entry into subcultures for the purpose of engaging in critical evaluation. Of course, when the critical approach is applied to people who are sympathetic figures there is sometimes a backlash. In effect, given the intimacy and proximity of researchers to the objects of study, how can they report on these interactions from the perspective of critical sociologists? Because of this, I think the best critical ethnographies usually pull off a difficult trick in that they make the participants in a culture fully human: they treat people with sympathy as a means of understanding them. But researchers also place motive and meaning within a larger context. This often includes an investigation of the harmful aspects of a culture. Hopefully the critique is insightful enough, and sympathetic enough, that it does not reduce the people studied to caricature.

Overall, the fact that sport can be regarded as both ennobling and destructive is a theme in the sociology of sport discipline.[17] In fact, this is a common paradox that sociologists confront when they study other aspects of social life. That a social act can have benefits for some and negative consequences for others is a fundamental idea within the discipline, as is that this contradiction can be embodied in the experience of one person.[18] A highly trained athlete such as a professional football player probably finds meaning and dignity through participation in sport. He likely finds camaraderie with the team. He may receive accolades associated with his skill, perhaps even associated with his sense of fair play. A lucky few receive college scholarships and other opportunities. But a critical inquiry into sport is likely to focus on the destructive and corrupting aspects of the enterprise. It may find that administrators, coaches, agents, and trainers use athletes for their own means. It may make clear that some sports cause athletes considerable physical harm.[19] The researcher may discover that some players find meaning in their ability to systematically commit violence toward others.[20] Perhaps violence sanctioned in organized sport makes other types of violence in the larger society more acceptable.[21] Perhaps some sporting cultures preclude people from expressing their sexuality, unless, of course, it is the heterosexual norm that many associate with men's sport.[22] And perhaps the athletes themselves, later in their lives, evaluate their past careers differently than when they were active participants.

My intention is to undertake a critical evaluation of lifestyle and adventure sport, but I also want to account for why individuals attach so much meaning to their participation. I should also confess that well before I became an academic sociologist I was inclined, probably more so then most athletes, to regard some aspects of lifestyle sport with skepticism. For instance, I wondered why so many of the women athletes I knew informed me that they were former bulimics. I wondered why so few racial or ethnic minorities participated in these sports. Even when I raced well I often found the total experience—the money and time spent—not particularly satisfying. At the same time, I remain fully aware that many participants in lifestyle sport are dedicated to it in an unselfconscious manner: indeed, it is at the core of their self-identity. I also know participants who find aspects of the sporting culture problematic. In some respects, the vantage point of a former athlete is helpful in expressing both the ennobling and the troubling aspects of sport. I obviously retain affection for my former activities, and certainly for many of the people I met along the way, but I tried to cultivate a relatively detached and critical perspective during certain periods of this study.[23]

But when I began this research my questions were more straightforward. Why did Scott enjoy racing? Why would anyone do this particular race? At that time I was also curious as to why I had begun to feel so much better about myself after deciding to engage in what, on face value, was a rather pointless exercise. In the end I realized I was excited (nearly ecstatic) because I was going to get to do something that might be considered play. But why did some people find this play so compelling? Many participants in these races have a near-evangelical enthusiasm for endurance and multi-sport events. When I began this study, race promoters had started to bill multi-sport and endurance races as "lifestyle sport," a trend that continues to this day. Was this really a lifestyle choice? And if so, what kinds of people adopted it?

A Primary Question: Agency and Social Structure in Sport

Much of this study is related to a question, once foundational within the sociology of sport but not much discussed currently, as to whether these sports should be regarded as "liberating" or "constraining" for those who practice them. I think this debate is also related to another question that has preoccupied many social theorists: How much of our life is determined by social structure, and how much through individual agency? Of course, this is a "big" question, one that has occupied some social theorists for their entire careers.[24] I want to be clear that my goals here are modest. I am not offering a new way of thinking about social structure and agency in people's lives. However, sport does provide a useful field for thinking about, and clarifying, how aspects of social structure and individual agency interact with one another.

Here it is appropriate to discuss Pierre Bourdieu's concept of social fields and to offer the example—as Bourdieu himself did—that social structure might be conceived of as a field of play. More specifically, let's make this allegorical "field" one where soccer (or *fútbol*!) is played. Bourdieu assumed that a social field concerned the rules of the game—in this case, the number of players, who can touch the ball and who can't, how play begins, when it ends, and how the winner is determined. Absent this structure, it would impossible to identify the game, so, to some extent, soccer is always played in much the same way.

But within the context of rules that structure a game, the players often act differently. In fact, if the game always looked the same it would not be much fun to watch. Within the context of the rules, players clearly make decisions and exercise some level of agency. At the same time, the object of the game—to score more goals than the opposing team—organizes all the action and the roles that players adopt. We would expect the strikers to play up front and try to score goals, for example. Some players are clearly better than others, perhaps because they possess some innate ability, but also because they may have grown up with advantages that helped them refine how they play the game. The rules may favor a certain type of player, too.[25] Here, soccer is a somewhat imperfect analogy in that Bourdieu's theory assumed the players within a field—of politics, work, or the like—would actively try to change the rules of the game to their advantage. For the most part, athletes nowadays appear to have very little power over how the game is played.

Bourdieu regarded both structure and agency—the rules of the game and how people decide to play—as inexorably linked. Notably, he used the terms "freedom" and "constraint" when he described how the best players acted within a game: "Nothing is simultaneously freer and more constrained than the action of the good player. He quite naturally materializes at just the place the ball is about to fall, as if the ball were in command of him—but by that very fact, he is in command of the ball."[26]

Importantly, Bourdieu regards a person's social life as consisting of many different, and interacting, fields of play associated with their work, education, and leisure. So, in modern life, the need for specialization within, for example, a person's work was a common field that also affected other areas of their life, such as their leisure.

This text regards the modern market as a structure, a dominant field that all have to navigate and that constrains almost all sporting action. This is often detrimental to athletes, although they have some limited agency in terms of how they play their sports. To some extent, who is playing the game, and how they decide to play, determines the degree to which lifestyle sport can be considered "liberating" or "constraining." Probably more than Bourdieu, I think the market in advanced Western economies largely acts to constrain human freedom as practiced within sport and leisure. Athletes seem to have little agency—maybe less than in the past—in changing the rules of the game. In fact, in lifestyle sport these rules can actually bar people who lack resources from even entering the field of play. Even players who are able to purchase a ticket and play anywhere they might want to are increasingly constrained by, and captured by, market norms.

Organization of the Book

In the chapter, that follows, "Social Life and Sport," I will provide a brief review of important studies related to sport in general and adventure sport specifically. This section discusses a few prominent theories, in particular, those that have used studies of sport in an attempt to reconcile the "structure/agency" conundrum that was briefly introduced above.[27]

Chapter 2, "Looking for Adventure and Authenticity," describes the meaning of adventure in modern life and the quest for authentic experiences among athletes. Chapter 3, "Disciplining Bodies in Lifestyle Sport," generally applies perspectives associated with Michel Foucault to how acts of disciplining the body are now normative in triathlon and mountain biking.[28] Chapter 4 provides a simple typology of characteristics that I associate with many adventure sport athletes and then applies it to my "Touch of Grey" team from the 24 Hours at Snowshoe mountain bike race.

Chapter 5 examines resistance to acts of sporting discipline. One of the problems associated with postmodern and critical approaches is that they can implicitly deny people individual agency. At the extremes, some critical theorists may discount that individuals possess any agency at all: they argue that social structure, the capitalist system, dictates our identity to us, tied largely to the range of consumer choices we make. Others in the postmodern tradition have crafted a model of resistance, essentially a path that allows for individual liberation based on resistance to consumer capitalism.

Sociologists have routinely found that ethnic and racial groups have different perceptions of sport and also differ dramatically in their use of the public land where some lifestyle sport is practiced. Chapters 6 and 7 explore the intersections of race, class, and gender with respect to participation in different adventure and endurance sports. "Why So White?" explores why lifestyle sport in the United States is dominated by the white professional class. "Where Are the Women?" first looks at the hypermasculine culture associated with professional downhill mountain biking. It ends by exploring changing concepts of masculinity in triathlon as women's participation has increased.

1

Social Life and Sport

• •

Much sociology of sport has been devoted to formally defining different kinds
of play and sport.[1] The play that interests me is a *physical activity* undertaken
by individuals because it gives them pleasure. Because it is so often a non-
utilitarian enterprise, many scholars regard play as a genuine expression of
human creativity and freedom. I have limited my inquiry into play and sport
to physical (as opposed to mental) pursuits and also separated sport from ritual. Nonetheless, it should be recognized that some rituals are institutionalized forms of play and sport. In many cases, these symbolic hunts, simulated
battles, and the like are games, could be considered sport, and once helped to
teach important social skills. In many cases they are a means by which cultural
norms are taught to individuals.[2]

Definitions of play, games, and sport can be expanded to include almost any
human enterprise. For instance, politics is often characterized as being a form
of sport and is highly ritualized, a reason why many people intuitively believe
that participation in sport helps impart practical social skills. It is within this
context that people state that sport teaches discipline, perseverance, and hard
work, all of which serve individuals well in other endeavors.

Many social theorists order the concepts of play, games, and sport into the
hierarchy presented in Figure 3.[3] In general, play is considered more spontaneous and less confined by rules than sport, planned activities governed by considerable rules.

One debate concerning play and organized sport is the degree to which
spontaneity is important to realizing individual freedom. Rules, obviously,

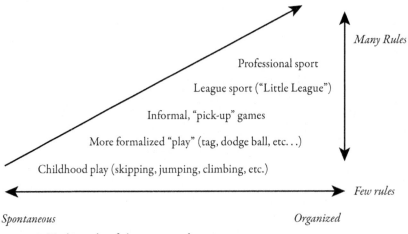

FIGURE 3 The hierarchy of play, games, and sport.

curtail both of these. But rules also allow for play to be organized and shared among a collective group of people. And collective play is, in most cases, made possible only because rules exist. Children often create new games spontaneously, derive joy from these games, and then share the experience with other children. Inevitably, in describing the game, they establish norms about how to play. If absolute freedom and absolute spontaneity existed at all times, play could not be shared. The social aspects of the game would not be maintained.

That play and games are a reflection of society, and a means by which individuals are socialized, was among the first insights made in early sociological thought. George H. Mead used children's play to illustrate how both social structure and the interactions experienced during games were primary to the development of an individual's self. The sociological self is generally a person's idea of who he or she is, how she compares to others, and where she feels she fits within a society. If you have ever watched children negotiate their respective roles during play—inevitably chaotic as everyone tries to cajole, coerce, or otherwise bend others to their will—you are observing children actively crafting their selves.

While Mead explored individual motivation during the construction of self, he always placed these motives and actions within the context of a broader society, or, to use his term, the "generalized other."[4] Put simply, individual action and the meaning people attach to it always takes place within the context of larger social groups. Not surprisingly, other early social scientists investigated the idea that play, games, and sport were important during the socialization process. In effect, being taught how to play—and about the standards of fair play associated with sporting behavior—can also be regarded as the act of teaching people how to be civilized.[5]

Even spontaneous play is governed by some societal norms. After all, we have to learn how to invent games somewhere, from somebody or some institution. So, despite the limits imposed on individual freedom, some people regard highly organized sport as a form of play that remains a broad expression of freedom and creativity. One rationale for this perspective is that, as opposed to being forced to engage in societal activities such as work, people most often *choose* to participate in sport.[6] That people often derive great joy from their participation in sport as players and fans is of no small importance. In fact, sport may be one of the few venues left where this type of intense emotion or devotion is still normative.[7] But it is also clear that some people engage in sport for utilitarian purposes rather than because they enjoy the game. They learn to play golf because their boss does. They join the company softball team to increase networking opportunities. As children, they learn a game because it helps them gain acceptance from their peers.

Some scholars do not believe organized sport is play. It is not spontaneous, they argue: it is governed by rules, and these rules represent a social order.[8] Some professional athletes have perfected one specific element of a game (pitching to left-handed hitters, punting field goals) and may call their play a job. Many do not appear to be having much spontaneous fun when they play their sport, although they probably experience satisfaction from doing their job well. But, of course, other athletes are creative and do engage in spontaneous acts within the context of highly organized sport. Certain basketball players, for instance, are highly inventive. But even in these cases, coaches, rules, and other institutions systematically eliminate an athlete's ability to make decisions independent from a game plan. No one would describe a basketball game coached by Pat Riley as spontaneous. In this regard, a pickup basketball game using a bent rim with no net, played on uneven pavement, with vaguely defined out-of-bounds lines and an odd number of players of varying ability looks more like play than the highly organized games played in professional leagues.

Often, participants in lifestyle sport describe their endeavors as play. Indeed, a few of the specific activities closely associated with the adventure sport genre—mountain biking may be the best example—were initially conceived in terms of recapturing a sport's play element. But similar to the process Allen Guttmann chronicled in his seminal text *Ritual to Record*, before long it became normative for some people who rode mountain bikes to measure their skill, and the skill of those around them, in very specific ways.[9] One more general paradox I observed with respect to these sports was that many participants were doing an extraordinary amount of work in order to build the competence they needed to perform acts they described as playful.

Another obvious constraint with respect to the freedom to pursue sport is associated with the social class into which someone is born. Early critical theorists found sport and leisure to be useful topics of study. Thorstein Veblen analyzed the latter in the context of the different social classes in his renowned 1899 work *The Theory of the Leisure Class*. His primary argument was that the new rich in America tended to engage in "conspicuous consumption" in terms of their leisure activities. The grandiose forms of play and spectacle—the fox hunts, the horsemanship, the grand celebrations in extraordinary homes— functioned primarily to distinguish the behavior of the rich from that of the lower classes. They existed as much for others to observe as for those who directly participated in the events.[10]

Notably, much lifestyle sport is associated with the upper strata of society as it relates to avocation: that is, white-collar professionals who have the resources to participate in sometimes-expensive leisure endeavors. Economic class can create material constraints—the poor may simply lack the means to participate in certain costly sports. But social class can also be associated with specific sporting cultures. For example, most working-class people would probably not be much interested in "lifestyle" sport even if they had the resources to participate in them. People with high social status and considerable economic resources do not participate much in "proletarian" sports such as bowling.[11] A number of scholars have found that sport remains largely stratified along racial, gender, and class lines.[12] So while many people regard amateur sport as an egalitarian endeavor—a place where the field of play is level and where diverse communities might find themselves sitting together—this is most often an idealized vision of sport.

But an important question, particularly as it relates to new sporting endeavors designed to recapture a play element, is why people formalize them when this may actually decrease the spontaneous joy they once experienced. Perhaps, as we become more highly socialized, it is inevitable that play becomes a more sophisticated social act. This makes adult sport more complex than childhood play. By virtue of the fact that we have grown up, there is an increasing sanction against continuing to pursue or derive joy from childhood games. Adults come to understand that they are no longer allowed to skip.

Play is also formalized, then governed by rules and formal institutions, because that it makes it easier to sell people commodities. A friend of mine once quoted someone—I have looked for the source of this quote in vain— that there will always be the game of golf as long as there are boys, sticks, and rocks. This may be true, but it is still in the interest of companies that sell a golfing experience to formalize exactly where, how, and why the game is played. Companies cannot sell sticks—although I am sure some have tried—but they can sell golf shoes, golf clubs, and golf balls.

Postmodern Alienation, Superficiality, and Lifestyle

Interpretations of postmodernism, or the constitution of postmodernity, are contentious. I regard postmodernity as a stage of advanced capitalism[13] and am interested in how this condition, most associated with countries in the global North, affects the production of culture, particularly new sporting cultures.[14] Most scholars associate the postmodern condition with technologies and modes of production established in the past forty years or so, which dramatically altered life among people living in the most developed capitalist economies. Life has become faster in the sense that social change occurs more rapidly today than in the past. Modern life seems to compress time as people are routinely deluged by information that is sometimes extraordinary (war and revolt), but more often mundane (what celebrities are wearing). Importantly, this knowledge is often presented with little context regarding the relationship (if any) the events have to one another. In this respect, there often seems to be no sense of balance—no scale for measuring importance—concerning ongoing events. At least in terms of their presentation, celebrity trends may be considered as important as matters associated with life and death.[15] Likewise, time and space—the distance between each other and where events take place—is compressed by modern technologies that make distance less important than in the past.

All of these factors may make some people feel adrift: in the terminology of Karl Marx, experiencing some manner of alienation. Marx was concerned with alienation from work, the idea that people increasingly felt a lack of affinity with the products they made, but also alienation from other people and even themselves. Postmodern theorists have broadened this notion to include the feeling of being increasingly disconnected from religion, nationalism, community, and other rapidly changing social institutions. Perhaps these conditions are creating a new postmodern sensibility among some residents of the industrialized West. These people may not be concerned with the vagaries of postmodern life, but adapt to it by cultivating, even embracing, greater superficiality in their relations with each other. Certainly there is a growing ahistoricism— a lessening of historical meaning and context—in interpersonal relations today.

The chapters that follow explore the question of whether new sporting traditions are acts of resistance to the vagaries of postmodern life or if, like other human experiences, they are being controlled by the market. While the terminology I use is largely in the postmodern tradition, I regard this question as an extension of the debate introduced at the beginning of this chapter, which has long animated theorists within the sociology of sport. In this respect, this study is a continuation of the debate as to whether sport should be regarded as liberating and ennobling or constrictive for the people involved.

Central to this question is how we should regard the disciplining of the human body. Most Westerners feel intuitively that people who engage in bodily discipline, who train their bodies to an extraordinary extent, are laudable. This belief is likely directly associated with the post–Second World War period when individual fitness became closely associated with national strength.[16] Certainly, extreme acts of discipline like those displayed during difficult sport are still considered noteworthy. Highly trained athletes are most often regarded as physically beautiful, graceful, and competent. The public often considers them to be exemplary people, and to some degree, even exemplary citizens.

But while many scholars see bodily discipline as liberating, those in the postmodern tradition might also regard its practitioners as captured, perhaps even commodified, by modern market forces. In this respect, there is logic behind the idea that modern capitalism makes us value exemplary athletes not because they are free, but rather because they so thoroughly embody the norms we associate with capitalism. It was largely Michael Jordan's ability to create conformity—to compel admirers to buy the "right" kind of shoes and drink the "right" kind of drink to "Be Like Mike"—that made him such an effective pitchman.[17] In this regard, postmodern theorizing offers an opportunity to explore contradictions associated with modern sport. It is entirely possible for people to regard certain acts of bodily discipline as liberating—as making them more powerful and perhaps more "free"—even when these acts require them to conform, often to extraordinary degrees.

A Risk Society: Edgework and Adventure Sport

One recent articulation of the social structure and agency conundrum in extreme sport is the work of Stephen Lyng, who developed the concept of edgework.[18] As the name implies, edgework characterizes acts that exist at the outer limits of human control or ability. They involve testing one's physical mastery over an act, essentially pushing the envelope of what an individual might be able to accomplish. These are often physical acts. How far can I run? How fast can I descend a mountain on a bicycle? Can I BASE-jump off a bridge with a small parachute and land safely? Some edgework involves mastery over a machine, as in the case of test pilots. Some of it is less a sport than an aesthetic or artistic endeavor that presses against prescribed social norms.

Not surprisingly, people who have investigated edgework have also confronted the agency–social structure dilemma. Lyng believed that the best way to understand edgework was to combine the social-psychological traditions of G.H. Mead with the structural sociology most often associated with Karl Marx. He regarded this Marx-Mead synthesis as ideal for analyzing edgework activities.[19] Lyng's primary intention was to understand people who sought out, and enjoyed, risk-taking. Like Anthony Giddens and Ulrich Beck, he thought much of modern life was increasingly designed to minimize occupational, environmental, health, and other hazards that people might confront.[20] He placed the motivation to pursue risky sport within the context of a society that regarded risk associated with work as increasingly unacceptable. In effect, the growth of risky adventure sport—rock climbing, hang-gliding, skydiving—could be related to the fact that modern life had increasingly become an exercise in minimizing risk in all other areas.

After the introduction of the edgework concept came a modest burst of academic studies associated with adventure, extreme, and lifestyle sport.[21] Lyng himself later edited a book-length treatment of edgework that included studies of adventure sport.[22] Still, the number of sociologists who have investigated these activities—particularly compared to psychologists, kinesiologists, and tourism and leisure specialists—is relatively small.

While some studies investigate the unique characteristics of athletes who undertake lifestyle sport, others portray these activities as not much different than other aspects of modern life. Lori Holyfield, for example, clearly liked the river guides she studied, but one of her findings was that their jobs, like those of other modern workers, involve a considerable amount of emotional labor. From their point of view, there is usually very little adventure in shepherding people down a river. In fact, the river guides found it often an exhausting and contradictory enterprise. It was sometimes hard to manufacture adventure for clients while also routinely informing them, "The most dangerous part of your trip is over now that you are off the highway!"[23] Of course, the participants in these trips want their experience on the river to be real. They most likely prefer guides who are adventurers, or who at least have escaped their own humdrum lifestyles. They probably want people who excel at extreme sport to be different, set apart from—rather than captured by—the mundane routines we associate with modern life.

Concepts of Discipline and Michel Foucault

Much of this text depends on perspectives developed by social theorist Michel Foucault, particularly as they relate to the disciplining of the body.[24] During the past two decades scholars have applied Foucault's perspective to a number of sports that require bodily discipline.[25] The appeal of his ideas is that he placed the body at the center of his work, describing the routine acts of controlling it within the context of modern life. Importantly, Foucault identified the training of "docile bodies"—through discipline—as normative. In this regard, the institutions of law and medicine that now organize human life routinely use modern science to prescribe very specific routines of bodily discipline.[26] We are now educated, reformed, and ultimately redeemed in relation to how we discipline our bodies. If we fail to discipline ourselves correctly, we are punished in subtle and sometimes unsubtle ways.

Foucault's larger, more audacious program was to undermine the West's dominant philosophical discourse, associated with the ideas that reason and science had advanced Western civilization during the period of the Enlightenment. Taking exception to the idea that scientific reasoning had increased individual freedom, Foucault argued—using acts upon the body as one example—that Enlightenment ideas often acted in ways that curtailed individual freedom. One way he demonstrated this was to explore how the body is now disciplined, essentially scientifically trained, as a routine consequence of modern life. This discipline is enforced by constant surveillance enacted by modern institutions—the hospital, the school, the prison—associated with the advancement of society. Importantly, Foucault regards disciplinary power as dispersed throughout modern Western society. In effect, no one institution or person determines how a body is disciplined. Because ideas associated with discipline are literally integral to the maintenance of society, this discipline is an inescapable condition of modernity.

It does not take much imagination to see the appeal of this perspective as it relates to modern sport. As I stated in the previous chapter, people who have participated in athletic activities intuitively know they have to discipline their body. For the most part, this discipline includes specific programs—lifting weights, running sprints, and the like—usually associated with some manner of scientific training designed to create model athletes. Athletes catch more balls if they run efficient routes. They make more baskets when they are square to the hoop. They stop more running backs when they wrap up their opponents' legs. They can dig more volleyballs if they use the flats of their forearms. They are faster when they run intervals. They become stronger when they follow a certain diet. Indeed, the idea that an athlete *might not* be disciplined seems impossible.

Athletes are also under constant surveillance. My university employs a small battery of staff to organize the lives of collegiate athletes. As a teacher, I sometimes feel that I have less contact with the athletes themselves than with their caretakers, who call to ask if their charges are showing up for class and doing their work. I can only imagine how highly monitored these young men and women must be in regard to their athletic training.

Many scholars have also applied Foucault's concept of discipline to sporting acts that appear solitary. Even if we train on our own, we ultimately know that there is some normative standard of self-discipline we should follow.[27] We know this because the companies that design athletic equipment tell us how to use it. Indeed, they often employ experts who specialize in training the body. As Foucault described, this surveillance often seems omnipresent, built into the social system itself, with few people being exempt from bodily discipline.

Foucault was not explicitly concerned with structure and agency dilemmas, but when he was read by sociologists—where this debate is central to the discipline—there was a tendency to focus on the structural aspects of his concepts of power and surveillance. Foucauldian concepts of resistance were less discussed, perhaps because this topic was not as systematically developed by its author.[28] Michel Foucault was not much interested in sport, either, but many scholars interested in the sociology of sport read his works in a manner that orients his ideas within the previous debates associated with play vs. sport. Some stress the idea that aspects of modern life compel people, athletes in particular, toward conformity more often than the idea that participation in sport can be regarded as an act of agency and freedom. Others regard certain acts of training the body as a possible "resistance" to discipline.[29]

Some of Foucault's contemporaries argued that, while his assessment of modern life was compelling, it provided no meaningful path that people might take to combat the negative conditions associated with the postmodern condition.[30] At times, a deep pessimism pervades Foucault's early work, but he later made tentative attempts to articulate a path where individual knowledge of the postmodern condition might represent some manner of resistance.[31]

Feminist scholars interested in sport have been very active in appropriating and expanding postmodern theorizing. They have also used Foucault's ideas to plot a path of resistance to discipline.[32] Indeed, control over women's bodies has often been at the center of feminist theorizing and feminist scholars have long regarded bodily control—specifically women's ability to control their own bodies—as an area of active resistance against patriarchy. It was not so long ago that women were told, explicitly, that their bodies were incompatible with difficult sport, that they were temperamentally and physically "not built" for certain arduous activities. In this context, Foucault's notions can be turned on their heads in that it becomes an act of resistance for women to discipline their bodies through sport. By concentrating on resistance, feminist scholars reinvented the discourses of Foucault as a philosophy where active resistance became possible.[33]

I find the ideas associated with resistance to discipline compelling, but it should be noted that it is just as logical to describe aspects of these new sporting traditions as being utterly captured by the market.[34] The expansion of adventure sport is now probably less about resistance to corporate sport—as some participants claim it is—and more of a continuing expansion of the disciplinary power identified by Foucault into more areas of our lives. The creation of adventure sport might be regarded as an act of colonizing the last wild spaces in the world that still have the power to awe, and are relatively untouched by scientism. In effect, many people once entered the wilderness to get lost, to ramble, to be overwhelmed by the extraordinary sights they encountered. Currently, adventure sport often seems less about experiencing awe than imposing people's will upon an outdoor landscape. Moreover, the norms associated with corporate sport seem to have been largely embraced by those who practice these sports. In short, adventure sport often seems more like the act of bringing corporate values to the outdoors, as opposed to escaping from the vagaries of modern life.

In this text I ultimately describe both sides of this coin. I do think that outside spaces are being changed, both physically and in our consciousness, in response to modern life. In some places, these so-called wild spaces and adventures—the ski resort zip-lines and the managed rafting trips along a river—are really not much more than a version of Disneyland for adults.[35] At the same time, it is hard to ignore that many people I met were often clearly ecstatic during the times I ran around with them in the wilderness. Indeed, it sometimes seemed wrong, in some elemental way, to regard these individuals as being unselfconsciously disciplined.

The Nation-State: Discipline, Healthism, and Lifestylism

Academics have increasingly explored manners in which the nation-state promotes "normative" standards of discipline associated with "healthism."[36] State-directed physical education programs and the establishment of health standards were increasingly implemented as societies transitioned into modernity; this occurred during periods when the primary modes of production in the economy shifted toward Fordism and increasing automation. In the United States, the decades following the Second World War coincided with increasing concerns that Americans—many now liberated from physical work by new automated industries—were no longer as fit as they ought to be. Within the context of the Cold War, the supposed "muscle gap" with the Soviet Union was earnestly debated by U.S. scientists and politicians, enough so that both the Eisenhower and Kennedy administrations established and refined national fitness programs aimed largely at American youth.[37]

This was not just an American preoccupation: state-mandated fitness regimens and the idea that national fitness was directly associated with geopolitical strength and military preparedness were commonly embraced by other countries during this period. In authoritarian nations such as China and prewar Germany, the programs were mandatory for much of the citizenry. More common in countries with liberal market economies were the adoption of state-mandated physical education programs, usually undertaken by the state educational system, which codified and then actively promoted meeting certain standards of health. These once included, for example, the "Presidential Fitness Award." Now they may take the form of national standards or measures such as the amount of fruits and vegetables one should eat daily or legislation on nutritional content, such as whether trans fats can be used in processed foods.

On the one hand, this would seem a noble enterprise for the state to undertake. What could be more important—or even more altruistic—than a concerted effort to create greater health for the citizenry of a country? But, importantly, many of these national campaigns tend toward a rigid moralism in which the unhealthy are defined as immoral or lacking self-control. Variables such as occupational or environmental hazards or poverty are more likely to explain a person's poor health, but in these states, being deemed unhealthy becomes a personal failing. Petr Skrabanek, one early critic of healthism, stated:

> The pursuit of health is a symptom of unhealth. When this pursuit is no longer a personal yearning but part of a state ideology, healthism for short, it becomes the symptom of a political sickness . . . In the weak version of healthism, as encountered in Western Democracies, the state goes beyond education and information on matters of health and uses propaganda and various forms of coercion to establish norms of a "healthy lifestyle" for all.[18]

Skrabanek associated state intervention with the establishment of a "health ideology." This was often the creation of norms associated with a healthy lifestyle—a totality of living that he described as "lifestylism." As an ideology, healthism was particularly powerful in more secular societies because "it fills the vacuum left by religion."[39] Its appeal was described as greater among the middle classes because they had "lost their links to traditional culture and feel increasingly insecure in a rapidly changing world. Healthism is embraced eagerly as a path to surrogate salvation."[40]

More specifically, Skrabanek argued that the American fitness craze of the 1970s—mostly associated with the growth of jogging and long-distance running—was indicative of the "interplay between health concerns, morality, and politics." In this case, he saw this trend as an extension of the programs that promoted physical fitness in the 1960s, combined with the quasi-religious ideas and rhetoric that associated good health with individual self-fulfillment and renewal.[41]

More recently, there has been increasing debate as to the degree to which the nation-state remains the most important actor in maintaining the ideology of healthism. Nicholas Rose, in particular, has used Foucault's concept of "governmentality" to describe how healthism—described as the normative desire by nearly all citizens to "be healthy"—is now maintained by nearly all institutions that govern social life. This includes those institutions most associated with the market economy. In effect, much of economic life, quite literally the reason why people buy products, is explicitly tied to the normative desire to establish or maintain good health. Certainly, the food we buy is associated with this need, but the rhetoric associated with healthism is now far more pervasive and far more engrained in the market economy, so much so that what we drive, what we wear, and even our supposed vices (think of "light" beer or red wine) are now sold in a manner that appeals directly to the desire to be healthy. In this respect, healthism permeates much of modern life because the market, not just the government, constantly reinforces the idea that adopting a healthy lifestyle is the most important goal.[42]

Lifestyle Sport: Ennobling or Constraining?

This study is primarily an investigation of lifestyle sport, using triathlon and mountain biking as exemplars.[43] In this respect, the term lifestyle is useful for capturing the degree to which some athletes believe that their sport of choice constitutes an entire mode of living, even a life philosophy that is, in most respects, related to the norms associated with healthism. Indeed, lifestyle athletes often state that the practice of sport is among the most salient feature of "who they are." As the name suggests, lifestyle sport can sometimes constitute a mode of living that acts to distinguish these athletes from others. Their sport may order nearly all aspects of these athletes' lives: certainly what they eat, but also where they might choose to live or even their occupations. In effect, the adoption of an active lifestyle—as characterized by the athletes themselves—is a dominant feature of their lived experience.

Previously, the concept of "lifestylism," the desire to live a healthy lifestyle, was associated with the concept of healthism. This desire was common among many of the athletes I encountered, particularly the triathletes. Sometimes moralism was associated with the practice of this sport, most directly an expression that these are hard endeavors undertaken by exceptional people, and perhaps increasingly uncommon enterprises given the "softness" of so many people in modern societies. Of course, lifestyle athletes portray their engagement in sport as an important expression of their self—they say that it helps to define them as a person. (See chapter 4.) But, importantly—and in opposition to ideas associated with healthism—many of these athletes claim that the adoption of a healthy lifestyle is also an active attempt to combat the vagaries of modern life. While Skrabanek regarded healthism as a constrictive ideology that marked an end to humanism, many practitioners of lifestyle sport claim that these sports are a means through which life's indignities are made bearable.

The previous contradiction is an important question to grapple with. Is the practice of lifestyle sport an enabling or a constraining act? Is lifestyle sport liberating? Is it a means through which one might combat the degradation of postmodern life? Or is lifestyle sport, because sport is now expressed as a totality—a lived experience that orders the importance of nearly all acts in life—a *constraining and dehumanizing* endeavor? In this respect, there would appear to be some things about modern life that drive people to define sport as among the most important parts of their existence, or even to consider adopting a totalizing sport lifestyle as an aspirational endeavor.

It is not hard to see this totalizing system as a constraint to human experience—how meaningful can life be if it is only understood through sport?—rather than an activity that broadens human experience. The counterargument, often made by the athletes themselves, is that adoption of a lifestyle sport is better seen as a reaction to the indignities people now confront in the modern world. For example, given the increasing obesity rate of people in the United States, a condition often associated with an increasingly sedentary lifestyle, perhaps adopting a totalizing and healthy "way of life" is *the most human* way to combat modern conditions that compel unhealthiness. Or perhaps sport remains an avenue for individual self-expression, a more important one than before given the insecurities associated with postmodern life. As we do away with minor dangers, sport remains one of the few arenas where risk—even if it is only the risk of failure—is commonly accepted. Perhaps the practice of lifestyle sport constitutes a means of resistance against the monotony of modern life.

People (academics among them) often think in terms of dualities. In this case, there is a temptation to judge lifestyle sport as being either "good" or "bad." But I actually regard it as possible that many social acts can be considered simultaneously ennobling and destructive. This has been a common theme in sociology—the idea that some social acts are good for some people and bad for others—and one that is well-developed in the sociology of sport discipline too.[44] In this respect, the primary question posed in this text—is lifestyle sport good for people?—might compel readers to look for a "yes" or "no" answer. The answer I arrived at is more complicated. What I believe, and what the text explores, are the ways in which lifestyle sport can have both benefits and negative consequences for practitioners.

Defining the "Lifestyle"

Academic exploration of lifestyles has waxed and waned during the past fifty years.[45] Most fundamentally, an investigation of lifestyle choices usually assumes that individuals act to define themselves and their actions within the context of others in society. So, for example, lifestyle can be "understood as a self-interpreted pattern of actions that differentiates one person from another (or allies people through shared practice)."[46] Most often, exploration of a lifestyle involves a group of people who have self-consciously defined themselves in a certain manner—their mode of living, their life philosophy, their daily behaviors—that is in opposition to other groups in society.[47]

Use of the term "lifestyle" is a fairly recent development, associated with the fact that it has become increasingly common for people to self-consciously choose a certain manner and style of living as a matter of routine. In this respect, many scholars connect the adoption of certain lifestyles to consumer choices. In effect, the adoption of a lifestyle is directly associated with what people buy—the clothes they wear, the foods they eat, the music they listen to. Of course, lifestyles are often closely associated with what people choose to do during their leisure time.

Lifestyle Sport

It should not be surprising that the analytic concept of "lifestyle" has been embraced in sport and leisure studies. During the past few decades it became increasingly clear that some athletes were practicing a range of "new" or "alternative" sports that they associated with a lifestyle choice. Previously, these were sometimes characterized as "whiz" (for example, sailboarding and surfing), "extreme" (BASE-jumping) and "adventure" (mountain climbing) sports. The athletes who practiced these sports often seemed extraordinarily committed to them—more so than traditional athletes—and the term "lifestyle" nicely captured this commitment. These sports seemed different from traditional sport in other ways too. Often, the action appeared more self-regulated and self-motivated. In some respects, these sporting practices seemed more individualized than in the past—these were not often team sports—but there were also sporting communities who closely identified with them.

Over time, "lifestyle" has begun to serve as an umbrella term for these new sporting practices. It tries to capture aspects of these activities that appear "different." For example, when first established, some of these sports had a more self-regulating ethic. Rather than being practiced in leagues and governed by rules, they appeared to adopt an ethic in which the athletes governed their practice in an ad hoc manner. They used a "do it yourself" (DIY) mode of practice. Ironically, though, much of the DIY ethic one might associate with mountain biking, snowboarding, skateboarding, and the like has become increasingly less evident as these sports became more institutionalized and captured by the market. Street skating, for example, still exists, but it is just as common for skaters to practice their sport in specialized parks. Snowboarding is often governed by rules associated with formal competition, enough so that several sub-disciplines have been established (slopestyle, freestyle, slalom) in which athletes compete with one another at venues throughout the world, including the Olympic Games.

As adventure or extreme or lifestyle sports became more commodified, there was increased institutional bickering concerning their definitions.[48] Initially, JoAnne Kay and Suzanne LaBerge offered the most complete account of this process in an article that mapped the field of adventure racing as it existed in the 1990s, in relation to other sporting and commercial endeavors.[49] During this period there was considerable competition between many companies that were offering, and standardizing (to some extent) the adventure sport experience. For many observers, adventure sport was first synonymous with the Eco-Challenge races, initially televised on the Discovery Channel and organized by Mark Burnett through his company, Eco-Challenge Lifestyles. Burnett later become more closely associated with another television adventure, the reality show *Survivor*. But as Kay and LaBerge aptly chronicle, the definition of adventure sport at the time was contentious. For example, many participants actively resented the introduction of corporate sponsorship. The increasingly "made-for-TV" nature of the larger events was often considered inauthentic and not really adventure sport.

Practically, the term most often used by both academics and practitioners that binds these enterprises together is "lifestyle sport." This line of reasoning has been nicely plotted by Belinda Wheaton, who uses the term to capture a range of outdoor sporting practices generally considered outside the bounds of traditional sport. This designation tends to signify a certain level of commitment in terms of both time and money. It does, as the name suggest, closely associate physical activity as a primary endeavor in someone's life.[50]

The most complete attempt by academics to create a typology of these "new" types of sports has been offered by Wheaton and her colleagues.[51] They designated the term "lifestyle" as an umbrella for a range of new and alternative sporting practices that include both "alternative" and "extreme" sport. Alternative sport is that which is self-consciously constructed as different from—even in opposition to—aspects of traditional sport. Some examples might include early snowboarding and street skateboarding. At least initially, this difference was articulated as an opportunity for individual self-expression that existed outside formal competition. Importantly, the practitioners themselves often self-consciously constructed their action as an alternative to traditional sport. This did not prevent aspects of these sports from being rapidly captured by the market. Moreover, the practice of these sports has sometimes moved from informal practice into formal competition. This inevitably required an increasing amount of codification and rules that structured the action. In short, sometimes "alternative" sport does not look much different than more traditional sport.

Some alternative sports could also be characterized as "extreme," or associated with an increase in risk-taking. The latter might involve potential bodily harm, but also the danger associated with practicing sport in isolated areas. For example, surfing is a sport, and big-wave surfing may be considered an extreme or edge sport due to the risk involved. At the same time, some endurance events, such as ultra-distance running, although they do not involve extreme risk, tend to also be labeled, at least among organizers, as both extreme sport and adventure sport. Extreme sport is also sometimes associated with acts of transgression—of practicing a sport in an area defined as "off-limits."

Many of these alternative sporting practices were also quickly captured by the market. Some became "made-for-television" events, with the "eXtreme Games" and the "Eco-Challenge" being two prominent examples.[52] Sometimes they became directly associated with product brands, as when Mountain Dew and later Red Bull used extreme sport and athletes in their advertising. Many people see no incompatibility between an adventure experience and corporate culture. There are now camps throughout the United States that offer team-building exercises in which middle managers from large companies might find themselves strapped onto a zip-line, or in a climbing harness, or catapulting down a river, ostensibly for the purpose of making them more productive members of their firms.[53] In some respects, this is quite remarkable given that the initial point—made explicit by many of the most competent adventure sport participants—was to flout the orthodoxies associated with mainstream or corporate sport. Now, many companies that sponsor adventure races follow the same formula that Mark Burnett did when he deliberately wedded the adventure experience of the Eco-Challenge to his management consulting company.

Mountain Biking and Triathlon as Lifestyle Sport

I studied mountain biking and triathlon for a few reasons. Primarily, these were the sports I had the most experience practicing. As a result, I already knew a considerable number of triathletes and mountain bikers, many practicing sport at elite levels. In short, I had a considerable amount of cultural capital concerning the practice of these sports, which made my entry into the field easy.

These activities are also good exemplars of lifestyle sport. Both were created at roughly the same time, in the late 1970s. They were both loosely organized endeavors first established by "do it yourselfers" in informal competitions. Indeed, the first "mountain bikes" were most often cobbled together in people's garages from spare parts, and the competitions were usually ad hoc gatherings. Similarly, the first Ironman competition staged in Hawaii was a barroom bet among friends. It is now an annual spectacle, a tightly scripted race where any change in terms of distances, the course, or a sporting practice (for example, allowing drafting) is not even contemplated. It is also a commercial juggernaut. The Ironman name is now trademarked and used to sell all manner of sporting commodities, everything from supplements to gear. It is extraordinary how rapidly both triathlon and mountain biking transitioned from the DIY culture into more formalized competitions. Like other new sports fashioned during this period, both have, at different times, become mainstream enough to be included in the Olympics as trial sports. An exploration of these sports demonstrates how rapidly, and pervasively, the market acted to establish a "discipline" for the athletes who participated in them.

Importantly, the athletes I interacted with, particularly the triathletes, defined their sporting activities using language associated with lifestyle. More than a few of the races in which I participated were defined as "lifestyle" events. As stated previously, this term was used mostly because it implied a totality of commitment—a way of being that is constantly lived—and this was also how most athletes regarded their participation. I was drawn to the paradox that while the athletes saw these endeavors as unique, separating them from others in society, the totality of their commitment often made them particularly susceptible to Foucauldian forms of discipline. Compared to others in their sporting community, they tended toward extraordinary conformity in terms of what they ate and drank, how they trained, and certainly the products—apparel, equipment and so forth—that they bought. Triathlon, in particular, seemed to require its athletes to adopt a totalizing lifestyle commitment. This was how nearly all the triathletes I interacted with characterized their devotion. Commitment to this lifestyle was often a point of pride.

Far from the DIY ethic associated with the sport three decades ago, triathlon is now entirely structured in a manner that requires athletes to engage in almost constant discipline as imposed by others.

These two sports, but particularly mountain biking in wilderness areas, also tend to be associated with "adventure." The athletes themselves use the terms "adventure" and "excitement" when they describe their participation in these sports. To me, the expanding definition of what this constitutes was interesting. That these athletes regard being adventurous as a primary motivation for participating in sport was intriguing. Closely associated with this desire was the need to establish that their sport captured something "authentic"— something that does not exist in other sports.[54]

Overall, I participated in a reasonably broad range of lifestyle sports over the past twenty-five years. Most was as a triathlete. In the summers of 2000 and 2013, when this study was formally conducted, I competed mainly in sprint and international distance triathlon races. At the same time, I also took part in a few races that more closely resemble the adventure sport genre, among them the New River Trial Challenge, 24 Hours at Snowshoe, and the Tour de Burg. With the exception of the Tour de Burg, these were all one-day events. Through The Pineapple Pedalers, a company I established and owned, I packaged two-, three-, and five-day adventure travel vacations in the Blue Ridge and Appalachian Mountains. There were also a few times when I interacted with athletes who were practicing what might be considered extreme sport. The best example is the period in which I observed, and interacted closely with, professional downhill mountain bikers who were competing in the International Cycling Union/Union Cycliste Internationale (UCI) Downhill Series.

The Perspective of This Study

My inquiry into lifestyle sport follows much the same path trodden by those who have previously studied sport. Ultimately, this study is a sometimes-sympathetic, sometimes-critical inquiry into why some people participate in lifestyle sport. It investigates why the lifestyle sport industry has grown dramatically during the past decade: why sport is so intimately tied to the market and how this might affect people's motivation to participate. In sum, my study is an insider's critique of lifestyle sport, one meant to be gentle and one informed by past sociological perspectives. It is an attempt to describe people's reasons for participating in these sports, but also account for the structures that facilitate or restrain their participation. The "big" questions are relatively straightforward: Is lifestyle sport good for people? Are these sports really that different from traditional sport? Are they liberating—an expression of individual creativity? Or does the ever-increasing discipline impose a far greater level of conformity among the athletes who practice them?

As stated previously, this study is not going to offer an emphatic "yes" or "no" to these questions. This may seem unsatisfying, but I believe it best captures the contradictions associated with the practice of lifestyle sport. Take, for example, the question as to whether these sports are different from others. Well, of course these sports are different. Indeed, many of their differences were outlined in this chapter. But this is clearly not always true, particularly as these sporting practices became increasingly codified, regulated by sporting bureaucracies, and commodified by the market. Sometimes these sports, particularly as practiced in formal competitions, are not much different from their traditional counterparts.

Perhaps the question readers will be most interested in is whether lifestyle sport is "good" for people. More so than the others, this question may produce some contradictory answers. Ultimately, the orientation of this study assumes that it is possible for lifestyle sport to have both benefits and negative consequences for practitioners. Even the experiences of a single person can embody both the ennobling and constraining aspects of sport. But perhaps, given the totality with which some people now adopt sport as a lifestyle, the highs and lows associated with these sporting experiences—the achievements and the degradations, the freedom and the conformity—are more extreme than in the past.

2

Looking for Adventure,
Looking for Authenticity

• •

Participation in lifestyle sport clearly provides many athletes with meaning. Indeed, the triathletes and mountain bikers I spoke with routinely replied, when I asked why they raced and trained, "These races keep me sane!" This sentiment is well-known among race directors and the sport's governing bodies. In a study commissioned by USA Triathlon, *The Mind of a Triathlete*, sixty percent of respondents reported that completing a triathlon was an "emotional or spiritual experience."[1] It is also common for these athletes to associate participation in their sport with adventure.

When I first began this study, I encountered an article in the *Washington Post* that was written by a triathlete of average ability who had recently quit his job at the White House in order to train full-time for an Ironman triathlon. Although he was more committed in some respects, his story mirrored those of the other people I talked with about their participation in triathlon.[2] In particular, this athlete characterized his decision to leave his job and train for the race "as a chance for adventure." He wrote (italics added):

> Training for an endurance event offers something that—from what I have seen—corporate America and the corridors of political power do not: a chance to set a goal, design a plan, execute that plan, measure success and accomplish a goal.

The Ironman has liberated me—at least temporarily—from life's monotony of wearing a suit, showing up at an office, slogging my way up the chain of Democratic Party politics. It has banished the nagging feeling that I never was accomplishing much. The Ironman, above all, *has given me a chance at adventure*, and that—with or without Lance's[3] guidance—is what I have always craved.[4]

When I interviewed a founding member of the Virginia Tech Triathlon Club who, at the time, was also a graduate student, he said that he regarded his participation in triathlon as something he controlled and possessed, unlike other aspects of his life. He stated, "It's more up to me. And I enjoy the fact that I don't have someone else telling me, 'you have to do this, or you have to do this,' or whatever the situation may be. So with triathlons it's just ... I'm on my own."[5]

It was not hard to find people who assigned more meaning to their participation in triathlon than to their work. Indeed, for the author of the *Washington Post* article, the Ironman allows him to "set goals" and "execute plans," which is considered his standard for success. Apparently, despite working in the White House for a Presidential administration—where one would assume that plans and goals were being made and acted upon—this man never felt involved enough to believe his job mattered. Indeed, this athlete states that he was "missing out on life" as he "slogged" through graduate school and into different political jobs.

This reverence for the Ironman race is common among triathletes. Much of this feeling is related to the fact that this 2.4-mile swim, 112-mile bike ride, and 26.2-mile run was one of the first ultra-distance races to became well known to the American public, after being broadcast in the early 1980s on *Wide World of Sports*. Many people regard completion of an Ironman distance race as a major accomplishment. I could usually find a few athletes at races who had permanent tattoos of the corporate Ironman logo, affectionately referred to as the "M-dot." When I asked about these, I was inevitably told about the Ironman distance race their owners had completed, the point at which most had decided to get their tattoos.[6] It appears that race organizers have noted or even encouraged this trend. For example, the Tough Mudders website prominently features people with the event's logo tattooed on their bodies. Where local laws allow it, race organizers are currently making tattoo artists available so that finishers can get a Tough Mudder tattoo for a $70 donation.[7]

Conceiving of endurance triathlon as an "adventure," as the Ironman participant above does, subtly redefines what the word has meant in the past.[8] In general, conventional definitions of adventure include the prospect of encountering danger or a new experience. The element of danger, or at least the prospect of bodily harm, is also a defining characteristic of the risk behavior that has become associated with edgework.[9] In some respects, long-distance triathlon and endurance sport may be considered adventure or edgework insofar as they offer extremely difficult physical challenges that require practice. However, participation in the Ironman is not akin to putting on a backpack and lighting off into unknown territory. For an adventure, triathlon is remarkably predictable in terms of dictating exactly what the participants will do. Indeed, the race was designed to be predictable. In fact, if an Ironman race turned into an unscripted adventure for the athletes—if the course changed suddenly and people got lost—there would be considerable complaint. The race is actually a tightly scripted, well-planned, and well-monitored event that is shown on television. During the race traffic is cleared; the racers are carefully numbered, tracked, and monitored throughout. Nobody is left behind.

Nonetheless, the self-narratives of participants in the Ironman and other ultra-distance races tends to be associated closely with what others have characterized as the "adventure culture." For example, Bruce Braun has stated that, irrespective of the task at hand—"climbing, jumping, running, or plunging"—it is the "encounter and the challenge that matter."[10] Or, as Sarah Jaquette Ray summarized, "At the heart of outdoor adventure sports is the appeal of personal challenge." Moreover, the use and extension of the body is often at the center of this challenge: "Adventure culture locates the site of moral purity and connection to nature in the suffering body."[11]

While the Ironman race is not an expedition or a trek, and not fraught with the uncertainty that people once associated with adventure, its high level of physicality, even physical competence, now makes the sport an adventure for many. Along with the need for physical discipline is the idea that some kind of physical failure is possible. At the same time, when it comes time to sell the sport of triathlon, its organizers increasingly describe it as an adventure that "anybody can do." (Most people who participate in triathlon do so in much shorter races than an Ironman.)

In many cases, the editorial comments in the magazines that cover triathlon portray participation in the sport as something akin to a religious quest and employ the pop psychology one might associate with new-age religion. In fact, some academic studies have characterized participation in certain sports as modern religion.[12] Admittedly, even when I was an active athlete I would have been regarded as a skeptic concerning the quasi-religious nature of these editorials. This was particularly true when the search for adventure (or truth or enlightenment) was closely associated with the need to spend money. Note the text I have italicized in this extract from a fairly typical editorial, "Got Adventure," written by Mitch Thrower for *Triathlete*[13]:

It's been said that life is a multi-stage adventure race, and there are times when the challenges of life seem to overshadow the challenges we create athletically for ourselves. But there's the secret. We have our own lives laid out in front of us with an unknown finish line. We have a roughly drawn map and some clear course headings. *It's time to buy the satellite navigator, a mountain bike, a race bike, some spring-loaded, air cushioned running shoes, and a super-fast swim suit to help get where we want to go in this adventure.* Through the process of maturing *through adventure,* we've all likely knocked a few things off of Maslow's list, and are now left with an uncharted course and a rough idea of what's ahead in this *Indiana Jonesesque adventure* race called Life. Grab a flashlight—you're it.[14]

The tendency for some lifestyle athletes to portray their participation in sport as a kind of evangelical search for truth, literally imbued with a divine purpose, is notable. I was often struck by the earnestness of triathletes and their sometimes beatific nature when given the opportunity to talk about their religion. It was sometimes nonsensical—and some athletes seemed somewhat narcissistic—but I have no doubt that, like participants in religion, the devotees of triathlon were sincere when they told me the sport was the most important activity in their life. It clearly provided them with happiness. And many were evangelical too, quite literally proselytizers in the defense of their faith. They believed sincerely that anyone who "Tri-ed" would experience a joy similar to their own. Their desire for an adventure—or at least for people to see their activities as unique—was clearly associated with the motivation to do the sport. At the same time, it was apparent that most of their modern adventures—even the adventure races—were largely devoid of the uncertainty and risk one might have associated with adventures in the past.

Workplace Alienation and Authenticity

Many participants in lifestyle sporting events told me, in some form or another, that they were drawn to these sports because they were looking for a "real" experience. Most did not use the word "authentic," but I interpreted this quest for the real as a quest for the authentic.[15] One obvious irony is that the sports they were engaging in were actually no more real than other aspects of their lives. In fact, when these sports are deconstructed in terms of their meaning they are often, on their face, rather pointless. For instance, unlike some traditional sport, triathlon was not developed to teach the skills people need to know in order to survive, such as how to hunt or engage in war. People who do not participate in lifestyle sport are far less likely to feel that there is much real value to it: when one of my friends heard I was conducting this study, she asked me plaintively, "Why would anyone want to do that?"

Importantly, whether something is considered authentic is always a group judgment. That is, what is authentic at one point in time—a style of music, a type of cuisine, a clothing fashion—may not be considered authentic later. David Grazian has nicely characterized the quest for the authentic as existing at two levels. First, something authentic should look (or taste or feel) the way we think it should—like the real deal, so to speak. Second, authenticity can be associated with the performance offered by ourselves and others: a judgment as to whether someone is making a genuine effort to do something notable, or in a tradition regarded as noteworthy.[16]

In some lifestyle sport, authenticity is often judged by the challenge involved. A difficult endeavor is likely authentic. To some degree, the idea that there is uncertainty associated with the act, perhaps a prospect for failure that causes hurt—both obviously related to being adventurous—also helps ensure authenticity. At the same time, an authentic style can be found in the approach to sport (how one trains), the tools used (the bike one rides), and how one looks along the way (the clothing and the quality of the performance).[17]

Many scholars have noted an increased desire to experience authenticity in *all* our endeavors. As Gary Fine has written, "The desire for authenticity now occupies a central position in contemporary culture. Whether in our search for selfhood, leisure experience, or in our material purchases, we search for the real, the genuine. These terms are not, however, descriptive, but must be situated and defined by audiences."[18]

Most often, the realness and authenticity assigned to adventure sport races is closely associated with the physical demands made on the participants. Many of the people I observed in endurance and adventure racing were skilled athletes. Most were experienced mountain bikers; many had some paddling and climbing experience too. While more people are engaged in these types of sports than in the past, they do remain somewhat rare.

Importantly, the sporting communities I observed were incredibly strong and cohesive. They understood each other intimately because they so often shared difficult experiences. They also spent considerable amounts of time training with each other when they prepared for difficult events. The physical discipline associated with these sports—what the participants felt, the way their bodies ached, their pain, their discomfort, the concreteness of the miles they covered, the fact that other people around them were doing the same thing—combined with the prospect of failure, even if only the failure to reach a goal, made the adventure sport experience authentic.[19]

Given these experiences—the very real aches and pains athletes shared with one another—few considered it a paradox that adventure in this context was a tightly prescribed act. In fact, that athletes were actually being instructed to perform certain tasks, often within certain times that defined the experience as a success, in no way diminished the idea that these athletes were experiencing something authentic. It simply did not matter that the obstacles involved in this adventure experience were, quite literally, defined before they crossed the starting line.

Most people I encountered did not contemplate that adventure might be conceived of as a more singular endeavor, practiced in solitude and without the explicit markers—the tee-shirts, the pictures, the medals, the tattoos—that are often used to document participation within lifestyle sport. One athlete, a fifty-year-old woman with a demanding job who lives and trains in New York City, informed me that she preferred to race amid the spectacle of the biggest Ironman-sponsored events as compared to smaller venues. She said, in so many words, "If I am going to invest the time and money to do an Ironman race, I want the spectacle."[20] Still, the language used by athletes when they described their participation, even in these big events, was often extraordinarily personal. In fact, absent the larger social context, their accounts of athletic accomplishments might be read as truly solitary endeavors: individual quests, or at least individual tests. The idea that everyone has a unique experience when he or she raced is notable given that hundreds if not thousands of people were doing the same things at the exact same time. Importantly, the community aspect of the sport—the stories swapped over the post-race meal and beer, the sharing of unique experiences (which, paradoxically, many people found they had in common)—appeared integral to this new kind of adventure ethic.[21]

As others who have studied adventure sport discovered, it was sometimes important that the physical acts be thoroughly documented in order to give them meaning. BASE jumping off the New River Bridge on Bridge Day must be exhilarating, but making the preparations to film it is apparently an integral part of the experience.[22] I was shown many, many pictures during my interviews with triathletes, notable, sometimes, because there is really not much spectacle in this sport compared to BASE jumping. A person chronicling himself online during triathlon is not going to be a YouTube sensation. Most of the blogs I encountered appeared to be for the consumption of friends and family. Still, some athletes do go out of their way to construct narratives that they assume are compelling and that others might find interesting. And these self-narratives are very common. In fact, most adventure race websites have dedicated areas for athlete stories—inevitably tales of trials, of tribulations, and usually of athletic redemption.[23]

Some interview subjects and authors of blogs I reviewed contrasted their participation in these races to their workaday paper-shuffling and e-mail-answering routines. In fact, many juxtaposed the "unrealness" of their day jobs and the "realness" of adventure sport. Many experienced real emotion, real feelings, and a real challenge when they raced. By way of contrast, their jobs were usually a drag. Sometimes they did not really make or do much of anything. This, according to some athletes, necessitated that they spend their weekends and spare time in some kind of physical pursuit. In some cases their participation in sport was framed as a physical craving, most often described as a need for an "endorphin rush" or a physical "release" from a sedentary job. Many described themselves as "endorphin junkies."[24] In effect, the physical changes in their bodies (they became stronger and fitter) and the chemical changes (from their "endorphin fix") were what made endurance and adventure sport "real."

Just as important were my interviews with many athletes who felt their jobs were fulfilling. Many of the older racers were professionals who had experienced considerable success in their careers. Many enjoyed their jobs. Still, they sometimes described their participation in endurance sport as a way to break up their workaday routine. They were less inclined toward a negative evaluation of their job, but still felt that participation in endurance events was an integral part of who they were. Also important is that many of these people were often highly successful, and usually well compensated, in their professions. The group I interviewed disproportionately represented the medical professions, in part because these professions—in contrast to what many might think—allowed them some flexibility in their work schedules so they could train more. Often, these athletes characterized the goals associated with difficult sport—participating in an Ironman, for example—as closely associated with their tendency to plan and be goal-driven in their jobs.

As stated previously, the authenticity of an experience is often both an individual and a community judgment. In sport the authentic experience is often framed in an emotional context. The realness of the experience, as compared to more routine actions, often determines authenticity. The physical nature of endurance sport, the sweat, the increased heart rate, the blood, the aches, the injuries, were all very real in this sense. For the most part, physical challenges such as these no longer occur in modern white-collar work. Very few of these athletes are engaged in jobs that require constant physical exertion. Conversely, there are very few carpenters, farmers, or other hard laborers participating in these sports.

It is likely that the increased popularity of triathlon is related to the fact that much modern work has caused—at least for a few—an appreciable increase in leisure time, and also lessened the amount of physical toil performed at work.[25] Both of these changes allow people to engage in challenging endurance sports. Of course, people have always been driven by physical challenges. The difference is that a farmer two hundred years ago, although he might have found meaning in hard work, would never have systematically engaged in hard labor simply because he was looking for an endorphin rush. Work, hard work, had meaning insofar as it accomplished a needed task. And while this work had personal rewards—people took pride in building a straight fence or solid roof—most regarded their leisure time as a period when they could disengage from physical toil.

A Postmodern Critique

Some critical social theorists now use neo-Marxist and poststructuralist approaches when they critique consumer culture. From these perspectives, our identities are no longer determined by work, but often by our other pursuits, or sometimes what we might choose to buy. For instance, the Ironman participant quoted earlier in this chapter was clearly experiencing alienation from his job as a political operative in the White House. He felt a greater affinity with being an Ironman participant. One obvious irony is that sport—which is often regarded as liberating—has clearly become a commodity used to sell consumer identities.[26] Being an Ironman means something to many triathletes, enough so that some feel compelled to tattoo the corporate logo onto their bodies. In effect, modern sport is used to sell us a range of identities that are largely tied to our consumer choices. The primary point that most critical theorists make is that very little can remain authentic when "image" becomes increasingly important.

Others regard the development of new sport cultures as a human process where people have considerable agency. For example, Johan Huizinga regarded the "play-instinct" as a natural part of human existence that was responsible for the creation of many cultural norms.[27] In this respect, the play-instinct would remain important in the modern age: when it interacted with modern technologies (and modern capitalism), the result would be new sporting cultures. As discussed previously, critical approaches often take issue with the freedom (or "agency") that Huizinga assigns to individuals who engage in play and sport.[28] This criticism assumes that the production of new sporting cultures—the way play and sport are structured—still reinforces class and gender differences. In effect, Huizinga's critics state, scratch the surface and "new" sport does not look too different from "old" sporting traditions.

Capturing Realness and Authenticity with the Market

Sometimes it did appear that the multi-sport and endurance racing participants I knew were finding some greater meaning—authenticity, realness, perhaps even something they would call "truth"—related to the physical demands of these sports. My wife, Christine—who is largely mystified by the appeal of adventure sport—had something of a revelation while watching the 24 Hours at Snowshoe Race at Snowshoe, West Virginia. (See chapter 5.) The riders who were completing their laps near the end of the twenty-four-hour period were often covered with mud and had a dazed and glazed-over look of extreme exhaustion. If a participant wrecked, as even the best riders often did on this course, they had ripped clothing, scrapes, and bruises when they finished a lap.

Christine, largely incredulous at the spectacle she was observing and trying to figure out why people would subject themselves to this, turned and looked me up and down. She stated, with both chagrin and disgust, "You know what this is! It's *Fight Club*!" A month previously we had watched this movie, now considered a cult classic, which has sometimes been commented on by academics.[29] It is a graphically violent film that juxtaposes the malaise of modern life against the purity of fighting man vs. man.[30] In fact, we had found it so violent that we had not been able to watch it to the finish. But the movie had an interesting premise in that Ed Norton, playing the primary character, was clearly alienated from modern life. He had a job working for auto insurance companies wherein he went from car wreck to car wreck to see how motorists died in accidents. His primary purpose was to keep information concerning automobile safety hazards from becoming public. In effect, he had the absurd job of assuring that car manufacturers would continue to produce unsafe cars. He had an office cubicle. He had an irritable boss. He was also an insomniac who found he could sleep only when he experienced "authentic" emotions. As a result, he went to support groups for the chronically ill, where he likewise pretended to be sick so that he could listen to people bare their souls as they confronted death. After experiencing this raw emotion he wept openly and then slept like a baby.

In this movie the character has an alter ego who blows up all his material possessions, primarily an apartment filled with furniture from IKEA, then lives in a nearly primal manner in order to experience "real" life. Most of the narrative involves a Fight Club where postmodern, de-masculinized men—put-upon retail salespeople, waiters, and white-collar workers—get together and beat each other senseless. The more bruised and battered Norton's character becomes, the more beatings he takes, the better he feels about himself. He eats when he is hungry. He drinks when he is thirsty. He owns what he needs to survive.

In short, the movie described modern life and modern work as largely bereft of meaning.[31] The primary idea was that for these men, life became real when it was reduced to the base elements of human existence. Not surprisingly, given traditional concepts associated with masculinity, the producers of this movie had decided that standing in front of another man who was trying to beat you up was as real an experience imaginable. The fear was real. Getting hit was real. Pain was real. And it is easy to see why this analogy might fit the 24 Hour race because it was premised on the idea that not sleeping and riding over difficult terrain at odd intervals throughout a full day and night would help create an authentic experience—just like the beatings administered to Fight Club participants. (See the "Pain" section of chapter 5 for further discussion).

Buying Authenticity, Buying the "Mandatory Equipment"

I like the *Fight Club* analogy with one very important exception.[32] In stark contrast to the primary premise of the film, the 24 Hour racers had adopted a sport that required them to be model consumers. In many adventure races a list of mandatory equipment is included in the registration packets. Academic investigations of lifestyle sport are often premised on the idea that this type of consumption designates a person's lifestyle choices. At mountain bike races, which tend to be more eclectic when compared with triathlons, the parking lots are still littered with SUVs, expensive bikes, and expensive equipment. The entry fee for 24 Hours at Snowshoe in 2000 was $110 per person—a total of $550 for our team alone—which is actually cheap by today's standards. I would guess the average bike cost around two thousand dollars.[33] Most racers stayed in condos at the ski resort, which is one reason the resort helped to sponsor the race. So, most people at this race had money, or at least enough to scrape together what they needed to participate in the event. More than likely, a working single mother trying to make ends meet would not have found "meaning" or "realness" at the 24 Hours at Snowshoe Race. Indeed, some of these facts caused an increasingly number of people to regard the race as inauthentic. (See chapter 5.)

Overall, this adventure experience required less mandatory equipment than others—just the mountain bike and powerful lighting system needed to ride it at night. It was still an expensive endeavor. During this study I talked with many mountain bikers who routinely contemplated the irony that people who have considerable financial resources now dominate their once-alternative sport. Indeed, many of the mountain bikers I met who had succeeded financially seemed uncomfortable with their success. Others seemed sheepish about the cost of both their bikes and the new components they routinely tacked onto them.[34]

By contrast, most triathletes I encountered were not as uncomfortable with the fact that they usually had considerable resources. The most common refrain regarding the cost of the sport was that, while it was a very expensive hobby, it was basically the "only one" the athlete engaged in. Indeed, some athletes told me the ways that their hobby saved them money (for example, that they did not have cable television). Of course, I did meet some triathletes who were concerned with the cost of the equipment they bought, and recognized that other people might not be able to participate in the sport. But it seemed that triathletes were more likely to conspicuously consume, with expensive bikes and equipment being part of the appeal of the sport.[35] Indeed, triathletes routinely showed me pictures of the "transition areas" of a big race that they had participated in—a couple of thousand bikes lined up and ready to go—and then inevitably commented, with admiration, on the amount of cash this equipment represented.

The governing organization for American triathletes, USA Triathlon, has largely embraced the affluence associated with modern triathlon. They literally use it as a primary selling point to create greater corporate sponsorship. Their commissioned report *The Mind of a Triathlete* routinely details the consumer and spending habits of their membership and makes the point that these athletes continued to purchase sporting commodities at similar and even increased levels even during a period when the economy was contracting. The average annual income of triathletes—$126,000 at the time of the report—is another selling point used to entice greater corporate backing of the sport.[36]

USA Triathlon regards its primary obligation to athletes as "marketing" the sport, by which I mean there is an explicit call to increase the "market shares" and "revenue" associated with triathlon. The second of four core objectives adopted by USA Triathlon "to establish the foundation of the strategic business plan for our sport" is "Maximize revenue and resources—Increase marketing revenue by 50 percent. Develop fundraising capacity. Increase royalty revenues by 100 percent."[37]

All in all, the close association between triathlon and affluence is celebrated by the governing organization. In fact, *The Mind of a Triathlete* does not really discuss broadening the sport beyond this elite group. It would seem that triathlon is unapologetically a game played by the relatively wealthy. Obviously, high income does not necessarily assure that someone is good at the sport, but this is not as much a barrier to participation as one might think. In effect, given that simply completing a triathlon is considered an important accomplishment—one that athletes routinely characterize as an "emotional" or "spiritual" event—the sport is set up perfectly so that participants with modest skill can have an authentic experience and even be considered exceptional athletes.

Because lifestyle athletes are so welcoming to anyone willing to participate "to the best of their ability," triathlon and adventure racing often resemble radio show host Garrison Keillor's creation Lake Wobegon, "where all the women are strong, all the men are good-looking, and all the children are above average." Importantly, many athletes would object to the previous characterization—pointing out that what they do is "hard"—but my intention is to demonstrate that the "everyone is above average" ethic is an extremely appealing aspect of lifestyle sport. It makes the adventure sport community—like Keillor's "little town that time forgot"—a very welcoming place. Triathlon is filled with people who spontaneously applaud the efforts of last-place finishers, an act I observed at all three races I participated in during the summer of 2013. I would judge this sentiment as genuine; that is, the most competent members of this community were genuine in their encouragement for those who struggle when they race.

At the same time, the paradox that resources—as opposed to sporting competence, potential, and skill—is the most necessary component needed to "grow a sport" is sometimes evident to those on the front lines of retail establishments. I routinely interact with a highly skilled amateur mountain biker in Arizona who also works for one of the premier cycling retailers in the region. One of his responsibilities is "sizing" customers who have ordered specialty bikes literally built to fit their bodies. Triathletes account for much of his business and their bikes cost many thousands of dollars to produce. He likes his work. He likes his customers. But in discussions he has told me that he finds it ironic that many of his customers, clearly people with resources, are often middle-range athletes who lack the skill and fitness to use this equipment in the appropriate manner. Indeed, he assumes much of it is rarely used at all. In effect, these beautiful bikes, tailored for speed, are operated by people who are not well-enough trained to make them go fast. But that is often not really the point, which is that his customers have the resources to buy the highest possible quality equipment associated with their hobbies. Why would they not get the best bike available?

The marketing report commissioned by USA Triathlon acknowledged my friend's observations. Within the context of an economic downturn they reported, "These high-income consumers are, in ordinary circumstances, the most likely to buy the most expensive or elite equipment—even if they are not extraordinary athletes. So higher-end goods may be harder hit than mid- or lower-level products."[38]

Lifestyle Sport and Authenticity: "Posers" and Real Athletes

That lifestyle sport is fueled by modern alienation, and then also manages to perpetuate it, often appeared obvious to me. People active in these sports routinely debate what constitutes an "authentic" sporting experience. When I reviewed back issues of *Triathlete, Mountain Bike,* and *Bicycling* it was clear in every issue that the identity of a triathlete, road cyclist, and mountain biker came with a full range of necessary consumer choices, often quite literally described as "mandatory" gear.[39] (This is a clever play on the fact that a mandatory gear list is usually sent to participants in some endurance and adventure races.)

Sometimes, the writers and editors of these magazines produced articles where identity issues—who is a real mountain biker and who is a poser?[40]— were batted back and forth with a truly postmodern absurdity. Indeed, the term "poser" reflects many of the contradictions some cyclists feel as it relates to a consumer culture now closely associated with cycling. In short-hand, a poser references someone who has expensive tastes in gear but spends very little time actually riding his or her bike. In effect, these people are posing as cyclists—they have purchased the requisite gear, but actually ride infrequently. They lack authenticity.

The most astute writers for these magazines were also clearly aware of the absurdity of their enterprise. It was obvious that they wanted to write articles for an informed audience who shared their love of cycling, but, practically speaking, this put them in the position of shilling for—sometimes affably, sometimes ironically—the cycling companies that were buying advertising in the magazines they worked for.[41] I thought this contradiction was navigated cleverly in the tongue-in-cheek "Style Man" column (retired in 2009) that was once a staple in *Bicycling*. The magazine's Style section, indicative of the way lifestyle sport is increasingly being marketed, included the tag line "Look Good, Live Well—On and Off the Bike." It included reviews, not only of "stylish" cycling products and apparel, but also products such as espresso machines that a cyclist (at least a stylish one) might use "on and off the bike."

The "Style Man" advice column—"He Knows Everything (And Knows It)"—dispensed advice designed to make sure a cyclist did not commit a breach of fashion (clashing cycling apparel, riding a bike with a kickstand), or etiquette (wearing cycling gloves at an inappropriate place).[42] It also dispensed clearly absurd lifestyle advice that gently mocked some aspects of the cycling subculture. In effect, it was a continuation of the debate associated with who is and is not a cycling poser, along with the range of consumer choices that might be made by the real cyclists. I thought the column pulled off a very neat trick. On the one hand, it allowed writers to gently mock the norms and consumer culture associated with cycling, while on the other it simultaneously helped to maintain them.

Many of these magazines' regular contributors clearly regarded themselves, and their sport, as exceptional. Most were probably drawn to the sport because it was slightly odd, but they now found themselves selling a lifestyle choice—complete with fashion advice—that was designed to sell the products associated with their sporting identity. To facilitate selling these goods, advertisers offer many of these writers the opportunity to test a range of vehicles, bikes, equipment, and apparel, which are invariably, as in the fictional Lake Wobegon, judged as superior in their printed product reviews. Indeed, one staple of many of these magazines is a so-called "test" of apparel and equipment (bikes, shoes, swimsuits, components, wheels . . .) wherein nearly every product is reviewed favorably.[43] The other staple of these magazines concerns getting fit in an impossibly short period of time, or riding (training, eating, resting) like the pros, or otherwise being the best or best-looking athlete possible.[44]

Not surprisingly, many manufacturers, race promoters, and publishers (particularly Rodale Press) now define participation in sport as a lifestyle choice and use this as a marketing strategy. For example, in 2000 the promoters of the Xterra triathlon series advertised the sport as part of an "active lifestyle." Nearly all the larger races, including this one, promote imprinted gear and other products. The 2003 Xterra Race promotional material included an admonishment underneath the Xterra logo to "LIVE MORE—Challenge + Discovery + Style."[45] More recently, the company has simplified this statement to "Live More"—and trademarked it. One past sponsor of the Xterra races was the Paul Mitchell Company, known primarily for its hair care and grooming products. To be honest, I found their ads to be incongruent with those of most other race sponsors, which are usually manufacturers of products directly related to sport.

Authenticity and Risk: The Sometimes-Mundane Nature of Danger

Excellent studies have been conducted as to why some individuals are more inclined toward risky—or adventurous—sports.[46] Generally, these are social-psychological studies that attempt to differentiate between people's need for arousal and new experiences that can be heightened during risky behaviors. Not surprisingly, there have been strong correlations between younger people, more often men than women, and greater risk. By and large, I take it for granted that some people are more predisposed toward risk than others. But the focus of my inquiry, in line with others, is why adventure sport, which is sometimes associated with risk, is increasingly valued as a leisure activity.[47] At times—not always—risk seems part of crafting authenticity in sport.

One of the paradoxes associated with the risk of road cycling—a sport more dangerous than many others—is that people are most often seriously hurt in mundane ways.[48] Many people believe that the prospect of danger or risk is associated with an adventure.[49] But with respect to road cycling in the United States, a place more dangerous to ride a bike than nearly all other industrialized countries, the potential for harm is primarily due to cyclists' sharing the road with vehicular traffic.[50] (That, and the fact that road pavement is an unforgiving surface to fall on at the relatively high speeds that a bicycle can travel.) Nearly every cyclist I know has friends who have been hit or killed by a vehicle. So have I. Shortly after I began this study, an infrequent cycling partner of mine when I was in college, Joe Hiney—at the time a well-liked local teacher—was killed on his bicycle by an elderly man driving on the shoulder of the road. Later, also while I was writing this text, a triathlete was struck by a vehicle and killed while racing in a triathlon at Virginia Tech.[51]

The risk involved in mountain biking is different. When people mountain bike, they are soon confronted with terrain in which they routinely have to make decisions that are ongoing calculations of risk. Indeed, this is what makes the sport compelling for many. A running narrative takes place in people's heads as they ride: a constant, ongoing calculation associated with their skill and the prospect for harm. Do I have the skill to roll through that rocky patch? Is that ledge, perhaps followed by some other tricky piece of trail, something I can ride? How much speed should I carry through this downhill section? How close to the edge of my ability do I want to move? Mountain biking routinely results in bumps and bruises along the way. Importantly, the risk associated with this sport is almost entirely within the control of the rider, something not always the case when riding on the road.

To an observer, the practice of off-road biking looks more risky than road riding. But while this may seem counterintuitive, nearly all of my friends regard mountain biking as much safer than riding a bike on the road. True, they may get a few more cuts and scrapes when they mountain bike, but they also eliminate their primary concern, riding with vehicular traffic. Still, over the decade that I actively rode I was present when three people—two of them experienced cyclists—broke their collarbones in falls from their bikes. I watched many more accidents that resulted in bruises, contusions, and lost blood. When I rode with friends the implicit agreement was that we personally accepted the risks involved. If we fell off a bike or otherwise knocked ourselves silly, we could count on help, but we were clearly responsible for our own actions.

Notably, the practitioners of the most extreme cycling I observed—skilled downhill mountain bikers are exemplary in this respect—work quite hard to make these acts routine and practiced. Indeed, the experience seems similar to what Victoria Robinson found in her study of climbers, in that "what might be considered 'extreme' behavior by most people, such as courting injury or evident risk-taking, was viewed as more 'mundane' everyday occurrences by the rock climbers in the study."[52] In effect, the goal of riding a mountain bike fast downhill was not to make it an extreme act, but rather to make it second nature. Of course, experienced mountain bikers might move to the edge of their abilities, but these acts were always preceded by a considerable amount of practice.

Most athletes I knew who had decided to ride a mountain bike assumed that they might be injured, which ensured that they all claimed responsibility for their actions on the bike. One man I watched break his collarbone was an experienced rider employed by the International Mountain Bike Association's Trail Care Crew. He and his wife were traveling the United States doing trail maintenance clinics and other forms of outreach for the organization. On this particular day a group of local cyclists had worked on some trails and then gone on a ride that ended with a two-mile downhill run on some fast, narrow, off-camber single track. This man fell while trying to keep up with a rider of some local renown, and responded to his broken bone with the kind of sheepishness typical of experienced cyclists who hurt themselves. It was an "I know better and screwed up" world-weariness that comes with the bumps and bruises people accumulate when they ride a mountain bike long enough. When I came upon him, he was sitting up, shaking his head, looking plaintively at his wife, and stating something to the effect that he "really should know better than that." His job of instructing people how to do trail maintenance was made much more difficult given the brace and bandages, but he cheerfully soldiered on.[53]

During the six years I ran an adventure travel company I developed, out of necessity, a very acute sense of how people might hurt themselves. This was because, following the exchange of money, I was suddenly responsible for my clients' well-being. Moreover, some of them were novice riders and being safe was important with respect to introducing them to the sport. True, I was concerned about mishaps that might be considered dramatic—a spectacular spill that caused considerable harm—but what I quickly discovered is that people tended to hurt themselves doing mundane things, such as stepping on glass while exiting a canoe. During my bicycle adventure packages, my clients often assumed that I had eliminated most of the danger from cycling. Despite their having signed waivers, despite my cautions to "ride within your ability," I sometimes encountered people who assumed that because someone was guiding them, they were essentially bulletproof. To a modest degree, this was true. Depending on the circumstances I changed difficult routes, moderated certain steep descents, stood in sections of trail to force people to stop before they hit a trouble spot, and tried to lower the risk that they would hurt themselves.[54]

Agency and Adventure: The Curious Case of the "Adventure Travel" Industry and Manufactured Experience

I think people are drawn to lifestyle sport mainly because it helps them to create some sense of agency, taking greater control over their lives by acting and accomplishing something, usually some self-stated goal associated with the sport. They learn to ride their bikes, or run over long distances, or scale a practice climbing wall. Most often, I imagine, many become competent at their sport of choice. But there is one curious area of lifestyle sport—that associated with the "adventure travel" industry—where a number of contradictory impulses associated with the new adventure ethic sometimes crash against each other. On these adventure trips, the participants engage in sporting acts, often in the wilderness, but they tend to have little control over the action. They are, to varying degrees, dependent on others to "make" the adventure for them.

When I operated my adventure travel company I often tried to manufacture adventures for participants.[55] For example, I found that fording streams after the spring thaw—strong cold water at roughly thigh level—was always conducive to creating an adventure. It made for good pictures too. At that time of year even my easiest mountain bike ride in terms of terrain and elevation gain, along the North River Trail, still required participants several times to ford a stream that was very cold and moved at a reasonably brisk pace. It ran fast enough to stagger people—perhaps even knock them down—as they waded across, but none were going to be swept away by the current. Participants were told beforehand to bring along a set of dry clothes they could change into when these obstacles were cleared. Many of my clients found the fording exciting, likely because they had never done anything quite like it before.

Were those trips an adventure? I think the answer depends largely on the perspective of those involved. At that time, as someone responsible for people's safety, it was in my interest to make these trips as routine as possible. I worked actively to avoid anything out of the ordinary or surprising. But sometimes clients did veer off the adventure script I had carefully plotted. For example, I once had a mishap in which a novice mountain biker who was determined to ride fast broke his collarbone on one of the easiest rides I scheduled. Even after his accident I never considered that ride particularly dangerous. Indeed, what I found maddening about that event was that someone had been hurt on a ride I associated with little risk.

At the same time, the meaning of a social act is most often a collective judgment—a group decides what is adventurous—and because my tour participants were experiencing a new type of cycling in a wilderness area with which they were unfamiliar, they probably did have adventures. Not only that, they had already been primed to think of their experience as being adventurous because that was how I had sold it to them. Most probably would not have associated this with the prospect of risk, but rather the idea of having a new or particularly stirring experience.[56] I expected, or at least hoped, that these trips would rate as adventure because the rides could be physically demanding and went through beautiful sections of country that relatively few people see. And notably, I sincerely wanted people to have an adventure, or at least experience the joy of seeing a wild place on their mountain bike. That was the primary motivation behind establishing my adventure company.

But what I also confronted—as providers of adventure travel do routinely—was that, practically speaking, once there was an exchange of money I had to be concerned with liability. As such, I attempted to eliminate as much danger as possible during these adventures. I quickly bracketed people's ability and tried to assure that they rode within that ability. I had escape routes out of the mountains where I knew I could get help quickly if someone was seriously hurt. But for the most part, what I discovered was that people, even in the wilderness, tend to hurt themselves in very mundane ways. They stir up a yellow jacket nest and get stung repeatedly. They forget to put on sunscreen and end up with a painful burn. Perhaps my most serious scare was a client's diabetic "crash" during a difficult mountain bike ride.

At the same time, because I knew the participants wanted an adventure, I did "pump up" certain sections of trail. I increasingly told mountain biking stories whose moral stressed safety, but still made the trip seem potentially dangerous.[57] For example, I routinely let my clients know about the past tour participant who had broken his collarbone on the easiest ride of the trip. This was a perfect story because it reinforced both the need for caution and the idea that the trip was adventurous. The isolation and scenery helped in this endeavor. Indeed, many of my clients commented that the mountain bike rides reminded them of the pictures they saw in cycling magazines.[58]

Many adventure travel operators feel pressured to eliminate uncertainty while simultaneously trying to convince people they are experiencing an adventure. One exemplary sociological account of people in this industry who routinely manufacture excitement was written by Lori Holyfield, who investigated the whitewater rafting industry. Guiding people on rafting trips is a near-perfect exemplar for unpacking the contradictory nature of creating a business (which necessitates elimination of uncertainty and risk) and selling it as an adventure.[59]

What Holyfield found was that whitewater guides routinely "manufactured" emotions associated with adventure. Water sport can, of course, be dangerous. Solo kayaking, for example, has very high fatality rates relative to other sports. But any reputable whitewater guiding company has made a systematic attempt to eliminate nearly all the serious prospects of danger from their trips. Indeed, whitewater guides know every trouble spot on the river; nearly all the thrills participants experience are manufactured. At some point during a rafting trip the guide will invariably push the raft through some "big water" in a stretch of river with an appropriately menacing name. The raft will bend and buckle before being shot into calmer water. Often, the guide discusses this stretch of river earnestly as the paddlers approach it. Past tales of mishap are recited. Danger is evoked. Nearly always the treacherous section is safely navigated. The tour participants will usually find that some enterprising photographer—perhaps employed by the touring company—has set up shop at that particular bend of the river and they can purchase a picture of themselves navigating the trouble spot. Not only do these rafting trips manage to produce an adventure for participants, but they also provide them with documents that help demonstrate the event's authenticity.

As a former provider of adventure, and someone who knew more than a few experienced paddlers, I resisted entreaties by my friends to go on guided whitewater trips.[60] I mostly considered it too much like my former line of work to be enjoyable, this despite the fact that I live near the New and Gauley Rivers, some of the most remarkable whitewater in the United States. These are wild rivers that require skill to navigate. I actually did want to go down them, but also knew I lacked the requisite knowledge to do it safely. I assumed that someday—likely after a period of instruction with a friend—I might paddle down the difficult sections of the New or the Gauley on my own. To my way of thinking, this was the most authentic way to approach the endeavor, as opposed to being shepherded. True, on a guided trip I would be handed a paddle, but I regarded this as not much more than a prop. Safety concerns ensured that whichever company was creating our adventure, if it was competent, would have dutifully stripped nearly all the agency from the tour participants to protect them—and itself.

But during this study, in the fall of 2001, I did decide to accept an invitation to go on a guided whitewater trip down the New River in West Virginia. Of course, throughout the trip I did my best to go along with the epic narratives being crafted. But professional curiosity, as much as this study, made me acutely interested in how these companies would craft the "river experience." Other scholars have investigated how river guides create adventure through narratives and group interactions, and I expected this trip would be no exception.[61] I was not disappointed. Even the jokes had clearly been oft-repeated: for example, the most authentically West Virginian of the guides—at least that is how he self-presented—unspooled the following set piece when we stopped for lunch. He and the other guides laid out the food for their clients along the river bank. Then he announced, "Now, I know most of you-all are from someplace else and it is important that I introduce you to a few traditions we have here in West Virginia and on the New River. First, West Virginians are chivalrous, so I am going to insist that it is 'ladies first' in the chow line ..."

After this announcement the women in the group, a few laughing, moved toward the lunch spread. As they formed the line this guide suddenly feigned indignity and then amended his announcement to include the following: "Ladies, ladies, ladies. . . . Be sure to pick up two plates . . . That way you can 'make a plate' for your man too. . . ."

When the group was on the river I spent most of my time assessing the quality of our guide's patter, which inevitably invoked the epic, versus the actual numerous precautions that had been made with respect to safety. At the end of the trip I mostly felt relief, not because we were ever in any danger, but because I had so closely watched the difficult work of these guides. It reminded me that "emotion work"—the cheeriness, the need to be constantly upbeat, the continuous interaction with clients—was probably the hardest part of their jobs.[62]

Many rafting companies in West Virginia track the number of people a guide dumps into the river each year. Guides who routinely spill customers are first warned and then often disciplined if the trend continues. On the trip just described—in which I admired the constant patter of our young guide as he manufactured our adventure—one person did fall into the river. This was literally the last trip of the fall season and from the moment we started downriver I sensed that our guide was genuinely happy, borderline giddy. Everyone else assumed he was excited to be on the river, but it quickly became clear to me as I talked with him that he was mostly ecstatic that the season was about to end. Soon, he would be released from paddling down this particular stretch of river. His spirits were high because he could see the end of the season in sight. One more cruise and he was free, at least for a little while, from the mundane task of making adventure for other people. Our guide was also very young, easily the youngest in this tour group of four rafts.

Perhaps because it was his last day this guide decided to do something off-script. Largely on a whim—I watched as he checked whether his group leader could see him—he decided to swing us into a large hydraulic beside a tremendous boulder where the water was moving quickly counterclockwise. Before doing this he warned those on the far side of the raft, where the centrifugal force would be greatest, to brace themselves because when the raft hit the churning hole it would begin to spin. Still, one young woman was dumped into the river as soon as the raft hit the turning water. This was the only time I sensed genuine fear from someone on the trip. The woman in the river was fine—fortunately, she was spit out of the hydraulic immediately and was soon bobbing down a stretch of river that was clear of any serious hazards. But the guide was clearly desperate—wide-eyed and frantic—determined to get us to this woman quickly and haul her back into the raft. Basically, he was in serious trouble if his tour leader, a middle-aged woman with considerable rafting experience, noticed he had put someone in the river.

After the woman was pulled back in the raft, accompanied by hoots from the other passengers, I quickly informed the guide, by way of relieving his stress, "You should be fine, she did not see it." He looked back at me, smiled slightly, and said, "It's my last day and I don't want to get written up. I can't believe that . . . I told her to brace."

At the end of this trip, as we admired the pictures now available for us to purchase, I struck up a conversation with the boyfriend of the woman who was dumped into the river. He remarked, "I think that was really dangerous . . . I can't believe that guy did that." He was upset mainly because he sensed something was "off" about the event. From the perspective of the rafting company, that short time in the water was a dangerous period. In effect, because being in the water is a dangerous act, and because the rafters ultimately have so little agency on these trips, the company guides are, de facto, almost entirely responsible for their safety. Most participants on these trips are aware of this pact, and that was why the boyfriend was so upset. In effect, while people may say they want an adventure, they also want, somewhat paradoxically, for it to be safe. In some cases, they are happy to give up their agency—they have no desire to plan logistics or steer the raft—because it has been made clear to them that their river guide will keep them safe.[63]

Looking Forward

A primary goal of this chapter was to describe the search for adventure, for an authentic experience, that sometimes motivates people's participation in difficult sport and adventure travel. In the former, participants often regard their chosen activities as liberating and their participation as a means to combat the more mundane aspects of their day-to-day lives. Nonetheless, adventure does appear to be an increasing prescribed act, often choreographed and managed in ways that, for the most part, do not appear much different than how other aspects of life are managed. Indeed, market forces appear to be capturing and then commodifying the adventure experience, so much so that anyone who has the money can now purchase an adventure. It is now routine to encounter the contradictory message that adventure can always be safe. Adventure is also sometimes redefined to include a remarkable amount of conformity related to completing very specific tasks.

The next chapter investigates the considerable amount of discipline associated with some lifestyle sport. This often includes how and where the sport is played, the types of equipment used, the athletes' diet, and their adherence to specific training regimens. In effect, a capitalist "norm of efficiency" is often reproduced as play is formalized into modern sport. As a practical matter, perceiving joy in sport and being efficient at it sometimes become closely associated. Fulfilling the norm of efficiency associated with adventure sport often requires considerable personal expense. Moreover, it causes many people to regulate their lives, even their minute-by-minute existence, in order to become the most efficient athlete possible.

3

Disciplining Bodies
in Lifestyle Sport

●●●●●●●●●●●●●●●●●●●●

An interesting aspect of mountain biking and triathlon is that they offer an opportunity to observe the rapid development of lifestyle sports from activities that were once considered more spontaneous forms of play. Triathlon, in particular, is an exemplary lifestyle sport in that many assume participation requires an individual's lived experience to be focused on both training and racing. Moreover, the governing body of the sport in America, USA Triathlon, routinely refers to triathlon as a lifestyle sport. The development of both triathlon and mountain biking into official sports demonstrates how rapidly and pervasively the market now transforms largely unorganized play into a commodified experience.

Ultimately, sport places greater emphasis on both formal and informal rules, bodily discipline, and the importance of measurement—of documenting records—all of which become closely associated with the new sporting discipline.[1] As a result, many critical theorists have asked: Why is participation in sport considered a liberating or egalitarian experience when in the modern context it is governed by considerable structural constraints?[2]

Related to the establishment of these sports is the use of scientific norms for training the body to improve performance. John Hoberman observed in the 1990s that the "fixation with performance"—as opposed to "fair play"—had become the driving ideal among those who participated in professional and elite sport.[3] This chapter largely builds upon this proposition, but argues that the performance principle is now so pervasive that middle-range athletes increasingly decide that it is normal to train, as best they can, in the same manner as the professionals.

Establishing Discipline in New Sporting Endeavors

Much of the following perspective is informed by scholarship associated with critical theory, particularly Michel Foucault's conception of power in modern life. Many scholars have adopted this approach because Foucault so specifically described how Enlightenment ideals can impose discipline on the human body.[4] In *Discipline and Punish: The Birth of the Modern Prison*, Foucault described how disciplinary power—the means of correct (scientific) training—acts upon "docile bodies" and establishes societal norms of behavior. This disciplinary power acts to control those bodies and then dictates how they are used. Inevitably, nearly all modern societal institutions (churches, schools, hospitals, prisons) ascribe a means of "correct training."[5]

Michel Foucault's approach is a natural fit for describing the bodily discipline now normative in modern sport.[6] Another aspect of his work is the observation that individuals are under constant surveillance in order to ensure their compliance with science-derived norms. In a modern context, this surveillance might include the information collected by government, schools, health care systems, and so on, much of which forces us to engage in behaviors designed to make us model consumers.[7]

Using Foucault's framework, the structure of modern sport should act like other societal institutions and seek to control participants by enforcing a "means of correct training." This disciplinary power should be pervasive and spread throughout the capitalist system. From this point of view, modern sport should cause athletes to conform by establishing the most efficient means of training as a normative value. Previously, Max Weber had identified increasing efficiency as an important goal in modern, or "rational," organizations (or bureaucracies). Indeed, Weber was largely responsible for establishing the foundations that scholars use when they study complex organizations and the rationalization of human endeavors. Weber also tied rationalization to the development of the modern economy. While he was not as specific as Foucault with respect to how norms associated with efficiency act to discipline the human body, he did assert that modern bureaucracies, in their drive for realizing maximum efficiencies, created an "iron cage" of rationalism that was ultimately dehumanizing to the individual spirit.[8]

These perspectives seem particularly applicable to the development of the lifestyle sports of triathlon and mountain biking. I had an opportunity to chronicle, over the course of two decades, exactly how quickly spontaneous forms of play were essentially captured by the market. As mentioned in the introduction, I found it startling how quickly these acts, and the "do-it-yourself" ethos, were transformed into tightly prescribed sporting practice, often defined by companies that now sold the "official" equipment required to participate.

In order to have an industry there have to be standards. In order to have standards there must be rules. In order to have rules there have to be institutions to enforce them. In order to enforce these rules administrative bodies must have some power. All of the preceding help routinize and standardize new sporting traditions. These new norms are also affected by market pressures. For example, people cannot sell sporting equipment if there is not some formal purpose—usually associated with some kind of "scientific" testing—for which it is designed.

Mountain biking and triathlon competitions are now governed by informal rules related to training in what are considered to be scientifically proven programs, and numerous formal rules are applied to the equipment that can be used in competition. These rules are enforced by sporting federations that issue licenses to participants. Both triathlon and mountain biking now have professional athletes who make a living at subdisciplines within their sports. The equipment for each of these subdisciplines is different. For instance, people do not use cross-country mountain bikes in a downhill mountain bike race. And, of course, there are very specific rules in each of these subdisciplines that govern what is legal when racing.

The Commodity of the Mountain Bike

It is striking to realize that some lifestyle sport was recently regarded more as play than as routinized athletics. Mountain biking, in particular, initially had very few rules. In fact, it actually broke rules, one reason why people found the activity so compelling. The initial genius of mountain biking was that it took a piece of equipment designed for a specific purpose (riding on pavement) and adapted it to a completely new one (riding in the mountains). Because I began as a road cyclist I was conditioned to avoid any bump, uneven pavement, rocks, and the like that might ruin my lightweight road bike. The people who designed road bikes would have been appalled if I rode them through the woods or over curbs.

But with respect to how modern capitalism can commodify a common human experience, it is important to point out that people have been mountain biking for as long as there have been bikes and woods. As I noted in the opening chapter, as kids my friends and I merrily pedaled our banana-seated, fixed-gear bikes through the back woods of our neighborhood. We jumped off ramps and spun out in the dirt. Sometimes I would pin a playing card onto the spokes so it generated a rat-a-tat-tat engine sound that, although highly inefficient, pleased me to no end. Likewise, people in Europe, where cycling is often used as a primary form of locomotion, have often ridden their bikes through mountains on unpaved roads. In this regard, simply naming a previous activity, calling it "mountain biking," and then formalizing an element of play that had previously existed in a more unstructured manner, made it possible to sell people the commodities involved in the new sport of mountain biking. Before mountain biking existed there was no need to own a mountain bike and the gear that goes with it. It was in the bicycle manufacturers' interest to strictly define the parameters of this "new" activity so they could sell the specific equipment needed to have this experience. As a practical matter, people often define their experience (mountain biking, road cycling) based on the commodity they have bought, not the actual acts in which they have engaged. In effect, my friends and I were not "mountain biking" when we were kids because we were not riding mountain bikes or using mountain bike equipment.

During the early 1980s mountain biking was discovered by large bicycle manufacturers and the first mass-produced mountain bikes appeared. The Specialized Stump Jumper, introduced in 1981, was perhaps the most important early success at marketing a "mountain bike." Soon, the first professional cyclists appeared. Still, a primary appeal of mountain biking, at least for the people I knew, was that it was play. The people who introduced me to the sport in the mid 1980s framed it exactly in that manner. They said that the best way to approach it was to get in touch with the joy I had experienced when I was a boy and rode my bike through the woods and over curbs and off ramps simply because it was fun. It had been years since I had built a ramp and launched myself into the air. For some reason, somewhere along the way, I had stopped doing this.

The people I knew enjoyed mountain biking because it was conceived of as unstructured, wild, something done for the sheer joy that accompanied riding a bike through puddles, across streams, and over logs and rocks in the woods. At that time there was no standard-issue mountain bike uniform. I had friends who wore cut-off jeans when they rode mountain bikes. One carried a Boy Scout canteen strapped to his waist. Many of my friends—I would actually guess most of them—did not wear helmets.[9]

In mountain biking lore, the sport originated in Marin County, California, an affluent and mountainous community just outside of San Francisco. In general, the early mountain bikes were cobbled together from a variety of spare cycling parts. Most often this consisted of a beefy cycling frame and wheels from something like a newspaper delivery bike that was then outfitted with a modern derailleur and shifter that might be found on a ten-speed road bike. Many of the early California founders of the sport, most notably Gary Fischer, later established some of the first successful mountain bike production companies.[10]

The first mountain bike I rode, loaned to me by a friend, was literally custom-designed and built by Thomas Ritchey, a California frame-builder who was among the first to produce and sell mountain bikes. Ritchey mountain bike components are now mass- produced; they are easy enough to find on many modern mountain bikes and are still considered among the best components available. Gary Fisher sold his company, Gary Fisher Bikes, to a large American manufacturer, TREK Bicycles. As these early founders gained increasing national stature within the mountain bike industry, some people referred to them as the "Marin Mafia."

As a practical matter, these innovators are now credited as the founders of mountain biking because they were the first to make it into a profitable capitalist endeavor. Of course, mountain bikes have since evolved into a piece of equipment that is substantially different than what was previously produced by those large cycling companies. Indeed, one reason why mountain bikes were so quickly embraced by the major bicycle manufacturers was because they were significantly different, and extraordinarily popular, when compared to the standard bicycles those companies were producing.

Correct Training

In a remarkably short period of time—less than a decade—the bicycling industry embraced this activity and began to produce specialized equipment designed for the purpose of mountain biking. A similar process occurred in triathlon, associated with the development of "time trial" bikes designed for this particular competition. In both sports it was not surprising that what soon followed—in minute detail—were prescribed riding styles, equipment, and apparel.[11] Flip through any magazine that targets mountain bikers or triathletes and almost every article is dedicated to the "correct" way to ride (or to prepare to ride) a bicycle. More than that, they prescribe the correct ways to eat and even sleep.[12] These writers' admonishments are representative of Foucault's concept of discipline. They have informed riders of the correct positions and training methods for all of the following: seat heights, frame size, handlebar width, pedal rotation per minute, heart rate during exercise, perceived vs. actual exertion, and protein vs. fat vs. carbohydrate intake for "optimal" performance, to name just a few.

All of this advice is geared toward using scientifically tested methods to increase efficiency. And they do just that. If people buy the equipment and train accordingly, they become much faster and more efficient. But why do people pursue efficiency in what used to be play? Why is efficiency so important? These are interesting questions if we assume that people experienced just as much or even more joy when they participated in unstructured sport or play that did not require commodities or constant discipline. In this respect, it is evident that the capitalist system is closely associated with why people value efficiency in most aspects of their lives. (It is normative that people are supposed to work efficiently, for example.) Perhaps it is inevitable that people would also come to value the most efficient means of "correct training" during their leisure.

Currently, the rules and sub-rules of competitive mountain biking and triathlon are elaborated down to the minutest details. Many are related to both promoting and regulating efficiency. For instance, in triathlon a person may race wearing a wetsuit as determined by the temperature of the water. This is regulated because wetsuits make the wearers more buoyant and allow them to swim faster. Swimmers do not necessarily wear these garments because they are afraid of hypothermia: indeed, when the sport first developed many triathletes used them in very warm water—in conditions *exactly opposite* to those for which the suits were designed—because it gave them a competitive advantage. The suits made the athletes very hot, but many wearers calculated that they still swam more efficiently because the suits raised their body out of the water, causing less resistance. As a result, companies began producing wetsuits designed specifically to help people swim faster. In effect, the "norm of efficiency" took a sport that required nearly no equipment and made owning $200–500 polyurethane suits a prerequisite for participation in the modern sport of triathlon.

Conformity and Routinization

So what exactly is liberating about participating in the sport of mountain biking, and even more so triathlon, when it requires so much conformity? For a few athletes the answer is "not much." The rationalization of triathlon and mountain biking is much debated. I found these debates particularly evident in the editorial and opinion sections of the print magazines that cover these sports and the online comment sections of their websites. For example, it is a common rhetorical trope that the premium placed on increased conformity—owning a certain type of bike, buying certain clothes—can dampen the fun associated with a sport people once loved. Some magazine editorials may make this point as well, but not too loudly, and not for very long, because, as a practical matter, these writers are in the business of selling advertising space to companies that want people to value products that increase their efficiency.

People who work for these publications need people to train efficiently. They need people to buy the products associated with this endeavor. Indeed, their very livelihood depends on this.

This debate was evident in the "letters to the editor" section of nearly every issue of *Bicycling, Mountain Bike,* and *Triathlete* that I reviewed. For instance, in the *Bicycling* "Buyer's Guide" of April 2003 a letter takes "Style Man" to task for paying too much attention to style issues and reviewing espresso makers.[13] As mentioned in the previous chapter, this column was largely a tongue-in-cheek exercise, but also a useful mechanism for introducing readers to cycling products and other commodities vaguely associated with the sport. In this same issue there is also an indignant response from a "5,000 mile-a-year; 57 year old rider with a resting pulse in the low 50s" who is upset that he is not considered "highly fit" according to a March 2003 article entitled "So You Think You're Fit?" The editor's response to this man ends with the admonishment, "Start training!"[14] Annually, usually around August, *Triathlete* prints a series of articles organized under the heading "Mandatory Gear," which outline, in an explicit manner, the equipment considered necessary for participation in the sport.

Overall, my sense has been that mountain bikers tend to engage in the "play vs. sport" debate more often than triathletes. In particular, it is common to find debate concerning the merits of racing mountain bikes as opposed to the joy of simply riding these bikes for pleasure. Some of the most popular mountain bike magazines—*Bike!* and *Dirt Rag*—reinforce the play element largely to the exclusion of racing and efficient training. Moreover, *Mountain Bike,* which seemed most firmly entrenched in the market as related to its advertising and production, was recently folded into *Bicycling* by the parent company, Rodale Press.

Triathletes, more so than mountain bikers, appear to be completely ensnared by the market. In effect, it is normative that one has to race to be a triathlete. Indeed, to be a triathlete one must do more than swim, bike, and run: one must do these things in formal competition at a prescribed time and place with other people. Unlike many self-identified recreational mountain bikers, triathletes must always buy their way into a race—a typical fee is around $100—and then complete a course in the shortest amount of time possible. Some cyclists choose to ride recreationally, but there is really no recreational triathleting. For the most part, self-defined triathletes must race repeatedly before they consider themselves members of the sport. By way of contrast, mountain bikers and recreational cyclists can claim to be "cyclists" or "mountain bikers" but never race their bicycles.

But triathletes do sometimes engage in a variation of the play vs. sport debate, particularly as it relates to the distinction between professional and amateur athletes and the motivations for being a triathlete. Some attributed a decline in triathlon participation during the early 1990s to the fact that other less-competitive, less-costly venues (mountain bike festivals, noncompetitive road bike events) were siphoning people away. Many posited that people were turned off by the sport's spiraling costs and increased professionalization, which changed the goal from "completion" into "completion in the shortest time possible."[15] This concern was not long-lived: the sport has since experienced dramatic growth.

Many of the triathletes I knew and interviewed did not often contemplate that the sport they regarded as liberating required them to conform to an extraordinary number of formal and informal rules. This is not to say that I did not sometimes have interactions in which a triathlete seemed to intuitively understand that the edicts of the sport were constricting. On a number of occasions, I watched triathletes prepare for a bike ride by mixing their sports drinks, slipping into their skintight apparel, calibrating their heart rate monitors, and making sure they punched their cycling computers before mounting their bikes. Following this elaborate and time-consuming ritual, many offered comments such as: "Look at all this stuff . . . It has taken me nearly as long to get ready for the ride as to do the actual riding." To a lesser degree, mountain bikers and other adventure sports participants, including those in ostensibly noncompetitive pursuits such as hiking, have a similar experience and preoccupation with equipment. The types of equipment someone has—the bike, boat, backpack, tent, shoes, harness, ropes—are all important markers that determine their owner's entry into the outdoor adventure community.

Triathletes represent a group at the extremes: they are routinely surveilled in order to ensure that they comply with "norms" associated with efficiency. One example of this type of surveillance occurred routinely among the members of the Virginia Tech triathlon club.[16] Continual friction occurred between the club's serious athletes—those committed to a regimen of strict training geared toward specific outcomes at specific races—and those who were more inclined to view their participation in sport as play. Some of the serious athletes regarded the haphazard training habits of other team members as a personal affront and quickly went about indoctrinating the slackers on the means of "correct" and "scientific" training. The serious members began to harass these inefficient athletes in a usually good-natured way. They told them that being a triathlete was a serious endeavor and they needed to become more "disciplined."

At the same time, a common editorial theme in triathlon magazines is that athletes should remember to keep the sport "fun" despite the latest scientific advances in training. As a practical matter, this does not prevent these same writers from extolling the virtues of the latest gadget or chronicling the latest "revolutionary" training technique. In general, triathletes (and cyclists and adventure sport athletes in general) have wholeheartedly embraced the drive toward efficiency and the need for discipline as a requirement to claim membership in their sport. Many letters to the editor in triathlon and cycling magazines start with a description of the writer's ability, or the number of races they have completed (complete with times) as a means of describing their relative rank in the sport. For example, in the July 2003 *Triathlete* one letter-writer (who reports he has done 187 races in ten years and always finishes in the top three in his age group) argues for the establishment of a speed-based criterion for race events. He writes, "Let the racers race and the 30 minute 5k racers stay at home." Inevitably, this was followed by indignant responses in the August issue.[17] In fact, in my survey of these magazines it was rare to find an edition where letters of this nature were not represented.

My early participation in the sport of triathlon tends to mirror the period of growing professionalization of the sport. My first race was the Green Mountain "Steel Man" in Brattleboro, Vermont, in the summer of 1986. This was a half-Ironman distance race (1.2-mile swim, 56-mile bike, and 13.1-mile run). While there were people racing in this event, and even a few professionals who were trying to win the cash purse, most participants framed their goal for this event as "finishing."

At this time, individual athletes still provided their own support. For instance, my sixteen-year-old brother, who had just received his driver's license, was my support team. This basically meant that he drove my battered Honda Civic around the racecourse and occasionally handed me bananas and Gatorade. Today, aid stations are dotted along the course and outside support is completely banned. Safety issues undoubtedly contributed to this change, but so has the commercialization of the sport: these days, Gatorade might be the official provider of the racers' sports drinks.

In 1986 the very distance of the various triathlon races was in the process of being standardized. In the beginning triathlon was associated with the most commercially successful race, the Hawaii Ironman (2.4-mile swim, 112-mile bike, and 26.2-mile run). This race came about as the result of a barroom bet by a handful of local athletes. Its first participants—on their own and without any support, sponsorship, or rules other than distance traveled—engaged in this activity simply to see who could complete the distances fastest. It was not a professional event.[18]

Many people were drawn to the sport when they watched one of the first professional athletes in triathlon, Dave Scott, win the race. There was also a particularly dramatic early race in which Julie Moss, the event leader among women, collapsed near the finish and then began to crawl desperately before being passed, just yards from the tape, by another competitor. This was dramatic television and introduced many people to the sport.[19] Still, it would have been hard to turn triathlon into a professional sport if it had conformed only to the Ironman distance. Even the fittest athletes would have been able to compete in only a handful of races at that distance each year. But, just like the current debate over changing the rules related to "drafting" on a bicycle, at first many athletes (including Dave Scott) resisted calling any multisport event that was undertaken at shorter distance a "real" triathlon.

If Ironman distance races were the only venues for individual participation in triathlon, than the sport would not have developed much mass or commercial appeal. Triathlon does not function well as a spectator sport and companies that make sporting equipment need amateur participation to be financially viable. Soon sprint, international, half-Ironman, and Ironman standards of distance were established. These standards quickly became norms: race directors rarely deviate from them even if USA Triathlon does not sanction their event. The international distance races (1.5-km swim, 40-km bike, 10-km run) have become very common and allow professional athletes to compete more often. Sprint distance races (.75-km swim, 20-km bike, 5-km run) are also popular and draw the most amateur participants.

Disciplining the Body[20]

Few people enter triathlon as a matter of play; nor is this considered a desirable perspective to adopt in order to become proficient at the sport. Indeed, one reason triathlon is indicative of lifestyle sport is that it is premised on the idea that one must be dedicated to very specific training routines that require constant commitment, often a complete change in lifestyle. This lifestyle is designed mainly to fashion the athlete's body so that it can cover prescribed distances in accordance with strictly defined types of locomotion. Triathlon rules can be elaborate. For example, as noted previously, the regulation of wetsuits has become common. Theoretically, most any kind of bike can be ridden, but the standard quickly became a very specific type of road bike designed for time-trialing. As the sport developed the standard time-trial bike became an increasingly expensive and complicated piece of equipment. Triathletes often use different types of shoes for training and racing, and serious runners pick their shoes according to their body weight and running style.

Highly trained endurance athletes usually have an extraordinary corporeal knowledge. That is, they tend toward hypersensitivity concerning how they feel physically because they use their bodies so routinely, and in manners that require physical discipline.[21] Endurance athletes tend to be hyperaware of exactly what they can, and cannot, accomplish on a given day. Even the ones who do not obsess much about their weight and diet inevitably know their race weight. When I was a highly trained athlete I knew that when I was fit—I am a shade under 5'10"—I weighed about 157 pounds. I usually began the early race season as much as ten pounds heavier, but this is where my weight would settle when I was turning in my best times. Notably, all the sports associated with triathlon also have high incidences of "disordered eating" among both male and female athletes. In the few studies that have focused on triathletes there is an indication that this is particularly the case with new athletes who are entering the sport.[22]

As relates to discipline, all of these norms—particularly regarding appropriate ways to train—discipline a triathlete's body by establishing the "correct means of training." Soon after the sport was established many authors went about the business of telling triathletes what they were supposed to be doing and what they ought to buy.[23] From the beginning, triathletes were obsessive about training techniques, training regimens, training equipment, and diet. The sport often seems geared toward strict accounting for nearly every bodily function imaginable: many athletes keep logs of their daily mileage totals, how they felt during their training, and what and how much they ate that day. Other endurance and adventure athletes have similar rituals. A friend of mine who routinely participates in ultra-distance running events has kept such a log for over twenty years. During a recent vacation he entered all of this data into his computer so he could systematically plot his development in endurance sport. The original logs filled an entire suitcase.[24]

This is not play. In fact, it more closely resembles the manner in which people approach their work. The expert advice offered in triathlon magazines and self-help training guides commonly includes the counsel that triathletes be particularly vigilant against spending too much time on the discipline they enjoy the most. In effect, if a triathlete does not like swimming, then that is the activity he or she should clearly spend the most time working on.[25]

Triathlete Magazine has always been oriented toward advertising the products needed to compete in the sport. In the late 1980s, well before the Internet, I subscribed to *Triathlete* primarily because it had a race calendar that listed nearly every event scheduled in the United States. When I reentered the sport in 2001 and 2013 and began this study, I perused the most recent editions of *Triathlete* and *Inside Triathlon* out of curiosity. In terms of the tenor of their articles, the magazines had not changed much in the intervening years. More recently, I followed the online edition of *Triathlete* and, again, found that the content had remained largely the same in terms of the types of articles, advice columns, and editorial content.

But I did find one article, now over twenty years old, which was out of the ordinary. I will describe it because it is exemplary of how someone is disciplined if they deviate from a sport's prescribed norms. In the May 1991 issue of *Triathlete* an article by a regular columnist, Rick O'Bryan, described a technique called "curb running" supposedly designed by East German running coach Jurgena Hirt ("you're going to hurt"). Curb running required people to find a sidewalk curb and run so that one leg was on the elevated curbside, and the other on the pavement below. After describing the exercise, the author gave an account of the tremendous physiological benefits on athletic performance of running with one foot striking the ground six inches above the other. In short, the writer parodied the advice columns that continue to be, now more than ever, a staple of this magazine's content. In case people did not get the joke, beside the column was a ditzy cartoon character doing this absurd exercise. Given the self-seriousness of this magazine's readers and writers, even though the sport was just over a decade old, this piece of satire seemed extraordinary. As it turned out, in the next issue the managing editor made it clear that he was indignant the piece had been run in the magazine. He insinuated that the editors had been tricked and he responded in a predictable manner. The editor assaulted the integrity of the author (how could he tell people to do such a potentially dangerous exercise!) and informed the readership that he had been fired.[26]

Overall, as it relates to triathlon, it is apparent that norms were established quickly as to the "correct" methods of training. Challenging these methods—insinuating that many might be nonsense or unnecessary for an amateur athlete—was an offense beyond the pale. In effect, to be a modern triathlete today requires that one train in a specific manner. When swimming, it is best to train with a master's swim team or at least use the same type of workouts and equipment (fins, paddles, kick boards). When running, the optimum method is long, slow distance work (LSD training) combined with interval training, preferably track work. Don't forget to monitor your heart rate. Calculate your target heart rate zones. And taper before that big race!

With the advent of small GPS (Global Positioning System) units, it has become routine for athletes to literally track their rides in terms of elevation gained and miles per hour achieved, which they then upload to their personal computers. These variables now define the riding experience for most triathletes, particularly how fast and far they ride and their physiology throughout. If you ask a triathlete about a bicycle ride they will most often respond with information about its length and difficulty, their miles per hour, and whether they hit their targets. This is opposed to what they might have seen along the way.

Technologies of Discipline and Surveillance:
Strava and Heart Rate Monitors[27]

I began to routinely encounter people training with heart-rate monitors when I was a graduate student at Florida State University in the 1990s. In fact, I remember the exact moment I realized that athletes were using these devices to determine the pace of training rides. This occurred when I did a ride with another triathlete, a strong amateur who aspired to becoming a professional. Around Tallahassee there are a few rolling roads covered by tree canopies. At that time my natural inclination was to push through these turning and hilly sections because they were like little roller-coasters if you rode them with pace. And the more riders the better—in a pace-line the roller-coaster feel was even greater and made the riding more fun. So, as we hit this section of road, I motored through the turns with pace, expecting my partner to move along with me.

But my riding partner did not jump with me, although he clearly had plenty of gas in the tank if he wanted to. I quickly gapped him by a wide margin and then spun back while he caught up with me. He was "in the drops," staring at a computer mounted to his handlebars. His cadence had not altered in the slightest. I told him that he should have come with me through the earlier section—that it was a blast! He looked up from his monitor and told me this was his "long slow ride" and that he had to stay within certain heart-rate parameters. If his heart beat faster than his prescribed limit his monitor would start beeping and he would dial back his pace. In effect, he was not allowed—no matter how fun it might be—to exceed this rate. And practically, he could not go below a certain rate either. He was an automaton, steadily grinding though the ride within a predetermined heart rate in order to increase and maximize his fitness.

When I returned to competition in 2013 it was remarkable how technology had changed in terms of people's ability to monitor their bodies. The statistics associated with any ride—the miles traveled, speed averaged, amount of climbing, calories burned—are now very easy to chronicle. Moreover, cyclists can now do a direct comparison between their effort and that of other local cyclists whenever they ride. And the technology is no longer bulky and difficult to use.

Practically, training with a heart rate monitor was standard operating procedure for nearly all of the triathletes and self-described serious mountain bikers I interviewed. I did not encounter any "Iron-people" who were, in the least, freelancing as it relates to their training methodology. Almost all of them were using the exact same training regimen—sometimes literally and strictly proscribed in the identical texts[28]—which had them constantly monitoring their heart rates and time spent training in order to complete an Ironman distance race. Some programs prescribed riding inside on a wind trainer at times rather than on the road. I once returned from a ride on a beautiful day and ran into a neighbor whose triathlete husband was training for an Ironman distance race. I asked if her husband had gotten outside to enjoy the sun. She responded that no, even though it was a beautiful day, he was scheduled to "ride the trainer today."

The most extraordinary changes I noted were associated with the refinement of GPS tools that can track riders' progress and provide them with a direct comparison to others who ride the same stretch of road. I had never trained previously with anyone who used a GPS, but it became apparent during the summer of 2013 that Strava, a GPS application that can be downloaded to a smart phone, was now ubiquitous among serious cyclists and runners.[29] Often, riders who were also using a heart rate monitor had synchronized the device with the Strava program. This allowed them to know their heart rates during the different sections of the ride.

Increasingly, serious cyclists have installed power meters in the cranks of their bicycles that track the watts of power they generate during a ride. In 2013 this was considered the best measure of overall effort: a watt of power is always a comparable unit whereas heart rate will fluctuate slightly from day to day. In effect, some days an athlete might be able to push more watts even while maintaining the same heart rate. Obviously, if this is associated with some kind of discernible pattern—a certain pre-ride meal, for example—then the athlete can further refine his or her performance. Power meters are relatively expensive, about $500, but increasingly "must-have" devices for serious athletes. It seems inevitable that as their cost declines, like heart rate monitors and GPS, they will also be adopted by recreational cyclists.

I registered myself on Strava.com in order to understand the application, but did not formally use it during this study. Still, when I rode with other people the "Strava effect" on group dynamics was impossible to ignore. Unlike most of my fellow riders, I was not particularly disposed toward tracking and monitoring my riding and body so thoroughly. Still, I have no doubt that if I had encountered Strava when I was a young cyclist it would have quickly become a standard piece of equipment when I trained. The application allows riders to track their progress with little effort in some remarkable ways. It provides an extraordinary amount of information quickly. For example, when I decided to do the opening day of the Tour de Burg I e-mailed a friend, "What is that ride like?" My expectation was he would provide a written account of the trail. Instead, he simply forwarded a "ride profile" from Strava.

It was immediately evident to me why this application was both useful and popular. Basically, at a glance, I had an extraordinary amount of very specific information concerning a ride I had never done before. In the past it would have taken a lengthy conversation to get as much information and it would have been incomplete compared to the details offered by the Strava profile.

A friend of mine, an enthusiastic Strava user, sent me a profile from another ride we took in the national forest west of Staunton. (See Figure 4.) We had taken a road, dirt, and gravel ride in a somewhat-isolated area that not many cyclists know about. This was the first time I had explored this area, but parts of the ride had, inevitably, already been entered into Strava by a few local riders.

The Strava application is useful for mountain biking, particularly in very remote areas, as it helps assure that riders will not get lost even if they do not know the area well. People excited about a new ride can send extraordinary details about it to their friends instantaneously. Indeed, if they "follow" their friends, they can keep track of exactly where and how much riding they are doing. Notably, most of the features I have described above are free—and, given the isolated areas of the national forest where many mountain bikers ride, the benefits of the application were immediately self-evident. Despite all these advantages, there are a few curmudgeons, often veteran cyclists, who have misgivings about this technology. As reported in *Bicycling Magazine*:

> Like any other game-changing innovation, this one has its critics and pitfalls. Chief among these is, indeed, the charge of gamification: Strava-besotted cyclists engage in personal time trials whenever they mount their bikes, and with

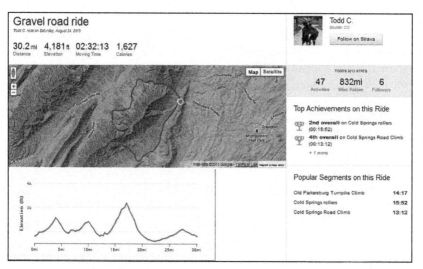

FIGURE 4 Strava ride profile of Todd C's North Mountain–Deerfield Valley ride.

so many users familiar with the locations of popular segments, formerly civil training rides now explode at predictable—if intangible—points.

The same article added:

> Wayne Lumpkin, owner of Spot Brand Bicycles in Golden, Colorado, and a longtime icon of the sport, summed up a common sentiment when he told *Bicycle Retailer*, "People call it social media, but I call it anti-social media."[30]

My most visceral response to Strava, notwithstanding the obvious benefits, was similar. In addition, I found the prospect of being confronted, as a daily routine, with my rank within the local cycling community as increasingly beside the point as to why I was riding a bicycle. Even when I was actively training I wanted mostly to continue to think about cycling, as much as possible, in terms of an aesthetic endeavor unrelated to how fast (or far, or high) I rode. I assumed this temperament would be harder to maintain if I used Strava, so I was never much tempted to use it as a comparative tool. While this was not so uncommon a response among a few veteran cyclists, it was not a point of view I found much evident among younger riders. And in fact, most older riders have also enthusiastically adopted the technology. Indeed, everyone I interviewed in 2013 used the application.

As I indicated previously, cyclists and runners have long tracked their mileage when they trained. This application tracks all the information that elite-caliber cyclists often struggled to manage in the past. For example, most serious athletes do interval training—timed sections where they increase their heart rate—and the Strava application has interval training built into its programming.

The Strava data that most dramatically changed the cycling experience are related to these timed sections, which riders can designate for popular rides. Some riders mount the GPS on their handlebars and essentially "race" even when they ride alone, a sometimes-dangerous endeavor. In fact, Strava has already been sued by the family of a rider in California who was killed while trying to reclaim his downhill record on a local ride. (He cut a corner and was hit by an oncoming vehicle.) Another rider, essentially "racing" with others on Strava on a San Francisco downhill that ran through a few stoplights and stop signs, crashed into an elderly pedestrian, who died in a hospital four days later.[31] Because Strava allows an individual to ride with everyone who is using the application in a particular area, it is impossible to ride alone if that person has his or her smart phone along.

At the end of any ride a Strava user's time (average speed) can be ranked against all other users who have carried a GPS device on the same route. There are, quite literally, hundreds of climbs in the region where I ride. Whenever

I have ridden with a cyclist who uses the Strava application there are always timed "King of the Mountain" (KOM) sections. Sometimes just a few riders have been clocked on these sections, but for the well-known local climbs times are listed for hundreds of ranked cyclists, including a few local professionals who train in the region. On routine rides, there are many users ranked against each other.

The KOM and timed sections of Strava rides are the features that have most changed people's riding habits. The cyclists I interviewed who routinely rode with others—on the weekly fast ride from a cycling shop, for example—invariably knew where the timed KOM sections of the course began and ended. One triathlete described how everyone "gets quiet" before the KOM sections—preparing themselves to push—and that it sometimes felt a little dangerous. "When everyone starts getting ready for the KOM," she told me, "it feels like they pay less attention to the people they are riding with, they all start moving around too much to get in position and it just kind of freaks me out . . . I want to scream at them to pay attention."[32]

This rider still used the application. Indeed, she was also proud to be the women's KOM for a few of the harder local climbs in the area. In fact, if someone beats her time she can sign up to receive an e-mail from Strava informing her of this fact. I found that Strava enabled an extraordinary level of Foucauldian surveillance on nearly the entire community of local cyclists. This surveillance had, quite literally, changed the way people rode their bicycles.

It also changed how people thought about their cycling experience. One of my steadiest riding partners during the summer I conducted this study is generally an early adopter of all technologies, so it was inevitable that he carried his smart phone with him when we rode together. After each ride, he immediately checked his statistics using Strava. Sometimes he sent me a post-ride e-mail with the ride profile. (See figure 4.). He would then dutifully tell me his rank: not just where he stood compared to other riders, but whether he had established any personal records. Often (really always), he seemed a little disappointed with his performance. After every ride he would reference his degree of fitness relative to a couple of years previous when he had "really been training a lot." This man does not race his bicycle and had no intention of entering any formal competitions, but still measured his experience as directly related to how fast he could ride. He was also intensely interested in who the strongest riders were on certain sections of the ride. "Tom is all over Strava," he once said with admiration of an acquaintance with whom he coached soccer. "He is a really strong cyclist." Remarkably, I later met Tom during the Tour de Burg—and interviewed him for this study—and even though we had never met before I had a reasonable level of knowledge concerning his cycling ability because it was so often referenced by my riding partner.

Tom was one of the more enthusiastic Strava users I encountered during this study. He is a professor at a local university and, like many academics, is clearly enamored with data. In the past, he had dabbled with competitive cycling and joined his college club team. At that time he had trained with a few national-caliber riders. Currently, by virtue of living in Harrisonburg, Virginia (see Chapter 5) he has continued to interact with top-level riders even though he no longer competes as a licensed category USCF racer. While his road riding career was relatively short—he described a series of disappointing races—he remains an avid cyclist. Within the context of the local riding community he is a strong road and mountain biker. He still routinely rides his road bike, but at the time I interviewed him was increasingly devoted to mountain biking, mostly because of the quality of the local riding.

Using Strava, Tom can compare himself to the best riders in the region, who sometimes happen to be among the best riders in the country. Perhaps the greatest current hope in terms of American international cycling, Joe Dombrowski, grew up near the Shenandoah Valley and has ridden locally. In effect, by using Strava Tom can sometimes compare himself to a world-class cyclist. He clearly finds this thrilling. Of course, the local professionals are faster, but he found this to be a motivation to go harder. Importantly, Tom also appreciated the cycling culture at Harrisonburg immensely: he routinely rode in groups with "real" people and particularly enjoyed the laid-back demeanor of the local cycling community as contrasted with those in other places he had lived. He was also thrilled that the inclusive cycling culture allowed him to sit in as best he could with the local professionals. But, he was also an enthusiastic Strava user because practically, even when he rode alone, it allowed him to ride with, and make comparisons to, these same riders.

For Tom, self-described as competitive in nature, the Strava application is an extraordinary motivational tool because of its ability to provide surveillance. He used Strava to discipline his body, and while I reacted negatively to this discipline, he and nearly everyone else I spoke with clearly saw the program in beneficial terms because it motivated them to ride faster.

Positive or Negative Discipline?: Technologies of Self-Realization

Here, the focus of this chapter changes, although it will continue to examine disciplining the body. Previously, I applied Foucauldian concepts to describe what might be characterized as a negative form of sporting discipline associated with increasing conformity and surveillance. Notably, Foucault also described acts of self-realization that might occur when people employed "technologies of self."[33] He sometimes stated that "ascetic" acts of care, using technologies of the body, could be venues of liberation from negative forms of discipline. He associated the act of knowing the self mainly with a level of expertise in certain knowledge areas, important for situating the self within the context of society and governance that increasingly acted to enforce negative modes of discipline. Ultimately, these forms of knowledge were regarded as useful for avoiding negative forms of discipline.

Not surprisingly, given his focus on the body, Foucault also outlined a program for being healthy—of caring for and maintaining one's body in order to maintain self-esteem and independent thought. This concept was later explicitly linked to "mindful body work" by other scholars. I have encountered studies that represent acts of sporting discipline such as yoga and bodybuilding, but these tend to be persuasively characterized as avenues of liberation, technologies of self-realization, by scholars who practiced and observed them.[34]

Similarly, triathletes and cyclists often know their bodies well. Some talk about their bodies, or specifically how they feel, nearly all the time. My tendency was not to interpret this particular preoccupation as liberating because for many triathletes, this intense focus on their bodies and the narrow goal of making them as fast as possible was almost the only thing they thought about. I sometimes thought that their preoccupation with disciplining their bodies led to rather debilitating social consequences and not toward cultivating an active program of resistance to discipline. It tended to narrow their experiences and views of the world. Sometimes discipline caused them to train so hard that they sustained very serious injuries over time.

One reason for different interpretations of bodily discipline may concern the word "ascetic." The word is sometimes associated with physical discipline and certainly with a pursuit of health and knowledge, but I tend to regard ascetic acts as creating a rich inner life. That did not seem to be the way many lifestyle athletes approached their sport. These acts seemed to me to be an extreme pursuit of one aspect of self-discipline, knowledge of the body, to the exclusion of others, such as knowledge of the mind.

But athletes' accounts of why they pursue these sports are important because, despite the extraordinary conformity I described previously, nearly all the people I spoke with regarded the disciplining of their bodies as an avenue for liberation. Triathletes characterize discipline as providing them with greater corporeal knowledge of their selves. One common narrative that I encountered among this population was that gaining control of their bodies made them machinelike. Eating and training right made them more efficient when they raced, but also allowed them to know their bodies to an extraordinary degree. On the one hand, making the body into a machine is perfectly in sync with Foucauldian insights about the direct relationship between increasing scientism and bodily discipline. Becoming machinelike seems like an extreme form of discipline for a human, although other academic and creative people have regarded machine/human interaction associated with cyborgs as a possible avenue for liberation.[35]

But among the athletes I interviewed, the discipline associated with being machinelike was regarded as universally positive. In fact, because they had wrested control of this body-machine, because they could now accomplish extraordinary physical feats—athletes regarded becoming machinelike as an addictive feature of the sport of triathlon. These men and women liked tinkering with their bodies, changing their discipline to see if it made them faster or more agile.

Pursuit of a Body Aesthetic: Discipline and Changing Self-Concept among Women Triathletes

As stated previously, all of the athletes I interviewed regarded their participation in sport as enabling. This was most often because it allowed them to assert some control over their bodies, which seemed, within the context of the demands of modern life, a particularly important act. In many respects it was the one domain over which they felt some control. As the corporeal knowledge of their bodies increased, which often corresponded with some notable physical accomplishments, these athletes often felt better about themselves.

Ethnographic studies of women in triathlon have often found that training the body is regarded as a very positive experience. These positive associations include a feeling of empowerment as women take control of their bodies and strong bonds created when training in both mixed and same-sex groups. Some researchers have even reported that women routinely have transformative experiences—that they fundamentally change with respect to how they perceive themselves. Often, as they grew stronger and became more competent triathletes they experience changes to their self-concept too.[36]

I often encounter women who have adopted such a strict adherence to discipline that the sport appears to be constraining rather than enabling. Indeed, other studies indicate that both men and women triathletes—but particularly the latter—tend to have high rates of eating disorders and be exercise-dependent.[37] In much of the interview reported below it will be self-evident that this particular athlete initially associated sporting discipline with certain unhealthy eating practices. In this case, participation in sport did not precipitate this athlete's bulimia, but sport was clearly related to it. A more general association between women athletes and higher rates of eating disorders is well established.[38] At the same time, all the women I interviewed who disclosed they had once had eating disorders also reported growing out of these conditions as they became immersed in sport.[39] They usually credited lifestyle sport with slowly helping them end their disordered eating, rather than causing these conditions to worsen. They also tended to state that participation in sport caused them to develop a greater acceptance of their bodies.

Initially, I tended to regard these women, like many of the men I interviewed, as being unselfconsciously disciplined, sometimes to the extent that their involvement in sport looked debilitating. Many of these people trained excessively and often hurt themselves, or they had such an intense and narrow interest in sport that they could think about little else. But, the fact that these interviews so often ended with a heartfelt account of how lifestyle sport had helped make them healthy, or had helped them to accept their bodies, was also a clear theme among the women I interviewed.

These accounts were often similar to a remarkable auto-ethnographic study I had encountered that described a recovery from anorexia through participation in triathlon.[40] Its author stated that she had been anorexic for eleven years and started training for triathlon after being released from a hospital. She assumed that her extraordinary workout regimen would pass for "normal" within the context of training for a triathlon. In effect, she believed that she might be able to train more and eat less because she would be considered a triathlete. But eventually, she began training with a group of athletes and slowly, over time, adopted their patterns of training and eating. She vividly recalls her distress when told that she sometimes needed to rest her body. To have the strength to train with this group she found herself eating the same kinds of foods they did. Over time, she developed a different sense of her body.[41]

I routinely collected similar, if less dramatic, narratives of transformation from the women I interviewed, particularly related to how they thought about their bodies. The women in triathlon often seemed even more enthusiastic than the men, and triathletes in general are as enthusiastic a group as I have ever encountered. Most of the other reasons that women offered for doing triathlon were not so different from the men's. They mainly reported that, given their work routine or other life stresses, triathlon training "kept them sane," or that exercise was "therapy." Both the athlete interviewed below and her husband (also an avid triathlete) were clinical psychologists, working in the same office, and most often counseled children. These children usually had psychological disorders considered severe enough that they had been referred by a state social welfare agency, the local schools, or the court system. They were living in home situations associated with poverty, patterns of abuse, fractured families, and the like that were, these athletes made clear, often very grim. Within the context of this job, this triathlete, referencing why she trained, stated (my italics): "*It's my sanity, you know?* At work I hear really awful things. I sometimes see really awful things. I often have to deal with really unhappy people . . . And then I come home and I ride my bike. And it's great. It's my therapy. I think I get my best processing done while I'm on my bike."

This was a very strong athlete who was routinely a top finisher in her age group at races. She trained seriously and had completed an Ironman distance race a few years previously. She had been racing competitively for about six years. But, as was common with the athletes I interviewed, she also described a series of somewhat extraordinary injuries by way of providing some context for her recent performances, many of which she regarded as disappointing. In this respect, even though she was a consistent top finisher, when she discussed her performance it was often within a context of how injury kept her from being more efficient. And many of these injuries seemed serious.

Like other women I interviewed, "Brenda" often related the eating disorder she was experiencing at the time to her injuries and overtraining. Indeed, she directly associated her past bulimia to "the dark side" of her involvement in sport. Like the other women I interviewed, she did not disclose her bulimia to me in response to a direct question concerning eating disorders. Rather, it came up during a discussion of past achievements, or simply in response to the question as to why the couple started to do triathlon. In this case, Brenda was chronicling a series of disappointing races that she attributed to injury before she disclosed her eating disorder.

> BRENDA: I have been injured [until recently] for the past three years. I have had two stress fractures. One was just in 2011, just after Ironman Louisville. And then I had another one this past year. So I spent a good chunk of the last two years on crutches . . .
>
> STEVE: So, is that the same facture or . . . ?
>
> BRENDA: Same foot, different bones. And then the year before I had a really awful thing going on with my hamstring and my I-T band, just some really awful muscular and bone friction. . . . So I have had just one really awful thing after another. So my run has suffered because I have been really conservative as I came back. But I was, at one point, getting really fast on the run, but then I kept injuring myself. I had some really serious knee problems, and a pretty haphazard training program for a while too. I had to take weeks off at a time when I was training for that marathon.
>
> STEVE: So you would run hard, hurt yourself, take some time off . . .
>
> BRENDA: Well, yeah, I had an idea that I was supposed to go easy, then hard on the weekends. I had read some books about training and knew this much. So sometimes I would run hard and then have to stop. And I ended up spending a lot of time before that marathon on an elliptical machine because it

did not hurt my knees... I actually ran the marathon in one of those J-knee brace things because my knee was rubbing the hell out of my I-T band...

STEVE: That sounds...

BRENDA: Yeah... I know. So I think the *dark part of my endurance sport history is that I got into the sport for some not very good reasons*... Issues related to an eating disorder, and stuff like that. *So all this [the injuries] are related to what might be considered the dark side of my involvement in the sport.* ...

STEVE: O.K....

BRENDA: So, this has actually been a very healing process...

STEVE: Uh... I can tell you this, and this is not something I ever asked other athletes about specifically, but this comes up pretty often with the women athletes I have been interviewing.... I often have women often tell me they are former bulimics. It is not something I ask about, but I probably should, given how often it is coming up.

BRENDA: Well, yes, it becomes a socially acceptable way to manage the disorder... So yeah, in high school I struggled with that a lot and got into running for, you know, not very healthy reasons. And then training with my friend [in college] for the ten-miler. Well, she had a very healthy self-image, but these problems were rampant at college. But Julia [this athlete's training partner] was just very nurturing and feeling in terms of teaching me how to run. To do it because you love it. Or because it is a beautiful day outside. But it took years, well... that marathon... I was just adamant that I was going to do that marathon and I was not healthy when I was training for it.

Later in this conversation this athlete indicated, like others, that when she began to ride a bicycle—in this case with her boyfriend (now her husband)—it became physically impossible for her to ride any distance without eating food along the way. Notable, though, was that Brenda believed her past bulimia, not the triathlon and marathon training, was to blame for the stress fractures. Indeed, at the time of this interview she was actively trying to get pregnant. She had recently visited a physician where she had detailed this past history concerning her eating disorder, which she worried might negatively impact their chances of conceiving.

Importantly, I cannot generalize from the relatively small number of women I interviewed to the experiences of all women in triathlon. But it has been commonly found, for example, that women in collegiate sports report higher incidences of eating disorders. Of course, causality—whether participation in sport can contribute to an eating disorder or whether the eating disorder may cause people to engage in certain sports—can be hard to pin down. Among the few cases in this study, the eating disorder often seemed to predate the participation in triathlon. Like others, these women reported that losing weight and creating a certain type of body was a primary motivation for entering the sport of triathlon. This is similar to the motivations that have been found in other studies of women's sports, and particularly true as it relates to workout routines like aerobics.[42] Notably, similar to the women I interviewed, other studies of women triathletes indicated that many women begin training for triathlon with an idea of losing weight, but as they became more competent in sport this became a less important reason as to why they continued.[43]

Among the small group of women interviewed in this study I encountered accounts in which participation in triathlon was first associated with an "unhealthy" relationship with food, but where participation in the sport was also ultimately responsible for eliminating some unhealthy eating practices and negative body concepts. In effect, many interviewees reported that the nature of training for triathlon made a sometimes-unhealthy relationship with food increasingly untenable as they immersed themselves in sport. They credited routine training with changing a negative association with food to an increasingly positive one. These athletes began to feel an explicit connection between the food they ate and how they performed. They came to regard eating right as necessary for competition. This trend is supported, to a modest extent, by another study that found it was mostly beginners who self-reported eating disorders. It may be that the women who remain in the sport have a greater tendency to grow out of these disorders.[44] For example, Brenda clearly associated her participation in triathlon as ultimately helping her overcome bulimia. She reported: "And you know, it's funny because when I was struggling with bulimia it was never a really an effective way to manage weight anyway . . . And now, doing triathlon makes me feel better. I am just much healthier. I feel much more healthy. And I am sure that a look much healthier too."

Most of the time, the women's body aesthetic portrayed in triathlon magazines is not so different than the men's, showing the same lean muscularity.[45] In a few cases, these women do appear dangerously lean. Brenda stated during the interview that she appreciated when the professional triathletes in the magazines had "normal" sized bodies. But in some respects, even the normal-sized women's body in triathlon is more muscular and lean then what was considered an ideal women's body not so long ago.[46] Still, all the women I interviewed ultimately regarded their body discipline as liberating. They clearly saw developing a strong body as enabling.

Importantly, there is an indication that an ideal representation of "healthy" women's bodies that generally appear in magazines for women, which also approximates the ideal body of many women triathletes, was developed during the 1980s. In this period—during the aerobics craze, for example—women were told they should be toned but not muscular. Some scholars have noted that these bodies were still fetishized and sexualized even though they look significantly different than in previous decades.[47] In some respect, it is an open question as to whether the women and the men I interviewed felt good about themselves as they disciplined their bodies because most had, to some degree, largely succeeded in crafting a body aesthetic considered pleasing to others even if it was not quite the ideal representation they had hoped for when they began training. But most often, the athletes themselves associated their now-strong bodies with their increasing satisfaction with themselves.

Pursuit of a Body Aesthetic: Discipline among Men in Triathlon

It was also clear that many men trained in triathlon as a means of achieving a certain body ideal. Like women, men triathletes have a greater likelihood of self-reporting eating disorders and being exercise-dependent.[48] Indeed, in print magazines associated with the sport the pursuit of an ideal triathlon body—how to get lean and muscular, for example—was apparent in every issue I coded. In this respect, the sport offered an opportunity to examine how men pursued an ideal body aesthetic that was, like women's, directly associated with disciplining the body. At least one article in each of the magazines I coded for this study dealt with how to attain the ideal body type of a triathlete. After perusing triathlon magazines published during the past twenty years, I came to regard the ideal body type among men in triathlon as "classic." By this, I mean that the men in triathlon admire and aspire to have physiques approximating a Greek classical ideal.

A photograph of Ken Souza, a well-known duathlete, was published in 1993 on the first cover of *Inside Triathlon*. (See figure 5.) In some respects, this image is not much different than the paintings and statues of male athletes participating in the gymnasium in ancient Greece. Practically, the body appears to approximate what is increasingly a standard representation in men's health and fitness magazines. (However, triathletes often appear somewhat leaner.) At the same time, I may associate triathlon with the Greek aesthetic because triathletes once routinely ran around in so little clothing. Indeed, most were not self-conscious in the least about showing people their bodies. It is notable, though, that many people commented on the fact that Souza's attire was often skimpier than his peers'. He was most often a duathlete (a run-bike-run specialist) in the 1980s and 1990s, so he did not have to wear a Speedo when he raced. He did so by preference. I think it is safe to say he felt comfortable in his body. Even those who took issue with his style probably admired Souza's physique. Indeed, he had crafted a body designed to go fast—he was among the most accomplished athletes in the sport—but was clearly content with his

FIGURE 5 Duathlete Ken Souza on the inaugural cover of *Inside Triathlon*.

physical appearance too. The "Speedo aesthetic" has largely disappeared in the sport as skintight apparel with greater coverage has been designed specifically for swimming and cycling.

Academic studies of how men employ discipline to craft body aesthetics have often focused on bodybuilding.[49] Comparatively, triathletes are probably not as self-conscious as bodybuilders in terms of their pursuit of a certain body aesthetic, but many clearly have very specific ideas as to how they should look. These athletes look closely at each other, often as a means of figuring out how fast the athletes around them might be. They keep track of their friends too.

One compliment commonly exchanged at the beginning of a race, if someone appears to have trained hard, is "You look fit." This is directly associated with the idea that the athlete looks fast—but within this exchange is the implicit assumption that the athlete also looks good.

I later regretted that I had not asked athletes specifically about body issues during my interviews, but even so these were always referenced by women (see above) and also, albeit more indirectly, by most men. Among many men, like women, it was common for weight gain associated with a job, increased commitments, or other stress to be related to the decision to pursue sport. The men I interviewed usually referenced their weight in offhand narratives probably common among many people, even those who do not do sport. Many indicated they had experienced life changes—had kids, changed jobs, or started a business—and gained some weight. So, they made a decision to take up physical activity. "Bob," the husband of the woman interviewed above—was in his early thirties and, like "Brenda," also worked as a clinical psychologist. But he described a period when he was working for a small newspaper as a sports reporter and had slowly gained weight on the job. He was clearly motivated to lose some weight when he started cycling, a sport he discovered after he covered a local race.

He indicated he had lost close to twenty ponds as a result of cycling and triathlon. He vaguely referenced how he looked before he began training, stating, "I was never obese, but I was getting pretty big for someone my size."[50] Most often, these types of narratives directly associated weight loss with the fact that the athletes now felt great, or had more energy. It was clearly regarded as a positive development in their lives.

Developing Function and Form: The Body as Machine

As stated previously, I often heard athletes—both men and women—describe another as "a machine." This was always a compliment: if someone said that Ken Souza was a machine in his prime, athletes would immediately recognize this as high praise. It describes the fact that Souza was a remarkably steady and dominant athlete when he raced and trained. He was so steady that he was a machine. So while body aesthetics are important to endurance athletes, they were usually also associated with very specific notions related to athletic performance. All knew, for example, that the best and most serious cyclists, over time, tend to develop bodies that are "stripped down." They are often very lean with highly defined muscles because they train constantly and low body fat makes them more efficient on a bicycle.

The athletes I interviewed often chronicled their body "deficiencies" in both clinical and funny manners. "My ass is tremendous . . . which seems to be great for the bike, but it slows me down when I run," reported one woman, laughing. In another case a man told me he was so lean that he did not have enough fat to be buoyant in the water when he swam: "I just sink like a stone." Many also made references to their sporting bodies as machines that they were actively trying to refine. Or they sometimes called others they admired "a machine" or described them with machinelike language.

I interviewed one man—a strong cyclist who did the Tour de Burg—who was described as a "hammer" by another rider. In general, this meant that "Tom" pushed "big gears" and was a powerful rider. This description also fit his physiology. He was about 5′6″ in height and relatively stocky for such an adept long-distance cyclist. During the course of our conversation he referenced his stature in a simultaneously funny and self-conscious manner. Basically, he said that if the other athletes he rode with were lined up beside him, he would always win the game of "who does not belong in this picture." But my impression was that Tom was not overly concerned with creating a certain body aesthetic. He knew he was never going to affect the "long and lean" aesthetic often associated with long distance cycling, but he was happy enough with his body because he had fashioned himself into an athlete considered fast by others.[51] Indeed, he seemed to enjoy the fact that he did not fit when compared to other cyclist's bodies.

So it was routine for athletes I spoke with, both men and women, to reference their bodies as directly related to performance. Triathletes, more than others, tended to describe their bodies as machines. Some used the analogy to indicate that what they ate and how they trained were directly associated with their performance. One can regard this tendency to describe the body as machine as related to Foucauldian concepts of discipline as described above, but the athletes clearly regarded making themselves machinelike as enabling, an act of taking control of their bodies. In some respects this narrative seemed more evident among the women I interviewed. Some said they entered triathlon to pursue a body aesthetic, but as they became immersed in the enterprise they increasingly changed their ideas of what they should look like and even embraced, to some degree, what had been considered liabilities in the past. (Think, for example, of that "tremendous ass" that was useful for cycling.) Often, these athletes increasingly came to value function (how fast they went) over form (what they looked like). When their bodies felt strongest and fastest they became increasingly satisfied with their appearance, too, even if it was in a body that was somehow different than an ideal they once associated with sport.[52]

Conclusion

Is becoming disciplined—sometimes to the extent that a person is described as "machinelike"—an enabling or a constraining experience? Earlier, I indicated that a single person could embody both the negative and positive aspects of a social act. Ultimately, this is how I came to regard much of the discipline associated with triathlon. Always, though, I regarded it as extraordinary. The conformity and the uniformity of thought associated with bodily performance—the totality with which scientific training is applied to an act regarded as leisure—all seemed to constrain these athletes' experiences. Sometimes it did not appear to be a very healthy endeavor either, particularly when athletes recounted their injuries. In this respect, discipline did not seem like an avenue for individual liberation. Indeed, it often appeared to epitomize the negative discipline closely associated with Foucault's well-known early work, *Discipline and Punish*.

But then there are the accounts given by nearly all of the athletes themselves that training hard and scientifically ultimately gave them greater control over their bodies, and even more strikingly, kept them sane within the context of their work. That training was "therapy." Indeed, these athletes clearly regarded their training as liberating. And despite their reports of self-injury, they most often directly associated training with the creation of a healthy body. In a country where a sedentary lifestyle and obesity are increasingly normative—a fact that some athletes referenced—is it possible that these extraordinary forms of discipline might be regarded as a liberating act, perhaps even a "healthy" response to the stresses of modern life?

Still, when I looked at the way triathletes train—or even as I watched a regular riding partner who was not a competitive cyclist flip through his Strava rankings immediately after we finished a ride—I most often thought that participation in these sports increasingly constituted a form of negative discipline. It constrained human behavior more, rather than less. With this particular cycling partner, one well-informed about this study, I developed the habit of asking him sincerely after we rode together whether he really needed to look at Strava to know how he felt about our ride. I asked this question in terms of the entire experience—whether the day was nice for example—but it included whether he felt strong and fast during the ride too. For me, the answer to these questions were largely unrelated to the information he might find on the Strava program. I felt that it was entirely possible he could feel good even if he rode slower.

This cycling partner, also my friend, regards this as thinking that only an academic might engage in. For him, it is self-evident that he is better in all ways when he is faster. Indeed, he is mystified why anyone would not use Strava, which is so clearly an enabling piece of technology. It is designed to provide more knowledge—not less—and it therefore has to be regarded as enabling. To him, it opens horizons, rather than narrowing them. In short, my riding partner consults his Strava times religiously because, to his way of thinking, it provides *exactly* the information *he needs to know* to in order to make a judgment about how he should feel about his riding. Feeling good about going more slowly, even if he is a recreational rider, is simply not logical.

Irrespective of whether the discipline described above is regarded as enabling or constrictive, it is self-evident that when an endeavor evolves from play (early mountain biking) into sport (competitive mountain biking) it becomes more highly structured. The change increases the conformity among those who participate. In my opinion, although triathletes often regard themselves as unique within the context of social norms—as being non-conformists—they actually demonstrate an extraordinary degree of group conformity within the context of their primary identity group. In other words, triathletes eat, drink, sleep, and consume products in a nearly identical fashion. And because they exercise such a high degree of conformity, manufacturers often find it easy to sell them the same products. They are model consumers. Indeed, even among other lifestyle athletes, triathletes are often considered to be the most methodical as it relates to their conformity to sporting norms.

In my estimation, the "scientific" means of "correct training" controls nearly every aspect (eating, sleeping, and training) of many triathletes' existences. This commonality of experience is what makes triathletes such a cohesive group, and perhaps explains their sometimes-evangelical enthusiasm for the sport. In effect, the totality with which they regulate and discipline their bodies in terms of what they eat and how they train is why they so closely self-identify with each other. Their level of group conformity is incredibly high, which inevitably increases the bonds—the shared experience—that these athletes feel with each other.

There are obviously benefits to group conformity. Moreover, it might also be considered an inevitable social condition. Conformity and norms help people to define a group ("We are triathletes"). It makes the group behavior cohesive ("We train together on Monday and Fridays for our 'fast' rides"). Groups define "us" ("We are highly trained, exceptionally fit and dedicated athletes") and then help distinguish "us" from "them" ("We are not like bowlers, golfers, and baseball players"). This can also help create a feeling of group solidarity and establish group pride ("What we do is notable because it is difficult"). Indeed, allegiance to any group norm, and participation with any sub-culture, can help people feel special. All of the rules of triathlon, and its informal modes of discipline, help create a group affinity, the degree of which is remarkable. Of course, people have long closely associated themselves with the sports they play, but members of this group appear to have a high identity salience with regard to perceiving themselves as being, first and foremost, "a triathlete."

4

Types of Lifestyle Athletes
and Team Touch of Grey

• •

In the previous chapters I described the considerable structural constraints that the modern economy imposes on those who participate in lifestyle sport. To a large extent these ensure that people conduct themselves in much the same way when they pursue sport; however, athletes also express some level of agency, individual decision-making, which distinguishes them from one another. In this chapter I construct a simple system of classification—a taxonomy or typography—that encompasses a few characteristics and motivations of athletes who participate in lifestyle sport.[1] I mostly conceived of this taxonomy using two variables. One was related to the participant's level of *conformity* with accepted societal norms, including those of the sports they were engaged in. The other was a general measure of an athlete's *past participation in physical activities*. I used the physical activity as opposed to participation in sport because some of the athletes I interacted with, the ones I identify as "Free Spirits," were highly active as children—they constantly rode their bikes, they skateboarded, many had motorcycles—but were seldom involved in more organized sports. By way of contrast, the "Method Athletes" tended to have considerable experience in highly organized team and individual sports. In particular, many were members of swim teams. I would have labeled past participation in physical activity in both these groups as "high," even though their activities differed dramatically.

Typologies are imperfect, and it is possible that some individuals possess characteristics represented in each of the different types, although some characteristics are exclusive to one group. I will later describe some specific details of the backgrounds of the Touch of Grey twenty-four-hour mountain bike team. To some degree, each member has characteristics associated with the groups below, but none has a perfect fit.[2] Following the general description of each of these athletic types I give a few examples of the individuals I used as models in the construction of these categories.

My impression is that participation in lifestyle sport is much higher among long-time athletes than those who come to these sports with little or no past physical activity. In fact, the majority of the athletes I knew and interviewed had continually engaged in sport. They often began mountain biking and triathlon after they had aged out of other sports. Relatively few athletes who participated in triathlon and mountain biking as a regular pursuit had little or no past experience with sport or some other physical activity. In fact, during this study I had to make a special attempt to find endurance athletes who had not been athletes in the past.

By far, most of the athletes I interviewed were highly conformist with respect to both societal norms and the norms imposed by their sport. I think this is likely related to the degree to which the modern economy effectively dictates how sport should be played. Still, it was not too hard to find a few nonconformists, particularly among mountain bikers, who seemed to derive some satisfaction from flouting societal norms and sometimes even the specific orthodoxies of their chosen sport. Triathlon is somewhat exceptional in this regard, being constructed in a manner that tends to insure near-absolute conformity. Indeed, nonconformity in this sport is officially and unofficially sanctioned in a number of ways. Given its emphasis on routine, standards of practice, and standard systems of training, it is actually quite difficult to both be a nonconformist and participate in triathlon.

Typologies are useful as a means of thinking about categories of people among whom we want to make comparisons. When we think about categories of people it is routine to construct an ideal type, an epitome. Ask basketball coaches about their ideal point guard and they will answer with a series of specific attributes concerning size, skill, and intelligence. Sociologists construct ideal types in order to organize information and make comparisons. Max Weber pioneered the use of ideal types, which he described an as mental constructions (that is, not describing a specific person or institution) with a number of variables that might be considered a perfect standard of this type. Importantly, these constructions are ideal in that no person can ever embody all their characteristics. Moreover, as many have pointed out, specifying and rigidly defining a "type" is a reductionist enterprise. It simplifies the world to a great extent.[3] So, rather than think of these types as set in stone, regard these two variables as a continuum along which an athlete might fall. And, importantly, depending on his or her temperament and specific sport, the athlete probably moves around in terms of their fit with the table in Figure 6.

The Free Spirits and Eccentrics

Although the type of athlete I call Free Spirits exists in team sports, a team-oriented coach might consider them selfish, or oddballs, perhaps even trouble-makers. These men and women seem to be motivated by an internal drive to succeed, but unwilling to succeed on other peoples' terms. Many of the athletes I associated with this type were in superb physical condition, but were primarily drawn to eclectic and obscure sports that they regarded as physically demanding. For example, one athlete I placed in this category had previously held a record in "distance" Frisbee events before becoming a mountain bike enthusiast. Many Free Spirits described themselves as active kids who participated very little in organized sports when they were younger. Those who did didn't always find it an enjoyable experience. The structure of participation in team sports is ill-suited for many of these individuals' temperaments, particularly if the sport involves any kind of inactivity between the action or extensive instruction from a coach. In some respects, many of these athletes seem to have a slightly, if not excessively, manic disposition that finds them most satisfied when they are involved in a difficult physical task. Sometimes it appeared that they became more manic the more difficult the physical conditions they encountered.

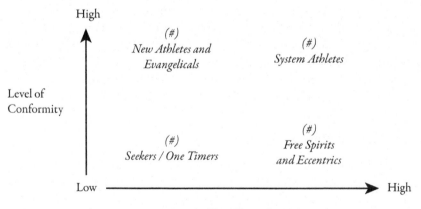

FIGURE 6 Typology of lifestyle sport athletes.

Free Spirits tend to be more creative and artistic in temperament than other kinds of athletes. Some routinely wear vintage cycling clothing. Some commute to work on single-speed bikes. They are more likely to have a hand-crafted bicycle frame made to their specifications. One athlete I knew ordered a custom Grove Innovations frame that glowed in the dark after she was hit by a vehicle while cycling at night. She never wore a helmet. Free Spirits are often iconoclastic in their beliefs and express a variety of opinions. Most of those I knew appeared to enjoy the company of other people. They are not extreme introverts, but many seem perfectly content to spend large amounts of time by themselves. If they are working on a project, particularly one that they regard as important, they sometimes appear manic until it is finished. They tend to see their participation in sport as an extension of their general personality. In many cases, these individuals spend much more time training in their respective sports than other athletic types, but are less likely to claim that they are serious or extremely dedicated athletes. In general, the ones I interviewed framed their participation in the sport as "fun" or as "play," even though a few performed at elite levels. They tended to not have extremely routinized training habits. They did follow general guidelines, and certainly prepared hard for some races, but they were generally ad hoc in their approach to training.

In direct contrast to the Free Spirits are the athletes who have a strict reliance on stable, largely unchanging, routines that characterize their approach to sport. In popular lingo, these athletes are "hard workers," "conscientious," "steady." What is interesting about these descriptions is that they are often applied to how athletes train and not their absolute dedication to the sport. Free Spirits may train continually and even harder than methodical athletes, but be considered undisciplined because they do not adhere to a specific daily regimen. Likewise, methodical athletes may train less, but their dedication to the sport is often judged to be higher because they have an easily discernable, easily identifiable regimen that is geared toward fulfilling certain goals. Free Spirits may be noncommittal concerning when they plan to race (entering an event at the last moment) or even which races they plan to do, and are not likely to be too concerned if they have a bad performance.

The Method Men and Women

Methodical athletes adopt strict training methods and are often prepping for specific races. All the triathletes I interviewed who were preparing for an Iron-man competition were highly methodical, for example. They tend to articulate very specific goals, usually particular interval times they want to achieve, and are usually concerned if their performance at a race does not fulfill these goals.

Free Spirits are unlikely to have adopted a specific regimen, a specific time frame, and a specific methodology as to how they train. They sometimes play it by ear, perhaps doing hard workouts when they feel good and taking days off when they feel subpar. Methodical athletes have strict regimens, have established goals, and engage in meticulous planning. They dutifully keep track of their physiology when they train. They are less likely than other athletic types to deviate from their training regimen. In general, even if they are tired or otherwise overtrained, they are likely to continue to adhere to whatever workout standard they have planned.

These are the types of athletes who ride or run along the exact same routes. If it is a circular route, they usually ride in the same direction. They know, to the nearest tenth of mile, exactly how far each of their training rides is. Furthermore, Methodical athletes are much more likely to keep training logs concerning their workouts. They are more likely to carefully monitor their heart rates, exertion, and average speed per mile. These are the athletes who never miss a master's swim workout, a planned ride with the bike club, or a weekly (or even daily) regimen of club running. They are familiar with a wide range of physiological studies regarding the most efficient ways to train. They adhere rigorously to the standard distances, seek out standard races, meticulously care for their equipment, and make judgments concerning exactly what they need to buy after very careful, and very deliberate, calculations.

While not completely immune to the scenery where they are training—these athletes have favorite rides or runs that they describe as aesthetically pleasing—Methodicals are much more likely to substitute technology for the beauty of nature. I interviewed several athletes, all training for Ironman distance races, who had adopted a cycling regimen that included using an indoor trainer. They dutifully followed their interior schedule even when the weather for riding outside was excellent. For Methodical athletes, once a routine is established—which they often do for every aspect of the training regimen, from stretches and warm-up periods to exertion rates at a specific point—they rarely deviate from their program.

For people who are not tied to a specific methodology, or who are not as methodical to the degree that these athletes are, these individuals can be both exasperating and entertaining. On the one hand, it is nice to have a steady training partner who is constantly aware of the time, miles per hour achieved, and distance traveled. But at other times this strict conformity to method can prove irritating. For instance, I interviewed a woman who was married to a "Method man." She tended to be highly methodical in her training too, but expressed some exasperation that her husband often refused to deviate from their prescribed routines: to extend a training ride, for example, because it was a beautiful day.

These individuals are not inclined to have nontraditional jobs. Among the group I interviewed were middle managers, engineers, and healthcare providers. In some respects, Methodical athletes' regimens lack any aspects associated with pure play. Their sport may look like a fairly joyless endeavor. In some of the most extreme cases this may be true, but I found that many of these athletes experienced considerable satisfaction from participation in sport, in particular when their plans worked perfectly. In this respect the sport was satisfying insofar as they met their goals. Indeed, many informed me that engaging in physical activity without a set of specific goals—cycling for the sheer joy of it, for example—was impossible. Indeed, a primary reason for their participation in sport was to have a goal. This sounds as if Methodical athletes are humorless, but this was not true for most of the ones I interacted with. The majority were extremely considerate, temperate, outgoing, and pleasant. Moreover, their affinity with their sport was every bit as strong as the Free Spirits'. They just needed to have a plan.

I also encountered an interesting subgroup of very methodical athletes who had become aware that their strict adherence to a routine was considered extreme by their peers. In some cases these athletes were attempting to incorporate more spontaneity into their training routines. Typical of Method Men and Women, however, they were doing this through planning: by scheduling a day during the month when they could "do whatever I want."

In one case, an athlete's strict adherence to training methodologies caused him to be routinely teased by his training partners, some of whom delighted in trying to make him break his training patterns. They might decide to ride together at a pace just outside this athlete's prescribed heart-rate zone for a particular workout to see if they could goad him into breaking his discipline. They might take the batteries out of his heart-rate monitor just before a ride. The athlete in question was remarkably self-aware concerning his training temperament. In effect, he embraced the fact that he was method-driven and could laugh about some of the more extreme routines he had developed over time.

New Athletes, Evangelicals, and True Believers

I found that most Evangelical and New Athletes tend to be highly methodical in their approach to sport, perhaps because they had so little experience with it until later in life. One common reason for their entry into endurance sport was related to health concerns. A couple of the athletes that I put in this category had become morbidly obese and were told to adopt an exercise regimen in order to reduce threats to their health. Others were heavy smokers and took up athletics once they quit smoking. Others had had cancer scares. In this regard, it is not hard to see why these athletes regard their newly found exercise regimen as an important activity, perhaps the most important in their lives. In many respects, it is directly tied to their overall well-being and their prescribed regimen directly relates to the most fundamental of all human endeavors: staying alive.

Other athletes may implicitly understand that they exercise in order to live longer, healthier lives, but many of these Evangelical and New Athletes had confronted very specific risks to their health. They had adopted an exercise regimen to negate these risks. Many believed their new lifestyle, one closely associated with working out, dramatically improved their quality of life. While many lifestyle athletes consider themselves fanatical concerning their need to exercise, it makes sense that those who have faced their own mortality and adopted exercise as a means of prolonging their life—which they often believed was in danger—would become more evangelical with respect to the importance of exercise.

Two friends of mine, whom I will call "John" and "Joanne," were primary catalysts for my creation of the Evangelical and New Athlete type. Both had been morbidly obese and adopted a multi-sport lifestyle as a means of affecting dramatic health changes. We were introduced during this transition and I watched them methodically take on the various attributes of the sporting culture. John and Joanne often hired other friends of mine as their personal trainers. When I first met them at a local race where they were spectators, they were wildly enthusiastic about triathlon. Indeed, they clearly regarded triathletes in the area as something of a template for how they might also approach the sport. During this period, they actually purchased a local bicycle shop that they eventually sold to a friend of mine. Both were in their middle forties when they adopted the sporting lifestyle. Neither had been an athlete or concerned with sports in the past. In their professional lives they were extremely successful; they often attributed their past physical inactivity to the fact that they had been busy building a regional company into a profitable enterprise.

The couple achieved varying degrees of success in triathlon. John, in particular, was a natural athlete who, as his body changed, affected the mannerisms of a man who had always been an athlete. He was about six feet tall, and dropped from three hundred pounds to about one hundred and seventy-five. In effect, he lost nearly half his body weight during the course of becoming a multi-sport athlete. More remarkable, he looked as if he had always been an athlete. He was fortunate in that his body seemed to adapt to the weight loss, which was accompanied by some fairly serious physiological changes. For instance, he told me that he felt fortunate his skin, which sagged a bit as he became lean, had remained fairly elastic. Had he been introduced to sport at a younger age I think it is likely that he would have been an exceptional athlete.

John completed the Hawaii Ironman in a very respectable time following his fiftieth birthday. From the time he began training, this had been a primary goal. As in the case of most methodical athletes I encountered, a specific goal was absolutely integral to his participation in lifestyle sport. While John never stopped training entirely, following this race his enthusiasm for triathlon did diminish. I think this was likely because of many variables. First, many of the primary group we were associated with began training less at this time for various professional and personal reasons. Also, John had used participation in the Hawaii Ironman at this particular age as a primary goal. Afterward, he was at a loss as to what his next goal should be. Furthermore, Joanne, due in part to a series of injuries, was not as enthusiastic about triathlon as when they began, and was gradually moving away from active participation. In general, while she experienced a dramatic physical transformation too, Joanne never had the same level of success that John did. She also struggled to maintain a constant weight after suffering her injuries. She once confided to me that she found triathlon difficult in that she knew, unlike other activities she engaged in, that her performance would inevitably be affected by physical limitations regardless of how hard she trained.

This period in these two Evangelical and New Athletes' lives might be regarded as a stage through which they passed. At the time I knew them they continued to exercise (more moderately). I think that the changes that resulted from their participation in triathlon made a lasting impression on their personalities. Still, over time they did become less evangelical with regard to the sport. I think that other athletes who go through similar metamorphoses—perhaps not as dramatic as John and Joanne's—often remain committed to the sport that helped them to effect physical changes they regard as positive. These activities are most often adopted as a lifestyle change designed to produce weight loss, but other types of change can also precipitate a devotion to a physical pursuit. Former smokers who have managed to quit for a long period of time and who have taken up an exercise regimen exhibit some of the same characteristics. I did not survey any cancer survivors, but they also seem to be well-represented in many lifestyle sports.

Seekers and One-Timers

Before I begin my description of Seekers and One-Times, it is important to reemphasize that these categories are not exact. Furthermore, as a proportion of all the athletes with whom I came into contact, these individuals should be regarded as rare. In effect, my descriptions of this type of athlete, unlike Free Spirits, Methodicals, and Evangelical and New Athletes, are based on very few people. In fact, during this study I found so few that I considered not including them in this text. Still, I think that more of these athletes may be out there despite the fact that I had a hard time locating them.

In general, I think that athletes in these categories may have maintained the highest degree of "play" in their sport participation. They are not methodical in their habits. They are not consumers of sport magazines, sport equipment, and sport paraphernalia. In fact, one athlete I interacted with tended to buy her equipment at yard sales and thrift shops. If they train at all, it is generally for a short duration, perhaps a week before an event, and even then they are not particularly methodical. Seekers and One-Timers care very little about their performance beyond completing the event. In many cases the impetus for their participation is an annual sporting event—a century ride, a canoe race, a triathlon—taking place in close proximity to their home towns. In effect, they participate because the event happens every year, does not require an extraordinary effort in terms of planning (for example, they can sleep in their own bed the night before), and they think it looks like fun. They would not frame their participation as a lifestyle choice. Instead, they would tend to say that the event was close by, supported a good cause, and was a nice way to spend the day.

Some types of events seem to attract these kinds of participants. I once routinely did a "fun" relay—a run, cycle, and canoe race that raised money for a local charity—many of whose participants lived close by. The race was a corollary to larger town events that were taking place the same day. While some very fit athletes showed up, many local participants were not serious athletes, knew they were not serious athletes, and actually reveled in the fact that they were not serious athletes. As some of them crossed the finish line they began joking about their poor state of physical well-being. I watched one man pretend to collapse from exhaustion, crawl over the finish line, and then symbolically kiss the ground. His friends—all ample in girth—quickly supplied him with some carbs (a beer) to aid in his recovery.

These folks are easily identifiable at these types of races. They ride obsolete bikes that they don't know are obsolete, perhaps with kick-stands and sheepskin seat covers. The bikes may or may not have gears; if they do, the participants may not know how to use them. I base this on the experience of a One-Timer I will call "Sharon" who once did a seventy-five-mile bicycle ride in Maryland because her friends talked her into it. She used a childhood bicycle that had been hanging in a garage for many years and was tremendously heavy. She had no riding equipment except a borrowed, obsolete jug of a helmet. The bike had gears, but she did not attempt to use them—she did not know how— despite the fact that she was pedaling through a hilly area in the toughest possible gear. After the ride ended someone showed her how to shift these gears. She laughed when she told me this story.

One of the other participants on this ride, a Seeker in his fifties at the time whom I will call "Gerald," had loaned Sharon the obsolete helmet. He had an assortment of minor physical ailments, but Gerald and his daughter had become cycling enthusiasts after taking a bicycle trip together through Europe. By the time I met Gerald his enthusiasm was largely an abstraction in that, so far as I could tell, he rode his bike very little. But when he did ride, I think it is safe to say that he enjoyed himself immensely. He later loaned my friend a bicycle seat when she complained about the one she had. Indeed, this was the one aspect of cycling to which Gerald had given considerable attention: he had a magnificent plush cover on his bicycle seat. Invariably, the few times I met Gerald we talked about cycling because he knew about this study and that I had raced in the past. On one occasion, when we were in his house, he showed me his bike. It was obvious that it had not been used in many years. The tires were flat, he had to move stuff out of the way in his garage in order to retrieve it, and Gerald was not quite sure where his equipment was. He seemed stunned at the bike's poor condition. I think, in his own mind, that this Seeker had simply put the bike away for the winter—although it was likely years—and he was waiting for a reason so that he could go zooming off again through the nearby hills.

But in many respects Sharon the One-Timer was every bit as much a lifestyle athlete as the other men and women I encountered. She clearly loved to ride her bike. She was actually very fit, in part because her bike riding was often woven into other aspects of her daily routine. For instance, she once lived near a rail-to-trail system that ended at the local mall and periodically used this route when she needed to go shopping. The round trip to this mall was over fifteen miles. Her bike had saddlebags to accommodate her purchases on these trips. Later, she routinely commuted to work on her bike. At the same time, riding her bicycle fast was most often beside the point. When I tried to hook her on riding fast, her earnest rebuttal was that when she rode fast she became tired and sweaty, and why would anyone want to make herself tired and sweaty?

The Touch of Grey Team

Reasons and motivations for engaging in lifestyle sport differ from person to person. This section explores some of these in greater detail.

In some respects, the five members of the Touch of Grey twenty-four-hour team who raced in the summer of 2000 are representative of the types of people who participate in adventure races. As such, providing a detailed description of each participant is useful for exploring the motivations of lifestyle sport athletes in general. One of the unforeseen benefits of taking my time to finish this text was that it allowed me to check in with the team more than a decade after we had raced together and update my record of their relationship with adventure sport.

Overall, I found that some people who participate in these sports as adults do so as a means of creating downtime from jobs that they sometimes regard as mundane, and at other times consider more "pressure-packed." In most respects, two members of our team—I have named them "Jim" and "Hanna"— were clearly using sport as a means of breaking up workaday routines and to sometimes relieve the stress associated with their jobs.

By way of contrast, another member of the team, "Chris," was a former professional mountain bike racer. Even as an amateur his association with cycling was among the most salient features of his identity. Cycling dominated his daily routine. He often took on seasonal work—usually a five-month contract as a heavy-equipment operator in Antarctica—so that he could ride his mountain bike as much as possible during the racing season. In effect, the time Chris spent on his bike was not downtime. It was time designed to systematically train and discipline his body so that he might possibly make sport his primary vocation.

When I first met Scott McDonald, the one-armed mountain biker who talked me into the twenty-four-hour race, he had no intention of making mountain biking his main activity. His participation in the sport was for largely therapeutic reasons. Indeed, Scott felt he needed to mountain bike as a distraction from the phantom pain he experienced, as a matter of routine, following his horrific accident. This was somewhat similar to Hanna's motivation to use sport to "feel better," but Scott was clearly evangelical with respect to his need to ride, likely because the pain he experienced was so considerable. But an argument can be made that every member of the team was trying to escape some manner of the mundane. Whether it was a simple escape from boredom or pressure or pain, perhaps we all pursued difficult sport to provide us with some relief from the vagaries associated with modern life.

Charles "Scott" McDonald in the Year 2000

Charles McDonald, whom we addressed as Scott, was a remarkable member of the Touch of Grey racing team.[4] As stated previously, Scott had lost his entire right arm at the shoulder after being run over, then dragged, by a slow moving train in West Virginia. In his account of this accident he indicated that it occurred when he and a friend were jumping from one train car to the next while the vehicle was moving. He fell, was caught underneath, and was then slowly dragged for a hundred yards or so before the train stopped. He was fortunate to have survived the accident. His friend—who immediately stripped off his shirt, wrapped it around Scott's body and then pressed himself against

Scott to stanch the bleeding—was credited with saving his life. Scott told me that the police officers who responded to the accident were not of much help because they were afraid to approach him when they saw how battered his body was. He thinks that one of the men may have become physically sick.

Scott's rehabilitation was not easy. To start with, people who suffer from this type of trauma generally have to redevelop their sense of balance: in effect, to learn how to walk again. Now that he has had to relearn what was once intuitive, Scott's balance is remarkable. The accident also left him with a considerable number of less-serious injuries. He lost parts of two fingers on his remaining hand. He also had to endure a series of skin graft operations and a long, painful rehabilitation. As a result, he was prescribed a steady diet of medication designed to negate his daily pain. He routinely experienced phantom limb pain well after the accident. He was resigned to living with constant pain for the rest of his life.

During a follow-up interview in September 2013, Scott indicated that he still experiences phantom pain. This sensation often occurs among amputees, in part because the mind still sends signals to nerves that once moved a now-missing limb. Other pain may be associated with the remapping of brain function—those areas that controlled the lost limb—following the amputation. Scott's pain was severe enough that he reported he had scheduled an operation that would have dulled the nerve endings at his shoulder. But at the last moment, literally as he was being prepped for the operation, he changed his mind. Scott had realized that, while his pain would be less following the operation, this might prevent him from ever having a mechanical prosthetic that could be activated by the still-active nerve endings at his shoulder.

There have been several attempts over the years to design a prosthesis that would help Scott ride with greater ease. A partial amputee would fasten a prosthesis to the stump of his or her missing arm, but because Scott's amputation took place at the shoulder, attempts at making a prosthesis that would remain in place during the rigors of mountain biking have not been very successful. Mountain biking with one arm and three fingers is a complicated enterprise. Basically, it creates what Scott describes as a "real estate problem" in that the brake levers for both the front and rear-wheel brakes and the gear mechanism are crammed onto one side of his handlebars. At points where mountain bikers often rest, Scott often has to work harder. On descents, in order to maintain his balance and control, he grabs both brake levers with his good hand, often pulling as hard as he can as he picks his way through whatever obstacles he encounters.[5] On a long descent the effort he uses to control his pace and balance can exhaust him. At the time I interviewed him, he preferred going uphill to going down. When I rode behind him on descents his arm became a gnarled, twisting network of veins as he fought to maintain his balance.

Scott was working on his technique when I first met him and crashed frequently. Often, to his frustration, he might navigate some tricky section of trail, a place where a two armed cyclist might fall, move into the easier section, and then suddenly find himself on the ground. He was remarkably good-natured about this. Obviously, practice had lent a certain balletic grace to his falls, but their unexpected timing—they might occur while we were holding a conversation on a smooth section of trail—still unnerved me. Most often, having buried his chin in his chest and rolled away from his bike, Scott quickly clambered to his feet and offered a wisecrack to the effect of, "I hate it when that happens." He was always battered and bruised, more so than other mountain bikers, and often showed off the scars he was actively accumulating. But in most other respects, Scott's background is typical of participants in mountain biking. He had always been an exceptional athlete and was on both the football and track teams in high school.

At times, Scott was endearingly belligerent. Given the nature of the accident that resulted in his amputation, he was probably always temperamentally inclined toward risk. He was also remarkably self-effacing. He did not go out of his way to attract attention, but being a one-armed mountain biker made him unique and he was usually happy to talk about his riding experiences. (Remarkably, one of the same years Scott raced at Snowshoe there was also a one-legged entrant.[6]) At the same time, he was somewhat embarrassed by the attention, but less so when I caught up with him in 2013.

Of particular interest to me was how Scott distinguished between his phantom pain and the pain that cyclists ordinarily experience when they ride their bikes. Scott actually used mountain biking as a means to negate the pain he often suffered during the course of his day. He told me that when he had made a decision to dump his medication, which he described as not taking away the pain but simply dulling his senses, he found he needed a physical release, a sport that required enough concentration and exertion to lessen the pain. Scott indicated that among the para-athletes he knows it is common to sometimes use marijuana to negate amputation-related pain. At the time, a post-ride beer (always Guinness) also helped. So, he mountain biked as a routine that helped him relax and sleep better at night. In effect, mountain biking, often described as painful by participants, was not regarded as painful by Scott.

It is impossible to know how much Scott's enthusiasm for cycling was directly related to his injury. He might well have been an enthusiastic cyclist had he never had an accident. However, his injury did, to a great extent, define the relationship he has with his bike and his place in the cycling community. My impression is that when we first met, Scott was largely reconciling himself to his status as "a one-arm mountain biker"—as opposed to just a "mountain biker." During our follow-up interview he seemed much more comfortable with the idea that to some extent, his disability defined his relationship to the sport, both to himself and to others. As Bill Hughes and Kevin Paterson have described, "The [impaired] body is not just experienced: It is also the very basis of experience. The body is . . . one's window on the world."[7] At the same time, Scott was always clear that he regarded his primary motivation for cycling as not much different than that of an able-bodied cyclist. The short answer for why Scott rode a mountain bike was that it was "a blast"—and that this was true whether someone had one or two arms.

Scott in the Year 2013

Given how important cycling was to Scott's sense of well-being it should not be surprising that he has remained the most active cyclist among the members of the Touch of Grey team. Indeed, it was not hard to find Scott in 2013 despite the fact that we had not talked in many years. I simply typed his name and "mountain bike" into the Google search engine and soon encountered an article titled, "The Badass of the Ohio Valley Cyclocross: An Interview with Charles Scott McDonald."[8] When I clicked open the article there was Scott, cyclo-cross bike shouldered with his good arm, bounding over some obstacle, not looking any different than when I had last seen him ten years previously. He was obviously still a very active cyclist.

In the initial draft of this text I had juxtaposed Chris's desire to become a professional racer with Scott's more personal motivations for riding. Ironically, Charles Scott McDonald is increasingly a full time cyclist. He rides for the Paralyzed Veterans Racing Team and has been trying to meet Paralympic standards in some road bike disciplines although he much prefers to race cyclo-cross. Like many mountain bikers, Scott does not like riding with vehicular traffic and on pavement. Falling off a road bike, which has happened to him a few times, causes far more bodily damage than falling from a mountain bike. He also rides for his local club, Covington Newport Cycling (CNC). When we spoke he had been invited to the 2013 CrossVegas cyclo-cross race, the largest annual racing event, which attracts elite and professional racers from around the country.

When I was tracking down Scott I also came across a website through which donations had been solicited to finally construct a prosthetic arm for him that might hold up to the rigors of mountain biking. When I excitedly asked Scott about this he somewhat sheepishly admitted that he had destroyed the arm during his initial test ride. "I grabbed a downhill bike from the shop where I work and I took it on a local ride," he told me. "I did get some air . . . but it was pretty much destroyed within the hour."[9] A friend at the shop had predicted as much, stating, "you're going to destroy that thing," when Scott first showed him the device. This same friend, something of an industrial engineer himself, is now actively working to build Scott's next prosthesis.

Overall, Scott reported, he was generally happier, more content, than he had been in past years. In part, his training regimen—now actively managed by coaches and a nutritionist—has made him feel better physically than during a period when he was working as a computer communications specialist in an adult education program. He is employed at a local bike shop and his combination of work and exercise appears ideal in terms of his ongoing pain management. When he was employed as a computer specialist he never stopped riding his bike (he routinely commuted to work) but he also reported that his weight had ballooned to nearly 280 pounds. As he became increasingly sedentary it became difficult not to self-medicate his pain with alcohol.

Scott also reported he is increasingly comfortable in his role as a spokesperson for people with physical disability who participate in sport. While he might prefer that his association with sport be more directly tied to his skill, he has increasingly recognized that his disability makes him stand out. He characterized this an opportunity to demonstrate that he is really not so different than other people who love to ride bicycles: that, like most of his friends, his motivation for riding bicycles is mainly to have fun.

It is difficult to place Scott into the typology above. I most respects I always regarded him as comparable to the Evangelical and New Athlete, but sometimes I thought of him as a Free Spirit too. Mostly, his experience seemed directly comparable to John and Joanne's—the once–morbidly obese athletes who were using sport to be healthier. In this regard, he had adopted cycling as a lifestyle change associated with his need to negate his phantom pain. As such, cycling was really integral to his sense of well-being. But he actually does not fit this type formally because he has considerable past experience with sport. Still, he is clearly a unique athlete who feels an affinity with a particular sport because of its positive health benefits regarding his disability. Notable, though, is that he appears to be training in an increasingly methodical manner, necessary in order to try and meet his goal of attaining the Paralympic standards for road cycling.

Jim in the Year 2000

I have known my fellow team member "Jim" since childhood. At the time of the 24 Hour race he was an engineer at a large firm that specializes in designing bridges that are often extraordinary in terms of their scale and cost. Of our group, he probably had the least amount of time to prepare. He had a demanding job and when I called him concerning the race was in the middle of preparing a bid for a large construction project that would directly affect his career. At the time, he also had a two-year-old son to help keep track of. Jim was a young, smart, aggressive manager trying to get ahead in a national engineering firm. Engineering a new bridge that is grand in scale is the most prestigious (and interesting) work that can be done. During the course of preparing this particular bid, a team effort that he coordinated, he informed me that he saw the process as a "roll of the dice" concerning his future with the company. Previously, the firm had lost a series of bids on large construction projects and now everyone was too shaken by the experience to put their personal capital on the line for this particular job. Jim was initially considered too young to be given the job of preparing the bid, but lobbied hard for it, knowing that if he won the contract he would be indispensable to the company in the near term. He assumed he could then wrangle a considerable increase in his salary. If he lost the bid, particularly after burning up the labor hours and money that preparing it would cost the company, he might be, in his own words, "marked." He considered that he might have to change jobs if wanted to get a crack at another big project.

This strategy corresponds with Jim's personality. He is generally even-keeled and self-effacing, but beneath this mellow persona is someone who enjoys calculated risk. In this respect, I did not regard his participation in risky sport as being too distinct from his attitude toward work. Some experts have asserted that risk in sport—or edgework in general—might be an antidote to the absence of risk in modern life.[10] In some cases, I think this is true. Jim himself characterized his needing to do sports—he is a nationally competitive J-24 class sailor—as necessary to keep him sane given the rigors of a sometimes-grueling work schedule. At the same time, he clearly enjoyed taking calculated risk at work too. In this case, if he won the job for his company he knew he would also become a company star. Why not take the chance? The worst that could happen was he would fail and move to another firm. Furthermore, if he went into this business to design bridges, he naturally assumed he should aspire to design the biggest, most interesting bridges possible. Jim liked his work and he liked a challenge.

The type of risk that Jim was taking was completely incomprehensible to me. The project's scale, the company resources that would be spent, the inevitable pressure that would be put on him throughout the process, were all considerable. Jim certainly experienced the pressure, but was also remarkably calm. The winning bid was unsealed literally the day before the 24 Hour race started. Jim did not seem too concerned. His response to me was, "Well, that's a big day, but my end of this thing will be done, so I should be able to make the race."

As it turns out, I was standing beside Jim the day before the race when he received the phone call that informed him that his team bid had not been chosen for the project. I watched as he involuntarily winced, shook his head a few times, and then quickly and quietly ended the call. After he hung up the phone he looked at me, smiled ruefully, and said plaintively, "We got killed." And then more emphatically, "Well, that's it . . . Let's race!"

Jim lived in Tampa, Florida. In terms of geography you could not pick two more dissimilar places than West Virginia and Florida. A local joke is that if West Virginia were rolled flat it would be bigger than Texas. Jim once told me that South Florida is so flat that you can roll a quarter across it. There was no appropriate place near his home for him to train for this event. Moreover, he did not own a mountain bike and intended to get in shape by riding his road bike in Tampa. He also had only been mountain biking twice, both times with me while visiting his family in Virginia.

Still, Jim had periodically done oddball endurance events like this in the past, and this type of race seemed to fit his style. He was never a very serious athlete as a kid, but now entered triathlons and long running races as a diversion to his workaday life. It seemed that he liked to take an extreme physical beating on occasion simply to break up his routine. Despite the obvious pressure he was under, it was not too hard to convince him to do this race.

Jim is a fairly good representation of a Free Spirit in the sport typology above concerning his participation in triathlon and endurance events. He dabbles. He enters events that look interesting. He is not much concerned with where he finishes. To some degree, he is even ad hoc when he puts together his sailing teams, although not to the same degree that I associate with his participation in other types of sports. When he was required to participate in sports at his private school he quickly decided to join the sailing club. In part, he had calculated that he would be left alone during the afternoons that the club sailed at a nearby lake. He and a few other club members quickly commandeered (and sometimes destroyed) equipment associated with the club as they whiled away their afternoons, largely under their own supervision.

Jim in the Year 2013

Since Jim's participation in the 24 Hour race he has maintained roughly the same pattern of participation in lifestyle sport. He remains a dabbler in various sports. He is a more enthusiastic runner nowadays and sometimes swims during his lunch break at work. He does about one triathlon a year—most often the St Anthony's Triathlon in Tampa—mostly because it is so close to his home. He has no aspirations beyond completing the event in the top half of his age group. Preparing for the race helps him stay in shape.

Jim is more serious about sailing and now routinely puts together national-caliber J-24 racing teams. He has qualified and competed in the J-24 class three times at the national championships. En route to a couple of these events, Jim stopped by my house in Virginia. The twenty-four-foot sailboat—not overly big when it is in the water—looks massive when it is in transport. Jim would not say his hobby requires much effort, but simply seeing that boat in tow and hearing about the preparation and training for the event made me realize that he has considerable devotion to this enterprise. The pattern I associate with Jim's sporting endeavors—and even his temperament generally—is restlessness. In effect, when he tires of one sport, when he needs a break, he enthusiastically embraces another for some period of time. With the exception of his sailing habit, which requires considerable commitment and skill, he has no grand aspirations with respect to his participation in sport. And, in some respects, his sailing goals are somewhat modest too. Mostly, once in a while, he likes to build a team that is good enough to qualify for the national championships. He still pursues sport as a diversion to his workaday routine.

Given Jim's temperamental restlessness and his stated concern when this study began that he might have to change jobs if he lost that large construction bid, it is notable that he continues to work for the same engineering firm. In fact, he later put together and won many bids for the construction of a massive bridges that would be familiar to residents in communities throughout the United States. In fact, at a reasonably young age he became a manager who now oversees the engineers working on all bridge projects within his regional office.

Hanna in the Year 2000

I sometimes saw "Hanna" a little stressed out by the demands of multiple part-time jobs and work as a graduate student, but she was also temperamentally easygoing. At the time, she told me that she always felt better in all aspects of her life when she made the time to work out. I came to know Hanna reasonably well during the period we raced together, but her somewhat-frantic schedule made her the team member about whom I ultimately learned the least. Like Jim, Hanna was a novice mountain biker. She was also the only woman on our team.

When she met Jim she found his mellow demeanor remarkable and was incredulous that he was largely unconcerned about doing a race in the mountains of West Virginia on a rented mountain bike presented to him the day before the race. She was much more diligent in her preparation. She and Scott trained together often and the three of us pre-rode the course at the Snowshoe Mountain Resort before the race so that she would know exactly what to expect on race day. Still, I regarded Hanna and Jim as similar in many respects.

For a novice cyclist participating in a difficult event, she was remarkably blasé about the whole affair. And while Hanna was nervous at times, throughout the event she seemed remarkably level-headed. She sometimes claimed to be worried, but always seemed to be smiling when she said this. She did not really hesitate to join the team once Scott asked her to. Although Hanna took training for the sport seriously, she was not nearly as fanatical as many others regarding her training regimen. It often appeared to me that her primary diet consisted of a half-dozen diet Pepsis during the day. She was often up for a post-ride beer too.

Hanna had a lot of experience in other sports. She often ran for fitness and had been a member of the inaugural cross-country team at her college. She was a serious field hockey player in high school. She enjoyed hiking. She sometimes followed a kickboxing workout routine. She was intrigued by sport and drawn to demanding activity. It seemed inevitable that she would become hooked (and later hook her boyfriend) on mountain biking. At times she was concerned about her lack of mountain biking experience, particularly the day when we pre-rode the course, but I was always confident that she was going to be fine and would enjoy the race.

Hanna most often framed her participation in sport as a physical need. She needed to run, she needed to work out, in order to feel normal. She had always been an athlete and when she quit training shortly after college she had felt horrible. She had reinstituted a workout regimen primarily because she felt better when she was engaged in difficult sport. Like many people who become involved in cycling, she was previously devoted to a running routine.

She also had a busy work schedule. Hanna was in an MA program in sociology and received some support from the department in return for working ten hours a week. But she and her boyfriend had also started a jewelry business and owned the small storefront from which it operated. For the most part this was her primary occupation and required a considerable amount of time. Combined with the demands of her graduate program, she often had little time to work out.

Hanna is not the perfect representation of a systems athlete, but she was generally inclined toward preparing, as best she could, for the endurance race we had entered. She definitely wanted to be ready and prepared. And she wanted to do as well as possible. I had an idea she felt some responsibility—perhaps related to the fact she was the only woman on the team—to do her best. She rode routinely with Scott and queried people about how to become a better rider. As the event approached, she became more diligent about her preparation.

Hanna in the Year 2013

When I caught up with Hanna after thirteen years I found she was the primary instructor in the sociology department at a Virginia community college. In fact, not long after we had raced together she had entered a Ph.D. program at Virginia Tech. During this period she also began to ride her road bicycle hard—she indicated this was to relieve the stress associated with being a graduate student—and completed a few difficult century rides in the Blacksburg area, the most notorious the "Mountains of Misery" century. She also continued to race in team endurance events. She particularly enjoyed a twelve-hour mountain bike relay race with a team of other women.

Hanna is now married to the boyfriend I met in 2000, a local builder, and they have a two-year-old daughter. Perhaps most notable is that she and her husband both became cycling regulars in a long-established local club, the Wednesday Warriors, which schedules midweek rides in the area where they live. Hanna indicated that this group of riders still constitutes her primary social network: even as her participation in the club waned after her daughter was born, they remained her best friends in the community. She and her husband continue to ride and run regularly: there is a local "rails to trails" cycling path that they sometimes pedal down with their daughter in tow. However, she no longer races. Indeed, she credited her husband with providing what she described as a "more healthy" sporting outlook. Generally, as Hanna became increasingly anxious while training for cycling events, her husband would ask her, "Isn't this supposed to be fun?" Over time, she increasingly adopted "fun" as the primary reason for participating in sport. To this end, she maintains a near-daily routine of running and riding outdoors most days, but has not raced for a few years now. She and her husband built their house at the trail access point where she and Scott began many of their training rides over a decade ago.

Chris in the Year 2000

"Chris" has considerable experience riding a mountain bike. In fact, he was ranked as the best elite amateur racer in the United States following the National Off Road Bicycle Association (NORBA) national racing series in 1995. The following year he became a professional racer with Jamis Bikes, the company that had sponsored him as an amateur racer. In his first year as a professional his finishes ranked him just inside the top fifty mountain bikers in the United States. This may sound impressive, but very few professional mountain bike racers—perhaps those ranked in the top ten nationally—were actually making a reasonable living racing their mountain bikes at the time.

So Chris had another job: he spent five months each winter working in Antarctica for Antarctic Support Service as a heavy equipment operator. Afterward, he usually spent a month (early spring in the United States) in New Zealand and then took part in U.S. races during the summer. He initially maintained this routine as a professional racer although his lack of training through the winter hurt his performance in the early part of the racing season.

Chris went to Antarctica for a number of reasons, but one was to make the money he needed to supplement his racing income. He regarded the job as a means of banking enough so that he could compete full-time during the summer. This was a different routine from that of most professional mountain bike racers who, despite the grueling training regimen and monastic lifestyle, usually do not take full-time jobs in the off season even though they are not often paid well to race their bikes. Instead many room together in warmer locales, do their best to preserve their dwindling cash—they sell their old bikes and perhaps borrow money from relatives and friends—until the checks start arriving again in the spring. Chris knew that despite some past success, his employment on a professional cycling team was tenuous in terms of job security. If he was injured or had a bad season or the team lost a big sponsor, he would likely find himself unemployed.

As it turned out, following his first year as a professional mountain bike racer, Chris was offered full-time employment with Antarctic Support Services in a job that he thought he would enjoy. This would have necessitated that he stop racing seriously. Whether to take this job was a hard decision in that he was twenty-six years old, approaching the age when many cyclists often reach their physical peak. He reluctantly turned down the offer. In fact, he decided not to go down to "the ice" that winter so that he could train full-time. Inevitably (or so it seemed), once he made the commitment to train hard through the winter his team decided not to renew his contract. In the past they had fielded a large team and provided him with good support as both an amateur and professional racer, but now the company executives decided they needed to scale back their commitment for the coming season. Chris, probably regarded as a dilettante because he worked in Antarctica rather than train, was among those dropped from the team.

By this time it was too late to hustle for a contract and Chris was coming off a mediocre year as a professional racer. He eventually found a sponsored ride from a small niche mountain bike company, Dean Bicycles, but his race support (from bike mechanics, masseurs, managers, and the like) was negligible compared to previous years. He largely fended for himself in terms of mechanical and technical support throughout the 1997 season. His goal was to perform well in a few races—he had always done well at Big Bear, California, for example—and then find a team that could support him better the following year. At the time it was clear to me, although he never said this out loud, that he was angry at his former employer, a fact that probably made him train particularly hard that winter.

When I saw him before the 1997 season the change in his physiology was dramatic. Always slim and somewhat tall for a mountain biker, he was leaner than I had ever seen him before. He had made major changes to his diet—high-protein diets were in vogue at this time—and it was clear to me that he had a body that was, more than ever, designed to sit on top of a mountain bike. I figured he was going to have the season of his life. His friends and former teammates also noticed the difference: he was clearly stronger than before. He seemed well poised to uncork a ride or two that would get people's attention. In the past, particularly as my participation in triathlon waned, I found it difficult to ride with Chris. The only way I could do it was during training rides on road bikes, and even if I spent most of them sitting in (riding in Chris's draft, which requires twenty to thirty percent less effort) I inevitably returned from these rides exhausted and beaten.

Surprisingly, Chris did not have a good year professionally. He had bad luck in general throughout the season, primarily a series of flats and other technical problems. He was most disappointed after a mass wreck at the start of the Big Bear race knocked him and much of the field out of the race less than a minute after it started. In the end, despite being markedly fitter, he finished at about the same level in the overall standings as his previous season. That winter, as Chris was preparing to go to Antarctica, he became sick with mononucleosis, probably exacerbated by the physical demands of racing. It kept him from making the trip. He spent the winter in Colorado driving a ski-resort bus that ferried people from a parking lot to the ski lodge. He also decided, having taken his best shot, to quit mountain biking. He put his bike away and did not ride for almost a year. Then I asked if he wanted to join the 24 Hour race.

I was curious as to whether Chris would participate. I knew that in the past his East Coast teammates had reluctantly done the 24 Hour Race at Canaan. Despite the publicity it garnered, some regarded it as a fringe event that negatively affected their performance at the more-important national NORBA events. Furthermore, compared with his previous racing companions our team was a motley crew. In fact, one of the reasons we all wanted Chris with us was that even if he arrived out of shape relative to his time as an elite racer, he would easily be our strongest team member. We were counting on him to save us from embarrassment.

He joined the team. Now racing as an amateur, Chris turned in times that were comparable with the professional entrants'. In fact, Touch of Grey enjoyed a (brief) moment of glory when Chris, despite having begun training only a couple of months previously, finished our opening lap with the leading professional riders. What I most remember about this was the race announcers indicating that Chris was among the race leaders and the beatific expression of joy on Scott's face as he bounded toward me as I prepared to do the next lap. "Did you hear that?! He's in the front!" he exclaimed, both ecstatically and incredulously. Even during the night rides Chris's times never fluctuated by more than a couple of minutes.

At the time I imagined that Chris still had some regrets about his decision to stop racing as a professional because, for the most part, he never experienced success at that level. After he quit he seemed to lament the fact that he had to start over again with Antarctic Support Services. Every once in a while he would say something to the effect of, "You know, I gave up a good job to race a mountain bike. What was I thinking!?" At this time he was working mainly as a heavy-equipment operator building a road in a mountainous area of Colorado. I would not characterize Chris as overly career-conscious, but it was also evident that he did not want to drive a bus for the ski lodge next winter. He was now in his late twenties and a little worried that he did not have a job that might be considered a career.

Within the context of other professional racers Chris was sometimes considered eccentric because he went to Antarctica during the winter to work as opposed to staying in the United States and training. Still, he is an exemplary Methodical athlete as described in the typology. This was particularly true the season he trained full-time and radically changed his diet to increase his performance. Indeed, even when he worked on "the ice" in the winters he designed a modest workout regimen to keep him reasonably fit during the off season. The month he spent in New Zealand before returning to the States was spent steadily building his cycling base—logging the miles he thought he needed to be competitive during the upcoming season—and he systematically picked up the intensity of his workouts when he returned to racing full-time in the spring.

Chris in the Year 2013

While Chris never stopped riding his bicycle he almost entirely disengaged from racing after his participation on the Touch of Grey team. His remorse over missing an opportunity with Antarctic Support Services turned out to be premature. He returned to the frozen continent as a contract laborer and was soon offered a full-time position managing the environmental policies at the McMurdo base, an international research facility. He described this position as being the "Head Can Crusher." In fact, as the primary environmental officer, one of his jobs was to direct a crew who ensured that the station's waste footprint was small, with every scrap recycled or removed from the facility by ship annually. He also later had the experience of "wintering over" in Antarctica—difficult because of the considerable cold and small amounts of daylight in the winter months.

Chris even, improbably, met his future wife in Antarctica. They actually decided to winter over together, living in small quarters during a period of near-constant darkness. Among the various ways that couples might test their compatibility, this is among the more extreme. Shortly after that experience they were married. By then they had already plotted out a strategy for their future employment and when they returned to the States both enrolled in a nursing program at Flagstaff, Arizona. Like other lifestyle athletes I encountered, they actually chose their profession, in part, because they knew nurses had considerable freedom concerning where they might live. Moreover, because twelve-hour shifts are routine, there would be large periods of uninterrupted free time that might allow them to hike, ski, and ride their bikes. They currently live in Boise, Idaho, with their two young children, in part because it has considerable outdoor amenities and a reasonable cost of living.

Conclusion: Agency in Lifestyle Sport

It is important to note that in constructing this taxonomy I used athlete characteristics and motivations often as expressed by the athletes themselves. My categories assume that they have some agency in terms of how they participate in sport. The taxonomy is useful for comparing different types of athletes, particularly their attitudes toward lifestyle sport. Nonetheless, all sport, including this type, is structured. This structure sometimes compels people to adopt very specific training methodologies and tends to punish people who do not. A Free Spirit, in some respects, still prepares for a bicycle ride in the same manner as a Methodical rider: they fill their water bottles, pump up their tires, wear the appropriate clothing, and bring the appropriate tools. I know many Free Spirits who can wax poetic on the Zen of the perfect pedal stroke, so they have obviously devoted a lot of time to thinking about the dynamics of their body, fitness, and ergonomics as it relates to cycling fitness and cycling comfort. So even Free Spirits find that their sporting activity is structured, confined by both formal and informal rules that order the practice of the sport.

The following chapter is also associated with athletes' agency as it relates to their participation in sport. In this case, I followed a group of highly skilled athletes—some of the best mountain bikers in the region—who sometimes flouted the orthodoxies associated with competitive sport. They have created a remarkable calendar of informal cycling events—ice cream socials, Super Bowl Sunday rides, mountain bike festivals, Do it Yourself (DIY) races—that have made Harrisonburg, Virginia, into the cycling center of the Shenandoah Valley. The group has also, over the past decade, actively helped to make a community once noted for its unattractive retail sprawl into a much more bicycle-friendly place.

5

Resistance to Discipline in a Cycling Community

• •

This chapter describes resistance to the commodification of lifestyle sport by a community of athletes who sometimes flout orthodoxies associated with modern sport. Many are also working to build and maintain a unique cycling community in Harrisonburg, Virginia. When I first encountered this community in the middle 1980s, they had recently discovered mountain biking and also established a nonprofit cycling organization associated with the League of American Cyclists. These were mostly road cyclists who were also among the first to ride mountain bikes in the nearby national forest. Soon, they were organizing community rides designed to introduce people to this new type of cycling. Their April 1984 newsletter reported:

> The first informal FTB (Fat Tire Bike) rides have already taken place. On Feb. 26, Bruce Werner and Mark Nissley rode down Hone Quarry on the trail from Flagpole Knob, the highest point in Rockingham County, and just missed Craig Mauck and Sue Rippey who had ridden up the trail for a picnic to just before the point in the road where the going gets nasty. Both teams crossed six streams on the way back. On March 4, Mark Nissley and Craig Mauck descended on the same trail again, this time there was a lot of ice in the streams to make it more interesting. Since the streams were frozen, everyone had dry feet. Stay tuned for rides on the town trails behind Madison and between Hillendale and Westover

Parks. There will also be downhill time trials on some local power line cuts too, after you FTB folks get used to your new machines.[1]

I was introduced to this community as a college student after I bought a road bike from Craig "Rearview" Mauck, at the time a national-caliber veteran (over thirty-five years of age) mountain-bike racer. The number of events sponsored by this small club was remarkable. Indeed, some of these rides continue to be annual events thirty years later. The "Super Bowl Sunday Ride"—an informal (no-registration) mountain bike ride to Flagpole Knob—has now been held annually for three decades and attracts upward of one hundred participants. This group also charted some now well-established road rides in the area: a local century (one-hundred-mile) ride has also been staged annually for more than thirty years and attracts several hundred cyclists. Ultimately, after periods of stagnation and growth, the club this group established evolved into the Shenandoah Valley Bicycle Coalition (SVBC), currently an activist nonprofit organization. Throughout, there has been a steady growth in the number of community cycling enthusiasts creating "do-it-yourself" (DIY) races and events.

I think one of these races, the Tour de Burg, offers a good example of sporting resistance. The event has retained a more traditional sporting ethos, one that reinforces fair play, camaraderie, and "challenging the self" with the intention of creating an esprit de corps.[2] It reinforces "play" among the participants, even though the athletes who participate are often among the best mountain bikers in the region. Founded by Mike Carpenter and Chris Scott, the Tour de Burg has been staged for nineteen years as I write this. Over time, it has gained a reputation as the most difficult mountain bike event in the region; its past winners have been among the fastest professional and amateur mountain bikers in the United States.[3]

Many of these riders live in Harrisonburg, Virginia, a town that has grown to about 50,000 residents, along with 20,000 students at James Madison University, and is considered a center for cycling in the Shenandoah Valley. Generally, the cycling community—from the period when I first encountered it to the present—has also been associated with efforts to revitalize the downtown after a long period of economic decline. In particular, they are closely associated with efforts to make the community more bicycle- and pedestrian-friendly. This chapter ends by describing how DIY events like the Tour de Burg are facilitated by this activist-minded culture, which contributes to the broader, ongoing community transformation in Harrisonburg.

Conceptualizing Resistance to Market Discipline

Previous studies of close-knit sporting subcultures that were sometimes unruly—in which participants often self-consciously broke rules associated with traditional sport—have been characterized as sites of resistance to corporate sport. Skateboarding[4] and other "whiz" sports such as snowboarding and windsurfing[5] have sometimes been considered sites of resistance, as have sports where athletes largely self-regulate the action, such as outdoor sport climbing[6] and surfing.[7] Often, observers conducted studies of these sports as they were becoming increasingly popular and grappled with the question of whether these ever-more routinized and professionalized activities were much distinct from more traditional forms of sport. This was particularly the case as these sports became increasingly covered within the popular media.[8]

On the one hand, it was clear that market forces were sometimes capturing and regulating these sports. There was increasing corporate sponsorship, professional events, and regulatory agencies that defined official rules associated with formal competition. But at least some athletes tried to maintain the more anarchic and self-regulating practices associated with the founding days of these sports.[9] In other cases, some of the best athletes might wade into the market for a while and be sponsored by corporate entities, but did so more on their own terms then other athletes. A world-class climber might, for example, document certain difficult climbs for which he needed corporate support, but then retreat into the more vagabond and solitary lifestyle many associated with sport climbing.[10] At least, some people argued, this represented a different interaction with the market than professional athletes in more traditional sports such as football and baseball.[11]

Others noted how quickly the market expropriated ideas associated with lifestyle sport and came to dominate these once-alternative sporting endeavors. Snowboarding was once considered a possible site of sporting resistance—it was initially banned at some ski resorts—but has been coopted by market forces to the extent that it is now, for the most part, a mainstream sport.[12] Indeed, it was often breathtaking to see the speed at which once-anachronistic ideas associated with these new sports were mainstreamed, sometimes as a means of selling commodities.

Some athletes thought that Eastern traditions of bodily discipline that emphasized ascetic "mindfulness"—a detachment from wealth and the physical world—were also at odds with the forces of market capitalism. Yoga, as it became increasingly practiced by Westerners, was considered a place that might become a site of self-conscious resistance to market liberalism.[13] But again, as one surveys the practice of yoga in the West it does not seem much associated with an act of sporting resistance or even an attempt to become somewhat less attached to the material world. Indeed, market capitalism has expropriated many of its practices and made it, by and large, another site governed by market rules. This is so much the case that the CEO of Lululemon, the largest provider of yoga apparel in the United States, believes that the hyper-individualist and pro-capitalist philosophy of Ayn Rand, whose quotes once appeared on their tote bags, should now be intimately associated with the practice.[14] What would the Yogi think?

The previous examples suggest that one should be cautious when describing any sport as a possible long-term site of resistance to market discipline. No doubt, there are still ascetics practicing yoga. No doubt, some skateboarders still reject the strictures of self-discipline associated with market norms within their sport. But, as a whole, subcultural sporting practices can be co-opted by market forces with remarkable efficiency. Indeed, that is largely what has happened to the sport of mountain biking in the United States and elsewhere. Still, my intention in this chapter is to describe acts of local resistance that I observed in a small mountain biking community.

Transgression

One idea central to Foucauldian forms of resistance is the act of transgression. Put simply, this is an incidence of "recalcitrance, refusal and unruliness" against some social norm now reinforced by increasing scientism and capitalism.[15] These can be individual acts, or sometimes more organized forms of resistance that try to "undo" narratives and practices associated with market norms. This chapter will focus on two acts of transgression in which strictures associated with corporate sport were either lampooned or ignored by participants. In one case, Team Hugh Jass increasingly engaged in modest acts of resistance "from within" as twenty-four-hour mountain bike racing changed over time. The other is a race, the Tour de Burg, which steadfastly ignores, and often makes fun of, some orthodoxies now associated with mountain bike racing.

Michel Foucault thought acts of resistance might "permit individuals to effect by their own means or with the help of others a certain number of operations on their own bodies and souls, thoughts, conduct, and way of being, so as to transform themselves in order to attain a certain state of happiness, purity, wisdom, perfection, or immortality."[16] That is a tall order, but it did appear clear that some of the anachronistic sporting practices I observed were an attempt to maintain, perhaps even recapture, the community-minded ethos that existed when these sports were first founded. But mostly, they were opportunities to ride hard and have fun.

The individual temperaments of the athletes who participated in these small acts of resistance varied considerably. Some were not much interested in racing in conventional settings or at venues where there was considerable corporate sponsorship. Often, instead of racing at "normal" venues they sought out more self-regulated events like the Tour de Burg. But there were also athletes who participated in these "off-the-grid" events who then moved easily into events sanctioned by governing bodies and held at more mainstream venues.

Cycling as Resistance

Bicycles have long been associated with social activism in the United States. For example, the League of American Wheelmen was established in the late nineteenth century as an advocacy group concerned with the construction of a national road system. More recently, some riders regard increasing bicycle use as a means of disrupting negative conditions associated with the "car culture" in many Western countries.[17] Indeed, some activists regard cycling as a potentially radical act. Some do not own cars for political and environmental reasons and argue that the American car culture has made people slothful.[18] Currently, even mainstream cycling advocacy groups argue that an increase in cycling will help to reduce air pollution, traffic congestion, and even the increasing obesity of Americans.[19]

Among the best examples of cycling happenings associated with recalcitrance, refusal, and unruliness—events in which thousands of cyclists around the world participated—were the Critical Mass rallies. These began as monthly rides in San Francisco in which cyclists decided to "claim" the streets during rush hour traffic to publicize cycling safety issues and argue that bikes should be more accommodated in urban settings. The largest rally occurred in 1997 following a comment by San Francisco Mayor "Willie" Brown that local cyclists were "arrogant." In response, the next Critical Mass event attracted several thousand cyclists who brought traffic in parts of the city to a standstill. Later, the movement's rides in San Francisco became more managed and less spontaneous, but Critical Mass spread to other cities worldwide. In some of these, it was credited with publicizing cycling grievances that were taken seriously and acted upon by local governments.[20]

Market Responsiveness to Subcultural Practice

The market associated with specialty cycling equipment is often more flexible and localized than many others. Many companies that make equipment for adventure sport are relatively small-scale manufacturing enterprises, often locally based. Dean Bicycles in Boulder, Colorado, for example, crafts highly specialized cycling frames locally. But even when the production of specialized outdoor equipment is a national or international endeavor, the manufacturers of quality outdoor equipment have tended to resist a move toward Big Box retailing, in part because small specialty shops better connect them to local markets. Indeed, in every community where I have lived there have been a few small retail stores—the rough equivalent of Mom-and-Pop stores owned by individuals or families—that sell specialty outdoor equipment. Many large producers of outdoor equipment still distribute their products through these relatively small, independently owned retail shops.

The fact that bicycles are often specialized equipment, necessarily maintained by people with expert knowledge who are employed by small shops, may make complete market dominance by a few large retailers more difficult. In particular, the production and selling of high quality bicycles looks similar to that of surfing equipment. While Rip Curl, Billabong, and Quicksilver dominate the surfing market, Mark Stranger has argued that these large firms are still responsive to subcultural practices that help "mediate the relationship between these companies and the mainstream market."[21] In effect, a large company's ability to maintain its "authenticity" is often intimately associated with creating a close connection to an anachronistic group of "end users" who judge equipment quality in very specific ways associated with performance. Bad products are quickly found out—often quite literally "broken"—by the steadiest end users. This may make even the largest companies relatively responsive to their customers, more so than in other markets.

Many of the best practitioners in both cycling and surfing tend to revere specialized production undertaken by small-scale producers. A custom-made bike, like a custom-made surfboard, is often regarded as superior to one that is mass-produced. Moreover, small retailers' close relationships "on the ground" with a community of active cyclists helps to ensure their success: this makes the buying, selling, and repairing of bicycles different from that of many other commodities. Importantly, it is common for small bicycle retailers to be among the community activists advocating for an increase in public space where people can ride their bikes safely. This has long been the case in Harrisonburg, Virginia, where local shop owners are intimately associated with efforts to make the community more bicycle-friendly.[22]

Making Authenticity in a Sporting Endeavor

I began this study in the summer of 2000 with the Toyota 24 Hours Race held at Snowshoe Mountain Resort. In many respects, it offers a nice comparison to the Tour de Burg, the last race I participated in. Initially, events like twenty-four-hour mountain bike racing attracted participants, in part, because it was considered an antithesis to corporate sport. It was one of many events where participants—usually relatively few in number—congregated in a wilderness area mostly to do something physically difficult together. When money was exchanged it was usually to defray some modest cost—for gas, for food, for beer—that the "organizer" had expended.

A few of the best racers in the early twenty-four-hour races later created the Tour de Burg. But unlike the latter race, the first events were quickly professionalized and commodified. The ones in West Virginia were initially considered unique because they did not conform to standards concerning distance and time. But soon enough, racing around the clock became increasingly normative within the new sport. Notably, as twenty-four-hour racing became increasingly commodified this changed how some athletes regarded it.[23] For example, as Tour de Burg founder Mike Carpenter observed the spectacle now called the Toyota 24 Hours of Snowshoe in 2001, he was quoted in a *Sports Illustrated* as stating, "It's not about freedom and survival anymore . . . it's about bling-bling."[24]

At the time Mike was associated with a team of racers who were flouting some of the orthodoxies increasingly associated with elite mountain bike racing. In fact, Team Hugh Jass (Huge Ass) had developed a form of burlesque theatre that routinely mocked aspects of corporate sport. At the same time, in discussions with me, they always characterized their primary motivations as having fun and riding hard. When I first observed the group they stood out mostly because they were so steadfastly determined to maintain the "play" aspect of mountain biking. For me, this juxtaposition—one where highly disciplined athletes self-consciously chose to have fun during competition—offered an interesting way to think about what distinguishes "play" from "sport."

Authenticity

I want to return briefly to the concept of authenticity. To some degree, both of the races in this chapter were conceptualized as creating something "authentic." Whether they ultimately succeeded, however, is a group judgment—in this case, by the people who take part in the events. Authenticity relies mainly on a determination that someone is making a genuine effort to do something notable, or to maintain a tradition that is regarded as noteworthy.[25] Both of these races have their genesis in the same early mountain biking ethos: they were associated with people taking their bikes into the wilderness, often in an ad-hoc manner, and trying something new.

I think both were considered authentic challenges when the races were first conceived. But over time, people began to question the authenticity of those associated with 24 Hours at Snowshoe as it changed from a small off-the-beaten-track race into a marketing spectacle. As it became commodified people regarded the event—even the motives of the race director—as inauthentic. Conversely, the Tour de Burg is still considered an authentic challenge by many. This is because the racers and race director have self-consciously stressed two points: 1) the race is hard: it is designed as a challenge to self, and 2) the motives of those associated with it, both racers and director, are genuine. The race director does not make money by organizing the event even though the logistics associated with setting up a multi-day stage race covering hundreds of miles are considerable. In fact, Mike usually has about $1,500 left over after staging the race, which he donates to the local bike advocacy group. In 2014, he bought SVBC memberships for all the tour participants and then donated the remaining funds. Related to maintaining the authenticity of the race is that a primary purpose is to showcase both the best and hardest trails in the region. And that the race is produced—as its Facebook page suggests—"Just for Fun!"[26]

Capturing Adventure by the Market: Twenty-Four-Hour Mountain Bike Racing

In contrast to the Tour de Burg, it is not hard to find mountain bike events that became increasingly commodified over time. For example, 24 Hours at Canaan—established by Laird Knight, who was inducted into the Mountain Bike Hall of Fame because of his success as a race sponsor—was initially loosely organized and sparsely attended. But soon, this race and others became part of a professionally run business dependent on considerable corporate sponsorship.[27] The early races were far from professional events, but by the time I participated it was called the Toyota 24 Hours at Snowshoe Mountain and had fully transitioned from an off-the-grid affair into a full-fledged marketing spectacle. (It had previously been the Newsweek 24 Hours at Canaan, followed, for several years, by the Toyota 24 Hours at Snowshoe Mountain.) The year I raced the many sponsors included Viagra, the erectile dysfunction drug, which also sponsored a team. Many racers found this hysterical. I was initially mystified by Viagra's sponsorship—it seemed incongruous with the adventure sport ethos—but apparently, at the time, there was increasing evidence that long-distance cycling was associated with incidences of erectile dysfunction.

Depending on a person's perspective, the two years I participated marked either the high or the low point of the race's history. In terms of corporate sponsorship, the cash purse, total participation, and media coverage, the years 2000–2001 were clearly a success for the organizers. In terms of the actual quality of the race course and the level of camaraderie associated with the experience, many found it to be an increasingly desultory affair. Initially, I was looking forward to the race—my first on a mountain bike—because I assumed it would be similar to the Fat Tire Festivals I had attended in West Virginia in the mid 1980s, but in the end my teammates and I were largely disappointed with our experience. The motives of the people who staged the event did not always appear authentic. My team members quickly grew to resent being nickeled and dimed for all manner of services that, in the past, would have been provided as a matter of routine. We resented the fee for parking. Similarly, pitching a tent near the race site had always been a way to defray the cost of participating; now there was a charge for that too. Many of these changes were associated with the fact that the race had been moved from the Canaan Valley to Snowshoe Mountain Resort. The organizers now assumed that most teams would rent a condo for the weekend or stay in the resort hotel.

That year there was a field of five hundred two-, four-, or five-member teams. There were even a few solo riders racing the entire twenty-four hours on their own. These numbers alone indicate that a continuous two-day race was no longer considered an off-the-beaten-path event. In effect, Granny Gear Productions had successfully institutionalized the offbeat nature of the first events, commodified the twenty-four hour experience, and now dutifully sold participation to those who could afford it. The race now attracted professional teams who competed for a cash purse. But the event was still being pitched as unique—"the Woodstock on Wheels"—during the period I raced. The 2003 press release below is indicative of how the race was being marketed:

> Now in its twelfth year, the 2003 24 Hours of Snowshoe (formerly the 24 Hours of Canaan) draws as many as 500 teams, 50 solo riders and more than 10,000 spectators. Sometimes referred to as "Woodstock on Wheels," it's one of the largest mountain bike events East of the Mississippi and has been listed as one of the top three mountain bike events in the U.S. by *Mountain Bike* and *Mountain Bike Action* magazines.
>
> Three years of rain soaked courses (add water, makes its own sauce!) combined with the extreme terrain of West Virginia's fifth highest mountain have made this event one of the gnarliest and most infamous races in the world—the arena of the hardest of the hard core mountain bikers.[28]

Importantly, it was also during this period that twenty-four hour racing was being discovered by the national media and used to represent the increasing interest in lifestyle sport. Both *Newsweek* and *Sports Illustrated* covered the event.[29] But, by this time, it increasingly appeared that the primary goal of the event was to make money for the promoter and the venue where it was held. The organizers' motives were regarded as increasingly inauthentic too. Importantly, many of the critics were often among the best racers in the field.

Twenty-Four-Hour Racing and Team Hugh Jass

Team Hugh Jass stood out for a number of reasons in the twenty-four-hour races. In particular, their gearless bikes—the type you might find at a yard sale—were directly at odds with the equipment increasingly considered mandatory for participation in the event. When I mentioned this to Mike Carpenter, the Tour de Burg organizer and an early Hugh Jass racer, he commented: "That was part of the deal behind Hugh Jass. Mostly taking on the idea that everyone had to be riding a branded bike and have sponsorship."

The team members also shared a pair of foam-padded cycling shorts that enhanced their backsides, which they passed along to the next rider after each lap. Their overall attire tended to be androgynous. This was a team inclined toward pink. A few members wore feather boas when they raced. Moreover, unlike nearly everyone else, the team members usually did not rest when they were not riding. Their campsite was an incongruous fun house of activity: beer, weed, and snack foods were liberally strewn about their camp site, along with games and toys. Indeed, the race often seemed largely beside the point. It was not enough to keep these men occupied for twenty-four hours, so they created other diversions to keep themselves entertained when they were not riding their bikes.

When I spoke with Mike Carpenter he indicated that he sometimes had a hard time embracing Team Hugh Jass' anti-competitor ethos—that it was hard for him to stop racing even when the idea was to "just have fun." Another rider, Tim Richardson, would generally rein him in. "He is a tremendous rider," Carpenter said of Richardson, "but he was also the anti-competitor. So as soon as we would get close to the podium he would see that it was kind of taking over what we were doing it for, and so he would go out and do a three-hour lap. Or he would not come in on time. Or he would come up with the idea that we would all ride the last lap together. . . . . He would remind us why we were out there. At the time I wanted to strangle him . . . but in the end it was great to have him there."[30]

Notably, as the race became more commodified the professional teams increasingly systematized their approach to racing twenty-four hours. They brought in masseurs, team dieticians, team mechanics, and team managers to support their racers. Inevitably, Hugh Jass decided it needed a manager too. Another team member stated:

> I remember one of the years at Caanan when the 24 Hours teams, the serious teams, all of the sudden had to have chefs and masseurs. That was the first year we had our own coach. He wore this full length pleather jacket. It was this silver, glistening jacket down to his ankles, you know? And it was great, because you

would be under the tent, drinking a beer, getting ready for your fixed gear lap, maybe eating bacon or something. And he would decide to give you a massage. And he would make it a point to put you right beside the professional teams that were doing the same things. Except they were all serious and we were.... We were kind of mocking them. It was really kind of a straight up mock [laughing]. And we knew them. They were our friends! And on another weekend we might be racing beside them just as seriously. So, in some ways we were mocking ourselves too....[31]

Sometimes the team's antics caused the race organizers some discomfort. While most found the spectacle endearing—it was clear that these were very skilled riders determined to have fun—the organizer was not always amused. Not only that, but the team sometimes had very specific complaints: for example, they were vocal about the fact that the women's cash purse was not nearly as large as the men's. Other times, the intermittent team nudity and libidinous nature of their campsite caused concerns. As Mike Carpenter put it, "We all had some conflicts with Laird for different reasons . . . He basically dis-invited us to the race for a couple years."[32]

During the 2001 race, the *Sports Illustrated* reporter covering the event also noticed grumbling by many of the race's long-time participants. He wrote:

In a field of $6,000 titanium-framed, full-suspension mudhogs, the Hugh Jass riders turn in strong laps on single-speed, fixed-gear track bikes that require constant pedaling—even downhill. "Everybody thinks I'm crazy for riding a 1974 Schwinn World," says captain Tim Richardson, whose crown of green and red curls frames a pale face, "but over eight years in this race I've never had one flat or mechanical. Even when I'm physically and mentally wasted, the bike still goes."

Old-timers like Richardson lament the yuppification and corporate drift of the event. When the federal government bought much of the Canaan course in 1999 and closed it to recreational mountain biking, Knight moved the race down-state to upscale Snowshoe. What the race gained in technical challenge, it lost in pioneering passion. "It's not about freedom and survival anymore," grumbles Hugh Jass mainstay Mike Carpenter, "it's about bling-bling." He means money.

"Now you pay fees for camping, parking, shuttles," adds Mike Ikenberry, a.k.a. Captain Endo of the Legion of Vroom. "What's next—a toll after every lap?"

Knight, who charges an entrance fee of either $160 (for pros) or $110 (for amateurs), dismisses such critics as "die-hard retro-grouches." He courts sponsors and quotes a self-commissioned survey that depicts 24-hour participants as older, better educated and more affluent than typical mountain bikers.[33]

I find it notable that resistance to the increasing professionalization of the sport often came from the best riders. Team Hugh Jass later demonstrated—during the one year they raced straight-up on standard mountain bikes, as the Shenandoah Mountain Team—that they were among the most skilled riders at the event. They finished first overall among the expert men, and ahead of all but one of the professional teams. But even that year they rode what they euphemistically called their "war machines," they continued self-consciously mocking the entire endeavor. For example, they distributed a supposed press release headed "All Good Things Come to an End" prior to announcing that they had decided to race on geared bikes:

> For the past 5 years everyone has feared it, now it has been done. Hugh Jass has finally thrown down the gauntlet, for the 2000 24 hours of Snowshoe they will put away the fixed gears and bring out the war machines. This last minute formation of team Shenandoah Mtn Touring is sending a message of fear throughout the competition. All four men have played key roles as team Hugh Jass members and now they plan on stepping it up to the next level. Their 6-digit sponsorship deal from Shenandoah Mountain Touring might explain the change of equipment but no one is questioning the team's discipline. This year Mike Carpenter and Tim Richardson; both past captains, will be the secret behind the success of the team. Carpenter has taken up the role of team "HIGH Priest." A role that is sure to make the honorary coach of years past look elementary. Richardson will be the bio-mechanical specialist, responsible for fine tuning the chemical levels of each rider and their race machines. It has been rumored that a crack team of 24-hour specialists has begun mobilization to the venue for this weekend's activities. To put these immortals upon the level playing field that is a geared bike will surely bring disaster to all that bear false witness.[34]

That year was the first time I participated in the race. In fact, I had purchased my bicycle from the above-mentioned "bio-mechanical specialist" a month previously when he and a few other team members opened a downtown shop. They were largely serious this time around, but I occasionally spied a costumed Mike Carpenter, apparently the Team's "High Priest," hurl invective at both his own riders and members of other teams. And the race continued to attract some other free spirits: people attempting, as best they could, to hold onto the early spirit of the race. During my night lap I passed a tandem team (on a two-person bike) whose stoker (the rear rider) wore a disco ball mounted to his helmet. As they pedaled through the dark the stoker propelled the ball in circles while illuminating it with a flashlight. This team also carried a tape cassette with the appropriate disco music.

It is notable that, while the increasing participation in twenty-four-hour racing was then being described as "meteoric," soon afterward it moved rapidly in the other direction. In particular, the Snowshoe event became steadily less popular among amateur mountain bikers, causing it to be discontinued in 2005. Eight years later, Knight shuttered another well-known twenty-four-hour race he organized at Moab, Utah. Perhaps this is an example of how local subcultural taste can have an impact on the practice of sport. In effect, many mountain bikers no longer associated twenty-four-hour racing with being different or authentic—at least at the prices they were being charged for the experience.

The Tour de Burg

There are still cycling events that have retained a more self-regulated and DIY ethos. Many of the members of Hugh Jass now help to organize the annual Shenandoah Mountain Bike Festival, a multi-day event where upward of one hundred volunteers organize the rides, make the community meals, and then clean up afterwards.[35] This type of event often schedules clinics, again run by volunteers—kids' rides, beginners' rides, women's rides—along with a few offbeat cycling contests, perhaps wheelie popping or some bicycle polo. This community also stages a few other local cycling "classics." The Harris-Roubaix, a dirt and gravel ride, is named after the French spring classic, the Paris-Roubaix. This is an increasingly popular community and family event, most recently drawing over a hundred riders of all ages and abilities who complete one lap on the race course before they settle in to watch more experienced riders participating in the three-lap race.[36]

This is a community of cyclists that promotes events that retain aspects of "play." I have long been intrigued by the Tour de Burg, now a notoriously difficult five-day stage race—it was once much longer—that takes place annually when the Tour de France is staged. The Tour de Burg is not officially a "race"—a designation that would complicate the undertaking in terms of costs, participant expectations, and insurance—but the participants are still timed in a manner that is impressive. Indeed, there were points and race jerseys awarded throughout for the Sprint Leader, the Super Downhill (Super D) champion, the King of the Mountain (KOM) and the final finisher or "Dead Fucking Last" (DFL). Placing in the "General Classification" (GC) indicates a top-five finish.

The timing often required considerable planning. Basically, a handful of volunteers synchronized their watches and were dispatched to the top and bottom of the surrounding mountains to keep track of the riders. By the end of the event the Tour riders could chart their daily progress on a spreadsheet that ran several pages long. In 2014, for the first time, the cyclists carried racing chips that monitored them electronically, but this system still required volunteers to station themselves throughout the mountains in order to "time in" the passing riders.

I first took notice of the Tour de Burg at the beginning of this study, in 2002, when I received e-mail race reports from the race director, Mike Carpenter, probably because I had recently bought a mountain bike from the Shenandoah Bicycle Company, whose owners were longtime participants in the event. The faux press release stated that director Mike Carpenter created the Tour de Burg as "an antidote for the whining, egos, and commercialism we have come to associate with bike racing and in life in general."[37] The following excerpt preceded the e-mailed course descriptions and schedule for the seventh annual race:

PRESS RELEASE

7TH ANNUAL TOUR DE BURG—JULY 5TH–JULY 10TH 2002

Addressing a rioting crowd of World Class cycling fans, the prestigious Committee of the Tour de 'Burg announced the dates and routes of the 2002 installment of the Grandest of Grand Tours. In response to the heightened security necessary in the post September 11th world and incessant whining about the severity and duration of previous tours, the Committee has shortened this year's Tour de 'Burg to 6 days. After a laborious 4 hour and 20 minute meeting, the Tour Committee determined that it cannot guarantee a suicide bomber or high-jacked short bus will not capitalize on this event to make one of the greatest political statements of all time. All tour riders will be subject to body cavity searches for added security. Complaints of grueling stages and race duration, mainly from the Team Clean camp, also weighed heavily on the Committee's decision to shorten the race. Although taking a back seat to these new controversies, the doping issues will not pass without notice, riders will still be subject to random and illicit testing at the discretion of the Tour Committee. Race directors hope the shorter format will bolster the number of racers battling for a placing in the General Classification. Regardless of the number of stages, the Tour will showcase the BEST riding on the East Coast and allow the top riders in the sport to battle for the crown jewel of the Grand Tours. An unprecedented sum of cash has been offered for this year's champion as well as single stage prizes, including but not necessarily limited to cars, children, pets, and hair styling products. Each stage has been adopted by notorious sponsors and will no doubt offer larger purses, better course marking, and "official" timing.[38]

Over ten years later in September, 2013, when I spoke with longtime Tour director Mike Carpenter, he indicated that the first race began because he was waiting for a notoriously "time-challenged" riding partner, Chris Scott, and was watching the Tour de France to kill some time. By the time Chris arrived, Mike had decided that they should stage a Shenandoah Valley version of the race over the next couple of weeks. So, the first Tour was actually a race between two participants with their friends periodically joining them as time permitted. At the time, both were interested in adventure and ultra-distance racing—in fact, Chris Scott sometimes competed as a professional. The idea was that each day of the Tour they would ride long and hard with the intention of mixing in as much cycling variety as possible. Chris and Mike apparently still argue about who won that first Tour de Burg.

Mike also created the Tour the year his daughter was born and over time it became something of a father–daughter affair. Indeed, "Lizzy" eventually became integral to staging the race. "She lives for this race," her mother informed me at one post-race dinner. "She basically grew up with it." Notably, during the 2014 race, "Lizzy Carpong," (her Tour nom de guerre), at age 19—easily the youngest participant in the event—did her first "full pull," a feat she was immensely proud of.

I have participated in the Tour de Burg twice. The first was during the summer of 2013[39] when I was formally conducting this study. That year I decided to "poach" two of the easier Tour stages. Indeed, "poaching" and "slumming"—riding "off the back" well behind the race leaders—are time-honored traditions for those too weak-willed to do the "full pull" of five daily rides. After riding a couple of stages I volunteered during the last two days of the event. That year, more than thirty strong riders started with the intention of doing the full pull and twenty-four managed to complete all five stages. Counting the daily poachers, each day's ride usually attracted forty to fifty riders.

The following summer, as I was revising this text, I made an impromptu decision to attempt a full pull of riding. This time around I did not participate for the purposes of research, I mostly thought the rides would be fun and a challenge. It was an opportunity to become a better mountain biker after many years in which I had only sporadically ridden. But mostly, when I thought about doing the Tour, I was looking forward to the "play." It had been a difficult year. I was "jammed up" with respect to several research projects, so when I spoke with my wife about participating I told her, "I think I could use a week with some silliness."

I had no intention of racing in the event—my goal was simply survival. I expected to be hard-pressed just to finish. I was in reasonable shape, but a modestly skilled mountain biker when compared to this group. Indeed, I had watched, a year previously, riders with far more skill quit the race for various reasons. The fact that I could contemplate participating in the Tour is also what makes the race unique. For some, it is a race that attracts the best regional riders. For others, it is a chance to "take inventory"—to try and get better at doing something hard—in an atmosphere with considerable esprit de corps. The event allows for, and celebrates, the fact that some entrants are going to struggle. I expected to be in contention for the DFL (Dead Fucking Last) jersey. And I would definitely be, within the lexicon of the tour, a "slummer"— among the group bringing up the rear.

At the Tour in 2013, signing in for the race involved finding Mike before the start of the ride and stuffing a couple of $20 bills into his pocket, my race fee for the day. The entry fee for five days of racing was $175. To poach a ride for a single day was $40. By way of contrast, the one-day triathlons I entered during the 2013 season had race fees in excess of $100. Mike was easy to find because he dressed for the part of Tour Director. One day he wore a canary-yellow

FIGURE 7 Rider style: the King of the Mountain (KOM) at the 2014 Tour de Burg (July 4, 2014). Photograph by Bryan Lewis.

track suit—many people referred to him as a "Smurf"—and spent much of the road stage riding in front of the peloton on a very fast moped. He donned a striking red, white, and blue ensemble—a vest and cut-off shorts—for the 2013 race on the Fourth of July. Other riders dressed for the occasion too.

Everyone who rides in the Tour is provided with cheap food and drink: peanut butter sandwiches, meat sandwich wraps, off-brand chips and sodas, Cheetos, granola bars, bananas. There is an abundance of cheap beer too. Tour participants eat constantly to fuel themselves through the race and many develop a taste for the soft drinks. I rarely drink sodas, but craved them during the Tour. Their popularity sometimes forced Mike to ration them. As he told the cyclists, "During the Tour you can have as many beers as you want, but only one Coke per rider during each stop." Each ride ended with a communal dinner, a couple of them held at Mike's house, which the participants often pitched in to prepare. So the Tour is a bargain: for about $35 a day a racer has meals and support over hundreds of miles. Many participants referenced the "cheap living" that the week on the tour represented.

The days I volunteered began with a trip to Wal-Mart, where we were dispatched to buy ample quantities of food, beer, and soda that would fuel the racers throughout the day. In the back of Mike's truck were several twenty-gallon plastic jugs—the sort that might be used to carry gasoline—which we refilled with water at intervals, sometimes mixed with energy drink. At points during the day some volunteers drove to points along the race course with synchronized watches to track the riders' progress. Sometimes these timers would sweep the course, riding on their own bikes behind the last rider and then later retrieve their cars.

Mike raced ahead of the group in his truck towing a trailer filled with supplies. On days when the race might cover sixty to seventy mountainous miles—much of it in wilderness areas—he sometimes drove twice as far in order to establish the "refueling" stations along the way. He and a few Tour volunteers would set up a tent for shade, along with a few plastic tables and a chairs. Soon after, volunteers might line up to begin sandwich production. When not in the race herself, Lizzy would station herself at the finish with a synchronized watch and dutifully write down the racers' times as they rolled into the rest area. Most grabbed a few sandwiches, some snack food, and a drink, and then rested until the next timed stage began. After they left for the next stage the volunteers quickly broke down the equipment, stowed it, and rushed to the next station for a hasty redeployment.

Mike sometimes claimed there were no hard "rules" to the race, only guidelines described as "rulish." These were designed to keep the group moving and also help riders stay in the tour if they were physically able to continue. For example, a person who had a technical problem with a bike might be "bridged" back up to the group. Given the distances being covered Mike could not let the group get too spread out, but wrecks, mechanical difficulties, injuries, and other Tour mishaps sometimes stretched the field. A rider an hour or more behind the others was often so tapped out that he or she would drop from the race. The course is difficult enough that strong riders are sometimes forced to abandon the race.

Over the years, a number of Tour de Burg traditions have evolved. For example, many of the participants give each other extraordinarily bad haircuts after the first day's ride. Over time, regional teams have been established, such as the "Cupcakes," a strong group of riders from Pennsylvania. Often, Tour de Burg participants adopt a nom de guerre during the race. I never quite worked out what they did when they were not on their bikes. For example, I enjoyed conversations with longtime Tour participant "Pedro Salsanongrata," but never bothered to ask his real name.

Notwithstanding the various extracurricular activities, the Tour is a difficult race. Even the fittest participants approach it with some trepidation. Given this reality, riders contemplating the race usually make reasonably somber evaluations as to their fitness. Practically, if they have not been riding much—and a few twenty-hour weeks in the saddle would constitute a reasonable amount of preparation—these riders are soon going to be "found out" by their friends on the Tour. In a manner typical of the Tour banter, they often express their nervousness in their letters to the director indicating their intention to participate. The following rider references a "Derecho" of the previous year: a storm with hurricane-force winds that knocked down trees throughout the national forest and had made for a difficult day on the Tour:

Carp—I've been having these nightmares though. Recurring, serious, PTSD dreams where I show up for my first ever stage of the Tour de Berg, and the route is littered with gigantic downed trees. All day, we're jumping them, trying to get around them, getting stuck in them, terrible. It starts to get dark, and things are pretty tense, and l'autobus is hungry and dehydrated, and then the moon comes out and it's wearing a yellow jersey, and all hell breaks loose, and the dream gets kind of jumbled at this point, but I'm pretty sure Thomas Jenkins kills me and eats me (he's VERY nice about it, talks to me the whole time, etc.)

What I'm saying is, I'm in for Sunday, two towers-derecho redemption. Gotta exercise these demons before they get fat.

Dave T.

Another, written by a long-time participant, comically inflates his preparedness for the upcoming race:

Big Carpong,

Count on me for a full pull! I have been Hitting the gym #tossingplates and transforming my Lower body into a freak show of muscles. I was even training with power, but I kept blowing up @garmin head units when I stood up because they are unable to display 5 figures! Ready to take my bike to the #ragecage and crush both up and downhill. See you in JULY!

> *—Dan*

P.S. I can wear any size leader's jersey as long as you have enough safety pins, and Nick Waite is there to tailor it up for me.

Often, these letters reference the pain—usually characterized as "slummin"—that the writers were anticipating:

Letter of Intent. . . . To Whom It May Concern—The Cupcakes are sending a small but determined contingent to maintain our franchise. Due to a high birthrate and an outbreak of responsibility our numbers have been impacted. However, I Pedro Salsanongrata intend to ride the full pull and give particular meaning to the term "slummin!" See you at high noon on the 3rd—

Dear Sir with the nickname of a large freshwater Cyprinidae, I was informed about The Tour's epic demands and rich history by a friend who claims himself a member of the "JV" squad. It both intrigues and scares me, as I have never been to the Shenandoah Valley and I know not the entirety of its beauty and peril. Based on folklore, I understand it to be a savage beast that turns boys into men and men into mashed potatoes. After decoding the lingo in the other posts, I can say with 51% confidence that I am in for a "full-pull" in the "rage cage." I am also well versed in what I believe to be slummin,' but up above the Mason-Dixon line we refer to it as Dirtnappin.' I also vow to provide a demonstration of stunts upon arrival.

I've included a brief portfolio for your review:
I hope you will consider me for this year's tour.

Thank you, Alex

Dearest Tour Director,

It is with tears of explosive joy that I submit this letter on my intentions to commit the act of full pull upon this 2013 edition of Le Tour. Over the past years my time has been squandered at lesser tours, all the while my heart longs for the heat and misery that only the 'Burg can provide. So many hours have been sacrificed in preparation for this event, millions of gravel pieces streaming under the tires.

Hundreds of trips through the rolling hills of my homeland dreaming of the Reddish mountain climb(s?). Oh, the anticipation is more than I can stand! Even now the pints of malt beverage pass through my hands at a feverish pace in hopes that this will prepare my soul for the crushing that is only a little more than a week away. Until then my friends . . . . Viva le Tour!!!

Joseph Von Blowseph[40]

The Tour participants I encountered were mostly men and had reasonably eclectic professional backgrounds. For example, the rider who ultimately claimed the "DFL" jersey in 2013 (actually among the most skilled riders when the course was technically demanding) was an airplane pilot who flew large jets out of Washington, D.C. In 2014, I encountered a lawyer who worked at the State Department. There were also a couple of youngish engineers, a social worker, and at least three college professors (counting myself). Other riders had recently graduated from JMU and were (kind of) looking for less-itinerant work than the part-time jobs they had taken in town. There was at least one stay-at-home dad. Some others were small-business owners. The eventual 2013 winner was a sometimes-professional road and mountain bike racer who had recently established a small company, Pro Tested Gear, which helped people to buy and sell outdoor sporting equipment online.

Pain: The Difficulty of the Tour de Burg

Participants in this race assumed there would be times when they would suffer. They spoke about this in Tour-specific terms: the aforementioned "slummin" (verb form: "slum" or "slum in") or fighting through some "very dark places," or perhaps "visiting the pain cave." For example, during a dirt-and-gravel climb over Shenandoah Mountain I encountered Pedro, who appeared to be struggling: "Right now," he informed me as he sweated into the dirt, "I'm in a very dark place." Nearly all endurance and adventure athletes routinely comment on pain and suffering, which the ones I spoke with described as a primary motivation for doing sport. Because athletes so closely associate pain with their pleasure—because they so commonly report, often happily, that they "suffered" during particularly difficult events—it became evident as I began this study that regarding pain and pleasure as a dichotomy was not useful for describing sporting experiences.

Other scholars who have studied endurance sport have made similar observations. Michael Atkinson noted, "The desire for suffering among triathletes, rather than indicating personal pathology of the mind, points to a dominant habitus categorized by intense self-control, pleasure seeking, foresight, and patience."[41] The "suffering" these athletes experienced was foundational to what made the sport meaningful. Atkinson believes one motivation for pursuing it is that it represents a "trial by ordeal" that connects participants to "neo-traditional communities." Researchers who have investigated certain sporting subcultures—endurance athletes, surfers, skateboarders etc.—have sometimes characterized them as "neo-tribal" groups who are bound together by a common sporting experience.[42] In the case of endurance athletes, one of the shared experiences would be the "pain" they endure as a matter of routine.

More generally, I often found the banter and unique lexicon that had developed among Tour participants to be very funny. For example, just before the prologue in 2014 as the riders were first encountering each other, one of them—a well-known local cycling advocate—made roughly the following impromptu declaration, likely inspired by the fact the race is held over the Independence Day holiday every year.

> Attention. . . . I would like everyone's attention please. . . . I would like to take this opportunity, since everyone is going to be gathered together this week, to talk about something important. Recently, a number of you have probably been hearing that 'Freedom isn't free.' . . . Well, I have been thinking about this and I have decided that *freedom actually is 'free'!* . . . That's why it's called 'free'-dom. So I think freedom is all around us, and that all we have to do this week is go out and grab some of it. . . . Thank you.[43]

In some respects, language closely associated with the event might appear crass, perhaps even confrontational in nature. At the same time, the terms closely associated with the tour—"slummin'," the "shit show," the "dead fucking last" (DFL) designation—were employed with considerable irony. They certainly reference hierarchy—they distinguish riders' ability—but I regarded them as acting to negate some of the same hierarchies. For example, in the Tour de France the "Yellow Jersey" is reserved for the race leader—but in the 2014 edition of the Tour de 'Burg it is was worn by the DFL. The DFL designation existed, in part, as recognition that whoever finished last had, in some ways, probably worked and suffered the most. And given the attrition rate—as many as a quarter of the racers attempting the "full pull" might drop out— the DFL was still considered an achievement. Bryan Lewis, the first-place finisher in 2014, was also a close friend of the DFL, Jeff Cheng. In his blog, he stated, "The relief of finishing [first in the General Classification] cannot be understated. That and seeing Jeff Cheng, who has been such a huge help in my cycling career and even more so with this race, slum on in [and] tighten his grip on that DFL jersey was great. We both came to le Tour with big goals and were able to achieve them."[44]

I found one term closely associated with the tour—"slummin"—somewhat mystifying until I participated in the race. Its original meaning is pejorative. It refers to the practice, in the late 1800s, of well-heeled upper-class whites in New York who went "slumming" as a leisure voyeurism in Black, Chinese and other ethnic neighborhoods.[45] Practically, that meaning was entirely disassociated with how the tour participants used the term, the one exception being that in a few cases it was used to characterize an attempt to "live cheap" for a week. In this context, "slummin" might mean sleeping on a friend's couch for the week during the race.

Mostly, "slummin" referenced those days, or moments, when a rider was at his or her lowest point physically and mentally. It could be a period when the self-doubt concerning the ability to finish was greatest, or when an otherwise stellar tour outing was suddenly upended by a malfunctioning bike, a revolt of the body, a hard fall, or some other manner of misery. Slummin described the periods when someone feels the worst: the point when a rider was "off the back" and alone, perhaps out of water and food, perhaps during the last "hike-a-bike" climb of the day. These were periods when riders worked hard just to hold it together. In some respects, nearly all riders experienced a low point and were forced to "slum." I came to regard the term as a way of referencing the Tour participants' shared experience of pain. As Mike Carpenter explained, "everybody slums" at some point during the Tour de Burg.

The Tour creates a community-minded ethos not common in many cycling events, but clearly associated with the cycling community in Harrisonburg. Mike Carpenter also regards this type of interaction between riders of different abilities as unique feature of the Tour. "It's nice to introduce people to the group ride dynamic of the race," he told me. "The periods when riders parade together are important . . . Sometimes, at the beginning, the fastest riders get jumpy when they have to wait for the slummers, but by the end of the race, as you saw, everyone has bought in and is part of the group."[46]

The Tour rides are difficult. Most take about nine to eleven hours to complete. Usually, the group has a peloton parade from downtown Harrisonburg for twelve to fifteen miles as a warm-up before they enter the surrounding mountains where the racing began. I thought the most difficult ride in 2014 was in the smaller Massanutten range that was on often rocky, narrow single-track that repeatedly climbed over the spine of the mountain. These were usually very steep three-to-five-mile climbs that gained 1,000 to 1,500 feet in elevation and, following some ridgeline riding, inevitably had a steep rocky descent. Sometimes, I quite literally had to fight for every pedal stroke. The total climbing that day was just over nine thousand feet. The day was made harder by thunderstorms: I received two separate severe weather warnings on my phone during the course of the ride. The riders left Harrisonburg at 9:30 AM and wearily pedaled back into town a little past 8:00 PM.

During this ride I encountered the gamut of Tour mishaps that can knock someone from the race. In my case, the day began with a wrong turn at the top of a ridgeline climb, which put me off the back of the last rider and forced me to chase (more than usual) the tail end of the race. Along the way I encountered the detritus of the tour—broken bikes and broken bodies—that occasionally pushed people from the race. On the "parade" back to town—a bumpy, rocky, and now wet ridgeline ride that a few riders described as a "death march"— the group I was riding with suddenly came upon the race leader, a highly skilled rider who had appeared to be breezing through the Tour. He was off his bike, sitting beside the trail, with several people gathered around him. He had wrecked on the final descent. He recovered, but if the wreck had occurred on a timed section of the course he would have dropped a few places from his position in front.

The next ride was the only "road" ride of the Tour de Burg, although much of it was on dirt-and-gravel forest service roads ideal for a "cross bike." The course covered a visually stunning 105 miles that involved a couple of climbs over the ridgeline separating Virginia from West Virginia. (A map of the ride and the elevation profile are included in figure 8.) It ended with a ten-mile dirt-and-gravel climb that summited Reddish Knob. That day, one I judged as easier than the previous ride, included over 10,000 feet of climbing.

The following day the Tour climbed Reddish Knob again, this time along a steep ridgeline trail that began at Hone Quarry, and then descended the

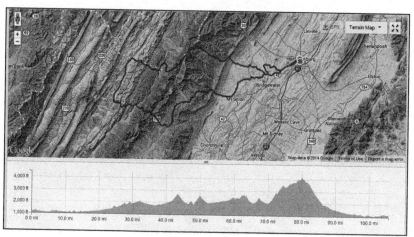

FIGURE 8 Map and elevation profile of the Tour de Burg on July 4, 2014.

mountain along Wolf Ridge. This ride included the longest timed descent of the event, along a narrow single-track trail about ten miles in length, which the fastest riders completed in about forty minutes. The beginning of this descent is pictured in figure 9. The final day included some of the most technically difficult riding, particularly along the ridgeline on the eastern ridge of Massanutten near Camp Roosevelt. It included about five miles of riding that I would characterize as an extended "trials" (obstacle) course. It was a stunning trail, but after five days of difficult riding I struggled to stay upright when I bounded into the first of these "rock slides." Overmatched, I resigned myself to "hike a bike" (not for the first time) through these sections. The most technically adept riders plowed through this stage, one that a hiker might judge as difficult, with few problems.

The Tour de Burg: "The Only Race That Matters"

Given the difficulty of the event it may seem remarkable that there is really no publicity associated with the Tour de Burg. While some sponsored riders participate, it is exactly the sort of race the corporate sponsors of elite and professional riders might ask them to avoid. Indeed, the tagline on the 2014

FIGURE 9 Riding the stairs at Reddish Knob during the Tour de Burg (July 5, 2014). Photograph by Bryan Lewis.

Facebook page claimed it was "Just for Fun." Tour Director Mike Carpenter's favorite motto—oft-repeated among some participants—is that the Tour is "The Only Race That Matters." When the 2014 winner of the Tour de Burg went on to win the national championship race in Category 1 cross-country a couple of weeks later, he posted a picture of himself standing at the top of the podium, with this commentary: "Hmmm . . . does anyone know what shirt that is under the Stars and Stripes? Probably the only race that matters!"[47] By way of contrast, the third-place finisher standing beside him was decked out in his sponsor's kit—literally a walking billboard for Hammer Nutrition.

So the race is something of a paradox in that only the narrowest slice of humanity, a small group of highly skilled mountain bikers, really knows about it. And while the Tour is not intended to be a secret, its reputation is probably related to the fact that so few people know what to expect when they first sign up to participate. Mostly, through rumor and perhaps second-hand (and even third-hand) gossip, they have discerned that the race is "hard," and that it will not be like any other they have done before. Of course, among the small community that does know about the race—and certainly those who have participated in the past—a win in the Tour de Burg is considered a significant accomplishment. For example, on one occasion in 2014, as I pedaled along with the peloton, I listened to a Tour de Burg neophyte exclaim to the person beside him, "This is completely ridiculous! This is the hardest thing someone could do that nobody knows about. Why does nobody know about this? It's incredible!" And then shortly afterwards, having contemplated the question himself, he added, "You know . . . It is probably good so few people know about it . . . If it got bigger it would attract a completely different crowd."[48]

The Women of the Tour de Burg

On the one hand, I found the Tour de Burg a space dominated by men—a sometimes raucous group engaged in a kind of modern *bonhomie*. At the same time, these men tended to be a fairly erudite bunch. Even the most outwardly bellicose members—those inclined toward speechifying and trash-talking, for example—did this with a clear sense of irony. And it is also notable that just as many of the participants were extraordinarily reserved—clearly friendly, clearly enjoying themselves, but not inclined toward verbosity at all.

Clearly, a normative male physicality is associated with mountain biking in general, and sometimes with the Tour too. Still, I encountered no men in this race who associated its difficulty as making it an explicitly masculine endeavor. It was never considered a "manhood act"—one that would distinguish men from women. In fact, it was taken for granted that attracting more women to the race would be a positive change. In some cases, participants were trying to increase women's participation in mountain biking generally. While there are relatively few women on the Tour—usually about five participated in the daily rides—they were clearly welcomed and fully integrated into the group. Most notably, Lizzy, Mike's daughter, had known many of these riders for years and had, quite literally, grown up riding with them. Indeed, much like her father, her very being seemed intimately associated with the race. Because she had grown up with the race, participants with the longest tenure often associated it with watching her grow up too. It was inevitable that Tour riders enthusiastically cheered her announcement in 2014 that she was ready to ride the entire event.

Sue Haywood is probably the most accomplished rider who routinely participates in the Tour in terms of her professional racing résumé. She is now semi-retired, but was once among the best cross-country riders in the country. She is certainly comfortable riding with men, but also sponsors a number of area camps, rides, and training sessions designed to introduce women to mountain biking. I did not have a chance to interview Sue, but came to regard her general temperament as an appealing mix of laconic and mellow. She is a woman of few words, but they always seemed to perfectly sum up the circumstances we encountered during the day. She seemed to delight in observing the action around her, which she often punctuated with some succinct observation.

Sue's personality was also reflected in the remarkable economy I came to associate with her riding: she routinely made very difficult things look impossibly easy. For example, one day when I volunteered in 2013 there was a descent off Reddish Knob that began with a roughly thirty-five-yard drop down a set of rock stairs. (See Figure 9.) In fact, Mike had informed the riders that they should probably "take a look" at the stairs before they began the descent. The riders were four days into the Tour and had just finished a six-mile climb. One of them wandered over, took a quick look down, and said to no one in particular, "Fuck that." And then most of the group—including the skeptic—began to consider whether they could manage to ride down the stairs. Some held their bikes and rolled them over different routes to see if they had enough clearance to make it down. Riding the stairs would be faster than running them, but for those who were tired, or "off the back," the latter was a sensible approach.

The race leader, who went down first, initially sprinted toward this obstacle, which caused a small murmur to rise from the assembled group. He initially appeared to be "going for it" and his speed—even for someone so skilled—seemed reckless. Then, just before he hit the stairs he starting laughing, quickly hit his brakes, and clicked out of his pedals. He began bounding down the stairs on foot, followed by some good-natured jeers from the crowd. He knew he had a few minutes cushion off the front and had decided to play it safe. A few observers, stationed at the top with squirt guns, sprayed him with water as he made his way down.

One of the next riders—someone who knew this descent well—rode the steps with considerable pace. It was a "bouncy" ride down but he looked in control throughout. He clearly wanted to move up in the general classification and had decided to go for it. The next cyclist also rode down—he cleared the stairs—but his descent looked rougher than the previous rider's. He appeared to just barely hold it together.

Following that descent, another rider walked to the edge and inquired as to "how it looked" so far. Someone watching the action replied, "Chris made it look OK, but then Buck made it look totally sketchy." Sue was the next rider to descend. It was always clear she was going to ride down, something she managed easily. Unlike the previous riders she did not appear to bounce much at all. She had clearly plotted the best line down. She stood out because she made riding down the stairs look remarkably easy, as if it were the most natural thing for someone to do. The rider evaluating the descents looked up from the action, clearly delighted by what he had just observed. Without hesitation, he continued his thought: "Or, I suppose, you just find a way to 'finesse it' all the way down." The rider standing beside him shook his head in admiration too.[49]

So Sue sometimes stood out in this community for a number of reasons, often related to the fact that she was so highly skilled, but sometimes because she was a woman mountain biker surrounded by men. On the first day of the Tour in 2013 she appeared for the prologue decked out in pink—a pink skirt was pulled over her cycling shorts, accented by pink knee socks. She had referenced her propensity toward the color with a creative stair-step rhyme in her letter of intent: "I'm tossing my pink Ass into the Tour de Burg slumtown browntown funkytown out of town downtown showdown."[50]

One man, as he encountered Sue, announced to a friend within her hearing, "You know . . . the fact that Sue is wearing a skirt on this ride is kind of freakin' me out." To which his friend responded, clearly joking and also loud enough for Sue to hear, "Hey, don't let her get to you . . . She's just doing that to psych you out." Sue appeared to find the exchange funny. At least she did turn and smile at them wryly.[51]

The Larger Project: Creating Community in Harrisonburg

During a review of this chapter I had one reader comment that various members of "Team Hugh Jass" and the antics associated with the Tour de Burg seemed closely associated with a masculine culture characterized by sadomasochism: that these riders were libertine men who enjoyed engaging in stunts designed to hurt themselves in order to demonstrate they were men. The reader thought their antics were comparable to those in the movie *Jackass*.[52] I had never seen the movie, but was concerned by this reading of the text. Notwithstanding the "stunts" associated with the Tour, this did not seem, to me, to capture the nature of why people participated in the race.

To some extent the stunts and various hijinks associated with the event seem associated with the desire, for some, to step outside or "take a vacation" from the confines of daily life now common among those in the white middle class. To some modest degree, the Tour created a space where acting outside the bounds of normal life—if someone wanted to—would be not only accepted, but admired. In some respects, I tended to regard the "Hugh Jass" spectacle and, to a lesser extent, the hijinks of the Tour de Burg, as channeling the same manic energy and pushing of norms associated with Ken Kesey and the Merry Pranksters' infamous 1968 "road trip" made famous by Tom Wolfe.[53] (Probably, this is because the costuming in both events—to my way of thinking—looked so similar.)

Later, when I participated in the 2014 Tour de Burg, a longtime Tour rider came up to me—we had spoken the previous year about this text—and he asked me how it was progressing. In particular, he was interested to know if I had described the Tour de Burg. Yes, I told him, I had described the race, but I was worried because one reviewer had decided it was akin to the movie *Jackass*. This rider—a stay-at-home father of two young children—was often closely associated with some of the Tour hijinks that I assume were the reason for the comparison. He had packed the shears and enjoyed giving particularly bad haircuts to other participants after the opening day's ride. I am not inclined toward bellicosity or profanity, but I personally found him to often be wonderfully profane in terms of the sheer inventiveness of his language. I expected he had watched, and maybe even admired, the movie. So my inquiry was not entirely innocent—I thought he was the best Tour participant with respect to evaluating the *Jackass* comparison. Given the brief grin that followed my statement, I imagine that he probably did spend a moment contemplating the stunts he had engaged in over the years. He eventually replied, "Well . . . there is certainly a bit of Jackassery on the Tour, but concentrate on that and people are probably going to miss the point . . . won't they?"[54]

So what is "the point" of the Tour? Mostly, what makes this race different is that it so clearly is anchored in creating and maintaining a community. The tour itself is just one race, one of many in Harrisonburg enabled by a culture of volunteerism. In effect, it is the sort of race where the Tour director contributes to the local cycling advocacy group and uses money left over from the enterprise to pay for participants' memberships in a local nonprofit cycling organization for a year.

This is not surprising because many of the members of Hugh Jass have, over the past decade, worked to actively transform the community of Harrisonburg into a more bike-friendly city. For example, several have been integral to the development of a "master" cycling plan and securing federal and local funding for the ongoing construction of bike and pedestrian infrastructure throughout the town. At various times they have all had leadership roles in the Shenandoah Valley Bicycle Coalition (SVBC). A couple of them helped to write and administer grants, the largest of which were two U.S. Forest Service allocations of nearly $300,000 to support trail-building projects in the George Washington National Forest. The opening day ride on the Tour de Burg often ends on the trail that was built from Lookout Mountain by volunteers connected to the SVBC. In fact, the staging of many events in the community is intimately associated with a culture of volunteerism. Put simply, an ethic of volunteerism is built into a number of local cycling events, the Tour de Burg among them.

The trail-building ethic was created informally during the "Six Pack" downhill races established in the area during the early 1990s. These were an expanded version of another ride, the "Dollar Downhill," in which participants each donated a dollar to buy beer and pizza at a local restaurant following the race. Over time, the Six Packs evolved into a series of downhill races held that culminated in a championship race. They were always held on Friday in the late afternoon and afterward there was usually an impromptu party (at which beer was consumed). Following the final race the party was known to be an incredibly raucous affair. As Thomas Jenkins, a sometime Hugh Jass rider and local bicycling advocate, put it:

> Yeah, without a doubt, that was the biggest thing. The whole thing behind the six pack rides was that there was a big final ride and a big party. And it was an out-of-control party. But to go to that party you had to do your trail work. . . . Which was kind of odd, but it was amazing what that did in so many ways. One, you always had that Friday ride usually followed by the party. And people partied hard. And then people got up early the next morning, and they were usually hung over, but they still got hassled to do their trail work. And then we were out there, you know, just slingin' tools. . . . But at the time, I don't think we really knew what we were doing, what we were developing. And now it has changed pretty drastically. Instead of ten people doing trial work, now we are doing projects that [cost] hundreds of thousands of dollars. . . .[55]

Thomas Jenkins, in particular, has always been an enthusiastic trail builder and someone I associate with being among the most proactive in building the

SVBC organization. At the time I first met him, in the mid 1990s, he invited me to join him and others during a trail maintenance session on Trimble Mountain. (Many of the local trails were underutilized and increasingly falling into disrepair.) I mostly remember this event because I was surprised that Thomas had secured a key to a regional U.S. Forest Service maintenance building, which he nonchalantly unlocked before passing out the shovels, picks, and other equipment that we used to clear a few mud slides that had drifted into the trail during wet weather. When I expressed some surprise that the Forest Service had given him a key to their equipment shed he explained that he had been talking with local personnel—who were increasingly stretched thin in terms of their responsibilities—and they were soon convinced that it was a good idea to let local mountain bikers use Forest Service tools for trail maintenance.

This cultivation of local Forest Service personnel demonstrated some remarkable foresight. In fact, at that time trail-use issues associated with mountain biking were becoming contentious in other regions of the country where different groups—ATV enthusiasts, hikers, equestrians—were sometimes coming into conflict with one another. In the case of George Washington National Forest the local mountain biking community had access to an extraordinary resource that was mostly unrestricted in terms of access. As such, Thomas wanted to ensure continued access by demonstrating that the mountain bike community was an asset, not a liability, as it related to maintaining and even improving the surrounding trail networks.

This is essentially the same mission of a recently established national nonprofit organization, the International Mountain Bike Association (IMBA), based in Boulder, Colorado. Not surprisingly, the network of mountain bikers associated with the SVBC actively supported the IMBA. For example, the IMBA periodically sent a "trail care crew"—a couple versed in trail building who worked with local mountain bike clubs—into the region in the summer. As successive "crews" passed through "the Burg" they were confronted with a group of local bikers who, even by the standards of the largest clubs in the country, were among the most committed to trail building. Eventually, Rich Edwards—a former trail care crew member and now an IMBA regional manager—was so impressed by this community that he decided to relocate to Harrisonburg. He has since become one of many people in the community who helped to take the SVBC to the next level in terms of seeking and administering grants related to bicycle advocacy.

Cycling, Community Activism, and Resistance

Harrisonburg has generally fared well during past economic shifts: the university always draws students and the local economy is reasonably diverse too. But near Harrisonburg are some very depressed rural communities that are also trying to take advantage of their proximity to the National Forest. They are at the base of the mountains, often along a river where one might paddle or fish, but these communities are not often regarded as appealing places for people to live or vacation.

It is notable that Harrisonburg has been successfully branded the "cycling center"[56] for riding in the Shenandoah Valley because, in the not so distant past, the community routinely failed to make a good impression on visitors. In particular, economic life downtown went through a period of stagnation in the 1980s and early 1990s as small merchants struggled to compete with the "big box" retailers that increasingly populated the periphery of the community. In 1995 a travel writer for the *Washington Post* ventured down the old Valley "turnpike" (Route 11), intent on visiting scenic towns along the way. She discovered that the road south of Harrisonburg was essentially a few miles of stoplights, strip malls, fast food restaurants, and big-box retailers. She then entered a mostly depressed and dull downtown. The resulting story included the sentence, "Harrisonburg definitely merited a detour on I-81, but unfortunately we made the mistake of following Route 11 through town and then past the unattractive sprawl that sets it apart from the other towns in this region."[57]

From the beginning, an important goal of those who founded the first community cycling organization was to make the community more bicycle-friendly. In fact, many were also active in downtown revitalization efforts directed by another nonprofit organization, the Harrisonburg Downtown Renaissance.[58] When outsiders peruse regional travel magazines or look at the community website, they invariably encounter a reasonably slick campaign— "It's Better in the Burg!"—that touts the amenities of Harrisonburg for those who might want to visit or move to the small city. A regional magazine, *Blue Ridge Outdoors*, in July 2013 featured the riding around Harrisonburg as one of its "eight best adventure road trips."[59] During the past two decades, Harrisonburg has become one of the livelier downtowns in the region.

Currently, the largest downtown retailer in terms of annual sales is probably the Shenandoah Bicycle Company. When I asked Thomas Jenkins, part-owner of the enterprise, about the decision to establish the business downtown over a decade ago he replied, "At the time it made no sense in terms of the things you were supposed to consider when establishing a small business. I had read a book that said I should sit at sites and count the number of people who went by in an hour. . . . That was not going to work here, not too many people went by this spot, but we were pretty determined to establish ourselves downtown."[60]

Notably, since the shop's establishment, life in this Virginia town has changed in some dramatic ways. There is more downtown living space, more restaurants, a new library and a few significant retailers too. And one important aspect of Harrisonburg's new identity is its increasing association as a cycling center. In effect, regional cyclists know that the Shenandoah Valley is an extraordinary place to ride and that many recreational cyclists and expert riders live in Harrisonburg.

Obviously, Harrisonburg would not be a cycling mecca if it had no places to ride a bike. At the same time, simply being located in a place where people might do outside sport does not assure that a community makes the transition to an amenities-based economy. To some degree, success depends on how people think about where they live—the town's history and the identity people associate with its past. In Harrisonburg the cycling community is now part of a larger group of activists who are trying to help people take advantage of the town's nearby outdoor amenities. In this respect, the Tour de Burg is part of a larger cycling and outdoor sporting culture now closely associated with the community. Of course, few people in Harrisonburg will probably attempt the Tour de Burg, but the race is indicative of a range of community events—the ice cream socials, the six pack downhills, the ride your bike to school program—that all tend to reinforce "play" and community aspects of sport.

6

Why So White?

• •

Race and Social Class
in Lifestyle Sport

Triathlon and mountain biking may be the whitest sporting spaces I have ever encountered. This first became evident to me at triathlons when the participants were massed together at the start of races. Of course, sport has long been stratified by race and social class—skiing, golf, and tennis being a few other examples of activities where participants are disproportionately white and of high social status. Indeed, the whiteness of these sports has often been explored by both academic and cultural critics, whose work I draw upon in much of this chapter.

When I began this study I wanted to interview a reasonably diverse group of athletes in terms of their age, gender, ethnicity, and race. If a group is underrepresented in a facet of social life it can make it particularly important to include them in a study. From my previous experience I expected these sports to be very, very white, but I was also planning to attend races where there would be hundreds, sometimes thousands, of people racing. Surely, I had thought to myself before the study began, I will be able to find a few people of color to talk with.

As it turned out, it was routine for me to attend races where nearly all the participants were white. Of course, it would be an exaggeration to state that I encountered no ethnic or racial diversity during this study. For example, one of the aspiring engineers in the Virginia Tech Triathlon Club was Indian-American, but I think he may have been the only club member who did not self-identify as white. I also routinely interacted with a racer whose family was from South America—one of a few middle- and upper-class Latinos I encountered in triathlon—but I found no meaningful participation by working-class Latinos in any of these sports. And the group that often seemed the most absent—people I was often quite literally at a loss to find among the masses at these races—were black athletes.

Perhaps it was this concerted effort to find athletes of color that made me start to think of triathlon—particularly during the race starts when everyone was together and waiting to begin their swim—as the archetypal example of elite white sport. The swim start in triathlon can tend toward spectacle: many people rushing into the water all at once is quite a sight. But soon, as I developed the habit of scanning the crowd in an attempt to find a black triathlete I might talk with after the race, what inevitably popped into my head was some version of *that sure is a lot of white people crammed together*.

And it was definitely a certain type of whiteness at these races. It was not the working-class/blue-collar whiteness that I encountered when I took my kids to the local county fair. Rather, it was an extraordinary concentration of a white professional class. The more I searched for diverse athletes to interview, the more I began to wonder if triathlon was perhaps the whitest sport on earth. Could it be whiter than tennis? Less diverse than golf? Perhaps even whiter than skiing? Indeed, I had a hard time thinking of activities that might be as white as triathlon and mountain biking.

Sometimes I talked about the whiteness of the events with friends in the sociology program at Virginia Tech. I once asked Tiffany, a young, black aspiring marathoner, if she might be interested in tagging along to a race in Richmond. Tiffany had recently discovered that a group of graduate students, myself included, had done a twenty-four-hour mountain bike race. Like some others, she had responded with a version of the refrain: "Why would you do that?" As we tried to answer her questions about what the race had looked like, we had finally decided that it mostly looked like a bunch of white people riding bicycles in the woods. During that race I had observed a single black men's team—indeed, among all those white men it was hard to miss them—and had wanted to talk to them, but never managed to track them down afterward for an interview.

Richmond, Virginia is a reasonably diverse city with a larger black professional class compared to other areas where I was racing. I was hopeful, but not optimistic, that its event could be a modest exception to the whiteness I had encountered so far. I figured Tiffany's observations would be interesting—and also thought that if we encountered the elusive black triathlete she might be, in terms of building trust, the better interviewer. As it turned out, the Richmond race proved no more diverse than the previous ones I had attended; we left without any interviews of black triathletes. Still, Tiffany was impressed with the spectacle of the race and the athletes too. And in the absence of athletes of color, she decided to talk with a few white men, chosen, it seemed to me, for their impressive physiques. She admitted as much afterwards. Later, as we were talking with another friend, she laughed and informed him, "Steve is studying beefcake on bicycles."[1]

Tiffany was joking, but I understood the reason for the comment. Basically, if one understands "beefcake" to refer to super-fit men in some state of undress, than the transition area of triathlon is as "beefcakey" a place as one might imagine. There was no shortage there of preening, half-dressed men with broad shoulders and six-pack abs—the type of men who populate magazines such as *Men's Health* and *Men's Fitness*. Indeed, the overall fitness of these participants, combined with the machinery they have to master, is probably one reason this sport is intimidating for many people. Still, this is clearly less the case for certain types of white men.

The Intersection of Race, Class, and Gender in the Creation of Sporting Cultures

The near-hegemonic whiteness of lifestyle sport offers an opportunity to think about how race and social class intersect with each other with respect to participation. Why are many of these sports so dominated by middle-aged white men with relatively high social status? The early strategy of this chapter is to account for possible structural and cultural reasons.[2] Feminist scholars have used the concept of intersectionality—how race, class, and gender connect with each other—in order to describe patterns of privilege or subordination experienced by different groups of people.[3] Generally, each of the previous can be associated with ordinate and subordinate groups within a society. In the United States men often have more power than women and blacks less power than majority whites. However, social statuses within all these groups can also intersect: not all white men, for example, have power in all social situations, particularly if they have lower social status associated with their occupation or social class.

Notably, I live in an area where white men from different social backgrounds—I will use the terms "white-collar" and "blue-collar" as shorthand descriptions—routinely practice different sports in the nearby national forests. Not all of the sports chronicled in this text are practiced in wilderness areas, but mountain biking is. The interactions between sportsmen in this rugged setting provided an opportunity to think about the motivations of mostly working-class white men who considered themselves more traditional "sportsmen" compared to those of the men in white-collar professions who were more inclined to participate in lifestyle sport.

Race and Social Class: Locality and the Expense of Adventure Sport

Obviously, it would be hard to find any sport in the United States that is entirely white. Gabby Maiden, a black woman, is a well-known professional snowboarder. Tinker Juarez, a somewhat iconic mountain biker, is Hispanic. But within these sports these two athletes are exceptions: they quite literally stand out among their fellow competitors. As for triathlon, at the time I began this study not one black man or woman had ever raced in the professional field. Just before this text was due to be submitted for publication, Max Fennell attained an elite racing license that would allow him to compete as the first black professional triathlete in the sport's history in 2015. Also notable is that during the period of this study the Black Triathletes Association was formed and formally recognized as a club by the USA Triathlon Federation. This gave me an opportunity to contact a few black triathletes and ask them about their experiences with the sport.[4]

Clearly, one barrier to participation in any lifestyle sport is the cost. To some degree, this probably prevents participation by the white working class as well as minority groups that are more predominantly working class. Caution is warranted here because there have been no empirical studies of the degree to which "cultural" vs. "economic" capital are barriers to participation in triathlon and mountain biking. But studies associated with other elite sport have often found that cultural capital is the greater barrier of the two.[5] Triathlon was probably the most costly sport that I investigated, although mountain biking equipment is often very expensive too. The governing organization for American triathletes, the USA Triathlon Federation, has largely embraced the fact that triathletes are affluent. A report commissioned by this organization, *The Mind of a Triathlete*, highlighted the fact that triathletes continued to spend money on sport even during a period when the economy was contracting. In fact, the organization used this as a primary argument for attracting greater corporate sponsorship to the sport.[6] In 2008, USA Triathlon commissioned the Tribe Group to survey their members. According to *The Mind of a Triathlete*, they contacted 150,000 athletes through e-mail and had nearly 15,000 responses. Online surveys have flaws—certain types of people are more likely to respond, for example—but this near ten percent response rate is quite good comparatively. That information is reproduced in table 1.[7]

Table 1
Occupations, Annual Income, and Annual
Spending on Triathlon by Athletes (2007)

Occupation	
49%	report white-collar jobs
19%	report professional jobs such as doctor, lawyer, or accountant
12%	are students or education workers
8%	are gray-collar workers
6%	are government or military
4%	are blue-collar

Income (Average: $126,000)	
12.9%	have incomes under $50K
14.5%	have incomes $50–74,999
16%	have incomes $75–$99,999
23.4%	have incomes $100–$149,999
12.1%	have incomes $150–$199,999
8.4%	have incomes $200–$299,999
5.5%	have incomes over $300K

Average Annual Spending on Triathlon	
$2,274	spent on bikes in the past twelve months
$564	spent on race fees in the past twelve months
$524	spent on bike equipment
$370	spent on training, running, and athletic footwear
$277	spent on nutritional supplements

NOTE: Reproduced from the USA Triathlon website. The percentages in each table do not sum to 100 percent. Judging from their *The Mind of a Triathlete* report these differences likely represent athletes who were not earning a wage (e.g. homemakers), were retired, or left these survey fields blank.

In the field of sociology, a discussion of demographics usually includes an accounting of the racial and ethnic composition of groups associated with a social phenomenon. This fact sometimes makes reading the demography sections in reports commissioned by Triathlon USA disorienting. I expected *The Mind of a Triathlete* to include a cursory discussion about introducing the sport to underrepresented ethnic groups as a marketing strategy—but there was, remarkably, no discussion at all of the ethnic composition of participants.[8]

Importantly, this information was reported in one table on the USA Triathlon website.[9] (See table 2.) Perhaps, given the cost of the sport, it should not be surprising that the people who race in triathlon are most often white men, mainly white-collar and professional workers who are close to the age of forty. *The Mind of a Triathlete* routinely notes that the composition of participants in the sport does not skew toward the young, but more often toward middle-career professionals with considerable disposable income. The report explicitly compares this demographic to that found in sports such as golf and tennis.[10]

Patterns of Residency and Access to Lifestyle Sport Amenities

Some activities require proximity to public land and wilderness areas, so patterns of residency limit access to certain types of outdoor lifestyle sport.[11] Of the sports explored in this text, mountain biking in wilderness areas may be most affected by this dynamic. Indeed, the amenities-rich rural counties of Western Virginia where this study was conducted tend to have the highest percentage of white residents in the state. At the same time, when I lived in Roanoke, the most diverse small city in southwest Virginia, I observed no appreciable difference in terms of the participation of people of color in lifestyle sport.

Probably, the whiteness of lifestyle sport like triathlon is reinforced by broader patterns of racial segregation within communities. For example, many suburban and urban triathletes live in reasonably diverse communities, but within these communities there are probably patterns of segregation that place white families closer to amenities associated with running, cycling, and particularly swimming. In fact, studies of swimming (and particularly rates of drowning) have long indicated that the black community in the United States

Table 2
Race and Ethnicity of Triathletes (2007)

88.2%	Caucasian/White
3.2%	Hispanic
2.1%	Asian
1.5%	Multiracial
0.5%	African-American/Black
1.1%	Other

NOTE: Reproduced from the USA Triathlon website. The percentages in this table do not sum to 100 percent. The difference (3.4 percent) probably represents athletes who did not answer the survey question, or whose answer was undecipherable.

swim less, perhaps because they live in areas with less access to resources where people can learn to swim.[12] Among the few black triathletes I surveyed, many stated that they believed that within some African American communities in the United States there was aversion, perhaps even longstanding fear, of open-water swimming. Indeed, one of the athletes surveyed identified "learning to swim" as the most significant barrier to her own participation in triathlon. But while residential patterns and the cost of sport explain why some ethnic and racial minorities spend less time in public wilderness areas, or less time swimming, there is persuasive evidence that cultural capital, more so than economic capital, also determines patterns of participation by different social classes in certain sports.[13]

Hegemonic Whiteness in Lifestyle Sport: Structure and Culture

The previous statement should not be read as a "racializing" of lifestyle sport and swimming—as supporting a now much-debunked idea that ethnic groups naturally "track into" the sports they do best. Rather, the varying rates of swimming and participation in lifestyle sport indicate the existence of both structural and cultural barriers to participation that are a result of minority communities' having unequal access to resources. Some of these differences are still built into the infrastructure of communities today. In my current home of Staunton, Virginia, it was not so long ago that there was a "white" public park (Gypsy Hill) and a "black" public park (Montgomery Hall). Of course, both parks are now integrated—and both now have swimming pools too—but swimming and golfing at Gypsy Hill Park are longstanding offerings, whereas the pool at Montgomery Hall Park is relatively new.

There is also considerable research showing that white Americans are more likely than blacks to engage in outdoor recreation associated with wilderness areas.[14] Many scholars believe that because of the history of slavery in the United States, African Americans do not share whites' positive associations with working the land and the cultivation of wild spaces that is often integral to American ideas. (Think "manifest destiny.") These narratives also underpin the U.S. environmental movement and Americans' supposed greater affinity with the "great outdoors."[15] Other studies indicate that black patterns of recreation are geared toward visiting places where they are less likely to encounter racism—the inconvenience of being targeted, for example, for "driving while black"—and also places where they do not expect to encounter more subtle forms of discrimination.[16] Some have asserted that a black historical consciousness—a "collective memory" that associates rural America with past patterns of segregation and abuse—may also be a factor as to why African Americans underutilize national forests.[17]

Often, these now well-established patterns of outdoor recreational use are routinely reinforced by media images. When the media show blacks engaging in recreation they usually appear in urban settings associated with traditional sports. People pictured engaging in recreation in the "great outdoors" are disproportionally white.[18] Similar patterns of racial segregation in media are also evident in well-established outdoor recreational sports. One of the most studied of these is the "unbearable whiteness of skiing."[19] While there have been few cases of private ski resorts barring blacks, advertising often associated skiing with highbrow European culture. This reinforced the notion that skiing was an elite white avocation.[20] Even after attempts to diversify, particularly as overall participation rates declined, skiing remained an almost entirely white sport. In Kwame Harrison's exploration of "black skiing"—or the lack thereof—he drew upon both historical and ongoing meanings of space as created by different groups. He was particularly interested in how ski resorts maintain nearly hegemonic whiteness even though explicit forms of racism at these resorts is not common. In effect, these are spaces in which extraordinary race segregation occurs without much consideration by the white groups who inhabit them.[21] These people are usually not explicitly racist; however, there is clearly a structure and culture associated with skiing that reinforces and maintains patterns of racial segregation and white privilege.

The sports I examined in this study—newer than more traditional white sports like skiing, tennis, and golf—are also most often spaces of near-hegemonic whiteness, so much so that many participants take the whiteness for granted. Notably, I observed the same patterns of minority-group representation in the popular print magazines associated with both triathlon and cycling. As in skiing magazines, the articles and advertising in *Triathlete*, *Inside Triathlon*, and *Bicycling* rarely show people of color.[22] In triathlon magazines I spotted only one notable exception to the hegemonic whiteness: a campaign that featured several "celebrity" Ironman participants in an advertisement for milk. One of these athletes was Ward Hines, a former professional football player, who is African American. He was sometimes the only black athlete shown in an entire edition of a magazine.

Mountain bike publications are—like triathlon and other cycling magazines—comparable in their non-representation of black athletes. This is so much the case that in the early 1990s a very small mountain bike company, Nuke Proof, created a minor stir when it featured James Bethea, a black mountain biker, in its advertising. In fact, the popular (and athletic) singer Janet Jackson contacted the company and inquired if she could purchase the same bodysuit Bethea wore in the ad. In the mountain bike magazines I looked at during this period, he was usually the only black athlete represented. The company was also sponsoring him as rider in East Coast races at the time. Later,

Bethea raced for Jamis Bicycles and was likely the first black professional cross-country rider in the sport. In a 2013 interview, Bethea reported that despite a few incidences of racism, his experience was overwhelmingly positive. He remains an active rider and amateur veteran racer to this day.[23]

Despite the lack of black athletes in modern advertising, triathlon and mountain biking are new enough that it seems doubtful a shared historical consciousness—memories of overt discrimination within the sports—would account for the small number of minority participants. The most likely explanation is probably that, like skiing, these activities are a field of hegemonic whiteness taken for granted as "white sport" from their inception. When white athletes enter these sports and consume this media, they help reinforce racism even though few of the participants are explicitly racist. Perhaps unconsciously, these athletes act in ways that reinforce patterns of racial segregation and that reinforce white privilege.

In a few cases I did ask white athletes why they thought their sport was so white. Because discussions of race and ethnicity can make people uncomfortable, I usually asked questions of this nature near at the end of the interview, particularly if I felt I had established a positive relationship with the person being interviewed. This strategy was undertaken with the idea that these athletes might be more forthcoming when they considered the question of whiteness in sport. As I have stated previously, triathletes are easily among the most enthusiastic people I have ever interviewed when given a chance to talk about sport—their passion is extraordinary. Most of my interviewees believed triathlon was self-evidently good for everyone involved and enthusiastically recruited people to the sport. Despite this, the most common response to my questions concerning the "whiteness" of triathlon was usually an awkward pause. Some athletes appeared to have never considered the question before. They thought about it for a bit, appeared to run through possible reasons, but mostly offered responses to the effect that they did not really know.

Backgrounds and Experiences of Black Triathletes

It was fortunate that a new triathlon club, the Black Triathletes Association, was formed during the period this text was written. This allowed me to contact a few members of the organization who filled out a brief survey of open-ended questions that asked about their experiences in the sport. I think many, perhaps most, of these athletes tended to see the barrier to greater black participation in triathlon as being related to the fact that there were so few examples of black triathletes for future athletes to identify with. The most common response to a question that asked if they had any insights concerning the low participation rates of minority groups in triathlon was a belief that some African-American communities were less inclined toward swimming. The next most common response was related to the cost of the sport.

My impression was that this new association was not conceived of as an advocacy group designed to, for example, press the national organization to actively recruit ethnic and racial minority athletes. Many members regarded the Black Triathletes Association as a resource—a place where a black athlete could find out how to do triathlon and inspire others. It was also clearly a place where the accomplishments of the group—and some in this small organization were quite accomplished—could also be publicized. Among the very few members I surveyed there was a decidedly mixed response to a question that asked whether the national federation should engage in outreach to increase participation among underrepresented groups. For a few the answer was "yes," and the rationale was largely economic. Outreach, these members said, should take place because there was an untapped resource, a community willing to spend money, who would likely find the sport attractive. Other members, because they perceived no explicit discrimination within the sport—and many went out of their way to describe the triathlon community as both welcoming and encouraging—felt that it was not the responsibility of the national organization to do this type of outreach.

Like other triathletes, many of the members of this association are avid bloggers and chroniclers of their triathlon experiences. This gave me an opportunity to compare their blogs to others that I had encountered.[24] Importantly, the members of the Black Triathletes Association are "self-selected": they make a decision to join the organization. This makes it likely that certain characteristics associated with people who are "joiners" are overrepresented within the membership. I had assumed that triathlon bloggers would be among the most enthusiastic supporters of the sport too. But judging from the blogs and the few surveys I administered, this group was diverse in terms of athletic ability (which ranged from novice to professional), gender, age, and profession. In most respects the group members were comparable to other triathletes. This was particularly true in terms of the "self-narratives" in many of the blog posts related to motivations for doing triathlon. Many of the middle aged women tied taking up the sport to the need to maintain their wellbeing and fitness, sometimes in the face of specific health threats. One of them was a cancer survivor. Many of the athletes also noted that it was increasingly hard to "eat healthy" and maintain a healthy lifestyle given the demands of modern life. In this respect there was the same strong association with triathlon as a lifestyle sport that reinforced healthy living. Some athletes, particularly the younger ones, were clearly looking for adventure or a life challenge, which competition in triathlon provides. Indeed, the overall enthusiasm expressed by Black

Triathletes Association members for the sport seemed, in almost every way, comparable to that of the other men and women who had adopted triathlon as lifestyle sport. Indeed, like most of the triathletes I had formally interviewed, these athletes reported that the community with whom they trained constituted their primary social network outside of work.

Like most other triathletes, this group was well-educated. Judging from their blogs, as well as responses to the survey, their occupations were diverse but disproportionately represented professional occupations. The members included health care workers, lawyers, a former stockbroker, middle and upper managers in large corporations, and a wide range of other mostly professional avocations. More than a few of these athletes had transitioned from professional careers to those more closely associated with health and personal training. The men, in particular, often reported that they were former athletes who had aged out of formal competition or been seriously injured in other sport and had then gravitated toward triathlon as a means of still competing.

In response to a question that asked whether the racial composition of triathletes had affected their decision to participate in sport, a few Black Triathletes Association members stated that they had grown up in majority white communities and that although the sport was very white, it was not so different from their previous life experiences. Some reported that they did not really perceive any barriers to their participation in triathlon despite the sport's lack of diversity, and that they had found the triathlon community to be both supportive and encouraging in general.

The previous characterizations should not considered typical of the entire community of black triathletes. I surveyed very few athletes and read fewer than twenty blogs, whose writers were, more than likely, the most enthusiastic of their group about triathlon. Other athletes may have had very different experiences. At the same time, I did not find it surprising that this group's members seemed particularly well positioned in term of professions, educations, and previous experiences. In effect, these few black triathletes possessed a considerable amount of cultural capital, which probably made navigating a predominantly white sporting landscape less intimidating.

Social Class and "the Great Outdoors" among White Sportsmen

It is also important to note the differences between white men of different social classes and how this is often reflected in their chosen sports. I think these differences may also affect how people think about wild spaces and public land. Sometimes, near where I live, I observe interesting interactions between men who share the same outdoor spaces but come from very different social backgrounds.

Some have speculated that white men in the United States have a common association with wild spaces because of their interpretations of American historicity. Their studies suggest that founding ideas and myths associated with U.S. history have helped to create a national reverence in this population for the men who first entered, then tamed a wild American landscape.[25] The narratives associated with this history helped create and maintain a mythology associated with "rugged individualism," manifest destiny, and the development of a unique American spirit associated with conquering wild spaces. Not all Americans—not the black men and women excluded from this narrative of conquest, for example—find this particular narrative convincing.[26] As such, some have argued that adventure and wild landscapes are resonant with white men because, from the time they are young, they are told the country was founded by adventurers who looked exactly like them.[27]

I do not discount the *general* idea that historical narratives associated with the American experience give meaning to people's conceptions of the "great outdoors"—but an *explicit* association with American historicity has never seemed, to me, a neat fit with the motives of those who do adventure sport. Perhaps this is because I live in an area where ideas associated with self-sufficiency, rugged individualism, and the ability to master practical outdoor skills are still regarded as noble, but more often associated with those who still farm and hunt in the region. In a few cases these are men who quite literally "work the land." Others have transitioned into working-class avocations, but they often remember—and likely romanticize—times when being outdoors, and hunting in particular, were communitywide activities. I am old enough to remember the expectation, when I was employed as a secondary education teacher in the region, that during hunting season truancy would increase dramatically. And to this day, in the region where I live, those who claim to be "sportsmen" are still most often associated with men who hunt and fish in the outdoors. Prior to statewide elections campaign signs on front lawns all over town—often printed on stock of the "blaze orange" color associated with hunting—proclaim "Sportsmen for Candidate X."

When I was operating an adventure touring company in the 1990s, watching interactions between these sportsmen and my clients was fascinating. This usually happened in the fall, when mountain bikers commonly encountered bear hunters running their dogs in preparation for the upcoming hunting season. There would be the four-wheel-drive trucks with gun racks, sometimes with the dogs yelping in their cages in the back. More often, the dogs would be running. Often, a few older men would be at the trailhead marking the dogs' progress with radio transmitters or GPS. The younger hunters followed the dogs on foot. If the dogs managed to tree a bear the older hunters might walk a couple of miles into the woods to join the others. The men tended to wear Carhart overalls, Red Wing work boots, and insulated plaid shirts; a few were usually in camouflage. The cyclists I guided had a different style. They were often decked out in skintight Lycra and usually some high-end sportswear.

I still routinely interact with hunters. For example, nearly all of my neighbors at our small family cottage in Nelson County hunt. These are good neighbors and we have some common interests. My wife has become an expert forager of wild edible plants, an activity some in the area have been doing for many, many years. But there are some differences too. For example, my family is the only one in the area that does not own a gun. At the last country store on the way to this cottage it is possible to buy an extraordinary range of ammunition, hunting knives, pistols, and rifles (along with groceries, cheap sandwiches, and beer). The store is directly by a main entry point for the national forest. This area was once a prime hunting spot. There are far fewer hunters now than in the past; still, one reason our neighbors have cabins is so they have a place to go during hunting season. One of the only fulltime residents on this mountain—a man who builds dovetailed notched-log cabins with timber from the surrounding forests—is a highly skilled hunter and outdoorsman. Nearly all the food he eats is wild.

I like going to this cottage, in part, to ride my mountain bike, which makes me the anomaly among my neighbors. Their most comparable avocation, mostly among their sons and daughters, is riding All-Terrain Vehicles (ATVs) on the surrounding trails. The mountain bikers who live in the surrounding towns quickly become aware of the local hunting culture. They sometimes encounter ATVs when they ride too. Among most of the mountain bikers I know there has developed an implicit recognition that all groups value access to the national forest. And there has been increasing accommodation—on all sides—with respect to the others' sporting pastime. While mountain biking and hunting may not have much in common, in my experience when the people who follow these pursuits find themselves together they get along well enough. For example, if I am with a group of mountain bikers from outside the area and we encounter bear hunters, I invariably inquire after the dogs. This generally ensures some good-natured conversation during the meeting. Most often, a query about where the dogs are running is returned by an inquiry as to where we have ridden from and might be going. This is usually followed with some expression of admiration with respect to our fitness, although sometimes accompanied by the observation that it would be easier to travel the distance on a vehicle with an engine. I had a version of this conversation about a month before writing this, when I encountered a young man looking for a lost dog on the top of Shenandoah Mountain.

Local mountain bikers usually interact with hunters enough to become comfortable with these encounters, although most I know avoid the woods for safety reasons during the peak of hunting season. But many of the people I took on trips who were from outside the region were incredulous after they encountered men who hunted bear. They were sometimes shocked that this type of hunting still took place in the Eastern United States.[28] More than a few of my clients simply could not understand the appeal of hunting. Sometimes, they contrasted their motives—associated with a love of nature—to these men's determination to shoot at it. Both groups clearly had a reverence for the outdoors, but expressed it in very different manners. Notably, while I do not hunt, it is clear that many hunters—other than the ones who run dogs—enjoy solitude and the stillness of the forest. Many have told me that what they mostly want is a quiet place to set up their tree stand and an excuse to sit in the woods.

In my interactions with hunters some have characterized their pastime as maintaining a human connection to nature, a style of living they assume their families experienced not so long ago. There is sometimes nostalgia—a reverence for the old ways—and some of this feeling is connected to past events in their lives. Indeed, the fact that young people are increasingly disinclined to hunt is a source of regret for many older hunters. It is an indication, for them, that people are becoming increasingly disconnected from the land and nature.

The differences between hunters and mountain bikers in terms of maintaining a connection to history are instructive of how they conceive of wild spaces. In some respects, these differences are associated with whether other members of their family were also sportsmen. Some local hunters revere the once-common hunting culture in which members of their families routinely participated. Some see hunting as maintaining a link to this past. The man who sold me the land where my cottage is built—who later put me in touch with local contractors and helped me when I worked on the structure myself—finds his adventure in an occasional weeklong hunting trip in the mountains of Western Canada.

Conversely, most of the adventure sport enthusiasts I interacted with were just as reverent about the outdoor spaces in which they played, but rarely connected their sport to the past. These sports were not handed down with the obligatory traditions associated with family practice. Mountain bikers enjoyed getting outside, but they did not associate riding outdoors as connecting them to a past sporting culture. In fact, one reason many of my clients found bear hunting so strange was that, to their way of thinking, it was an anachronism left over from a bygone age. They could not understand it because it was too far removed from personal experience. Unlike the sportsmen who grew up in the area, they did not associate it with a frontier spirit or self-sufficiency or man's conquest of wild spaces. These athletes still had a desire to connect to nature, but a nature more cultivated, and less wild, than in the past.

Some athletes I knew—certainly not all—had a curious detachment concerning the wildlife in these spaces. By this I mean that they made far fewer attempts to understand and observe nature. These new athletes revere the great outdoors, but to them the spaces are more strictly associated with recreation. At the same time, I have known mountain bikers who were very knowledgeable of the wildlife where they ride. Indeed, many of the people who introduced me to mountain biking were expert foragers—often a reason why it took so long to do rides together. There are still mountain bikers in the area with an intimate knowledge of the surrounding woods. For example, during the Tour de Burg I watched a group of local riders abandon their bikes after the first stage of the event and bound into the woods after a tremendous patch of "Chicken of the Woods," a particularly tasty wild mushroom.

But it also seems that the patterns of use in the national forest among adventure sport enthusiasts—white-water rafters and mountain bikers, for example—is often not too different from other, more cultivated outdoor sports such as skiing. And these sports do seem to have a special appeal to the white upper classes. So it follows that local ski resorts—Bryce Resort in Virginia and Snowshoe Resort in West Virginia—now cater to the mountain bike community when there is no snow.[29] In this respect, I think there is an increasing tendency for practitioners of modern sport in wildlife areas to regard public land as places increasingly cultivated, perhaps even groomed, as sites for practicing outdoor sport.

I also sense an increasing split among white working-class men in this regard. For example, the older aesthetics associated with hunting—the patience required to have a successful season—seems at odds with the sensibilities of ATV enthusiasts, although many of them hunt too. Indeed, if one observes the noise and conglomeration of humanity at some popular ATV trailheads it is apparent that observing wild habitat is largely beside the point for many of these riders.[30] Although ATV enthusiasts and mountain bikers have different motivations, both types of athlete are focused on the triumph over terrain. Both are mostly interested in covering miles, summiting peaks, and surmounting obstacles, and probably less with cultivating an intimate knowledge of the types of foliage, wild plants, and animals that are sometimes nearby.

Hegemonic Whiteness and Outdoor Lifestyle Sport

Why are triathlon and mountain biking so white? First, these sports often require considerable financial resources which, to some extent, stratifies participation by social class. To some degree, the cost of these sports is one reason they are so often practiced by the white upper class. But patterns of racial residence, combined with the meaning that wilderness has among different groups, probably accounts for much of the whiteness in adventure sport too. Indeed, past research has indicated that white Americans are more likely than blacks to engage in outdoor recreation associated with wilderness areas.[31] More specifically, I previously outlined a routine use of the national forest near where I live that makes it culturally resonant to many in the white working class community who live nearby. But the fact that public land is sometimes closely associated with hunting culture—with white men, in trucks, with bows and guns, in isolated areas—probably makes these spaces more inhospitable to many African Americans, particularly if they are not from the region. In practical terms, many probably do not have the same positive association with these spaces as the white working class men from the region.

In many respects, the whiteness of many lifestyle sports is directly comparable to that observed in more traditional white sporting spaces—skiing, for example—where extraordinary race segregation is maintained, often without much thought, by white athletes who have considerable privilege in terms of their social standing and social class. Triathlon and mountain biking are much newer sports than more traditional white sports like skiing, tennis, and golf—but they were also, from their inception, spaces of nearly hegemonic whiteness, so much so that many participants seem to take it for granted. The images in popular magazines associated with these sports reinforce the whiteness of the sport.

All of the previous factors help to explain the demographic statistics reported by USA Triathlon and even how their report *The Mind of a Triathlete* approached the study of these figures. The ethnic and racial demographics of triathlon were not much commented on in this report, although age, gender, and annual incomes were. Indeed, the report largely regarded the demographic composition of triathlon—the fact that it was mostly practiced by white men with considerable resources—as a marketing tool that could be used to attract greater corporate support. This may also explain why there appear to be no programs associated with increasing the diversity of athletes within either the U.S. Cycling Federation or USA Triathlon.

7

Where Are the Women?

• •

Differing Levels of Participation in Lifestyle and Adventure Sport

Just before the start of a multi-sport race—a swim, mountain bike, and run—in Richmond, Virginia, in 2000, I was talking with another participant in my swim heat and exchanging information about the mountain bike course, which was rumored to be very difficult. Before the start, as we were looking at the field and watching the different groups begin to swim, the women's field lined up directly in front of us. It was very small. This competitor turned to me and asked rhetorically, "Where are the women?" This has been a familiar lament in both the mountain biking and multi-sport racing community even though the number of women participating in triathlon has grown remarkably during the past two decades. Still, other adventure and lifestyle sports remain dominated by white men. In this chapter I compare and contrast how two sports—triathlon and downhill mountain biking—have moved in different directions as it relates to participation by women in the sports.

A little over fifteen years ago I had an opportunity to closely observe professional downhill mountain bikers racing at an International Cycling Union (UCI) World Cup Downhill event held at Massanutten Resort, Virginia. At the time I was covering the event for a local newspaper.[1] This close interaction with professional downhill racers occurred during a period when the image of the sport was actively being debated and renegotiated by the participants, who were increasingly embracing some of the cultural tropes associated with the eXtreme games and snowboarding. A well-known snowboarder named Shaun Palmer had recently entered the sport. He was increasingly its most recognizable figure and easily its best-compensated after securing a lucrative racing contract from Specialized Bicycles.[2] It was assumed that Palmer's willingness to challenge norms associated with cycling culture was because he had migrated from professional snowboarding, at the time an exemplary eXtreme game sport being marketed to young men.[3]

Next, I examine a lifestyle sport that has experienced a dramatic increase in rates of participation by women. Currently, men race more often than women in triathlon, but nearly forty percent of the triathletes in the United States who apply for a license to race are women.[4] As such, the sport of triathlon offers an opportunity to think about how increasing women's participation changes sport over time. In particular, it may cause some men to rethink ideas associated with their masculinity and sporting identity.[5]

In contrast to triathlon, other new sports—particularly the extreme varieties—remain dominated by young white men who have adopted a hypermasculine ideal. In the past, some practitioners of alternative sport—skateboarders and snowboarders for example[6]—affected the mannerisms and styles associated with marginalized white groups such as punks and even aspects of black hip-hop culture.[7] This strategy was often a means of crafting an "outsider" sporting status. Other times, it was to create a distinction between alternative and mainstream sport.

So here we have an opportunity to think about how two sports once dominated by men have moved in different directions. In triathlon, as more women entered the field it became routine for men and women to train and race together. Conversely, in one subset of mountain biking culture—that associated with downhill racing and free-riding—it appears the sport has increasingly embraced a hypermasculinized gender ideology.

White Masculinity and Extreme Sport: Downhill Mountain Biking Culture

Diverse masculinities are clearly being created within a range of new sports, and sometimes even within those sports' subdisciplines. Later in this chapter I will describe how one lifestyle sport, triathlon, has largely carved out a place where women's performances are routine. This may be changing how men regard their sporting performances. But other new sports, particularly those associated with high levels of risk, have adopted a hypermasculine sporting ideal where women are not much evident. Of these, sports identified as "extreme"—those once closely associated with the eXtreme Games, for example—seem to have most firmly embraced a masculine sporting ethos.[8]

The mountain bike community that I knew best in the 1980s–1990s was a mixed-gender group who rode cross-country bicycles. I was introduced to the sport by a veteran woman rider a decade older who took me on a very long ridgeline ride that was anything but easy. But even among this notably mellow group important distinctions were often made between men and women as to why they rode. Many of the women mountain bikers I knew were admirers of Jackie Phelan, a former professional cross-country racer who founded the Women's Mountain Bike and Tea Society (WOMBATS) to encourage more women to mountain bike.[9] Some women embraced a more noncompetitive approach to the sport. From their perspective, cycling offered a chance to create a social environment that created greater commonality—women who rode bikes together—as opposed to distinctions based on how fast the cyclists were. But I also knew very competitive women racers, at the time a few of the fastest regional racers. Moreover, most of the men cross-country riders I knew, even the best ones, were actively encouraging women to mountain bike more often. At the same time, a study that undertook a content analysis of mountain biking magazines during this period found that discourses associated with the mechanics of mountain biking took for granted that it was largely a sport "for men."[10]

Still, I was shocked by the hostile gender ideology of some racers when I was first introduced to the spectacle of professional downhilling while covering an UCI World Cup Downhill event as a freelance writer. This event, held at Massanutten Four Seasons Resort in McGaheysville, Virginia, was important for those associated with it. Most of the UCI Downhill races were held at ski resorts located in the high alpine mountains of Europe or in the western United States and Canada. Suddenly, an international event was being staged in Virginia, a place not commonly associated with mountain biking. At the time, I was operating a bicycle touring company only five miles from the resort. Considering me a local expert, the editor of the resort newspaper for which I sometimes wrote, the *Villager*, had asked me to cover the event. I ultimately wrote six articles that previewed the field and then followed the athletes as they prepared for the race.

Because I was still operating my adventure travel company I also made contact with a large bicycle manufacturer—the company I used for my rental bikes—and worked out an arrangement to house their downhill team while they trained and raced. The two men on this team—there were no women racers—were accompanied by their manager, a team mechanic, and a masseur. I spent a fair amount of time with these men as well as some other racers. Previously, I had pre-ridden the course (very slowly) with a couple of other local reporters and generally helped publicize the race in the local newspaper. I then watched the downhill racers practice their runs for a few days before the competition. By the end of the week I had been through a crash course in the professional downhill racing culture. Although there were a few prominent women racers at the time—Missy "the Missile" Giove was well-known—this remains the most hypermasculine subculture I have ever encountered.

Previously, I had considered mountain biking a mostly masculine endeavor in which the participants welcomed, even encouraged, more participation by women. This race was the first time I encountered men on mountain bikes who argued they were "made for downhilling" in a way that women were not. It was clear that many participants valued men's performances over women's. For example, the International Cycling Union (UCI) required an equal cash purse for men and women downhillers. The two racers staying with me—and many others I spoke with during the event—often complained about this fact. They argued that the men's field was larger, so the competition was far more intense. They said the small women's field allowed marginal racers to "get a ride" from sponsors. Even though there were no women on this particular team, they argued that this rule was going to push competent men downhillers from the sport because sponsorships would be reserved for women. To some lesser degree they implied downhilling was a "man's" sport, so they should obviously get paid more for practicing it.

More generally, it was clear that the downhill culture within mountain biking was very different than that in the cross-country discipline. Many of these differences were being negotiated during the period I was covering this race and one could watch this tension play out in terms of what the riders were wearing. The previous standard was skintight cycling apparel with greater padding and protection that approximated that being worn in downhill skiing. But at the time a small group of downhillers, the most well-known of whom was Shaun Palmer, who had adopted the more baggy apparel associated with moto-cross and snowboarding. In terms of the "made for TV" downhill events—those shown on the eXtreme Games for example—the moto-cross style was normative. "Men in tights" was not an image X-Games executives wanted to promote.[11]

In a study of the content in *Mountain Bike Action* (MBA) from 2000–2008, Sherry Huybers-Withers and Lori Livingston found that the magazine reinforced the "Televised Sports Manhood Formula (TSMF)."[12] This is "a master ideological narrative that is well suited to discipline boys' bodies, minds, and consumption choices in ways that construct a masculinity that is consistent with the entrenched interests of the sports / media / commercial complex."[13] They reported that "since the early 2000s boys and men reading MBA have been increasingly presented with traditional hegemonic ideals of masculinity, rather than an alternative masculinity whereby aggression and physical domination are not emphasized."[14] These authors closely associate changes in the downhill culture—including hypermasculinized ideas attributed to the racers—with the modes created as the sport became increasingly "made-for-television." They also regarded the increasing popularity of free-riding—largely made-for-television events featuring extraordinary cycling acrobatics—as particularly reinforcing a masculine ideal. I closely observed the professional downhill culture just before the period they studied, and it seems clear I was watching the genesis of the culture during the UCI World Cup Downhill race.

At this time some of the professional riders—including the two staying with me—found the intrusion of the eXtreme Game sporting ethos embodied by Shaun Palmer disturbing. They did not regard Palmer, no matter how skilled he was, as a professional. To their way of thinking, if apparel existed that made you faster than it was self-evident that you should wear it. They thought Palmer had ability, but also that his best performances during the previous season (when he had nearly won the UCI championship race) were unlikely to be repeated. He might do well now and again, in races particularly suited to his skills, but they doubted he would be a consistent top finisher if he did not train like a professional. And given his self-conscious flouting of cycling orthodoxy—he made it a point to say he trained less than other professionals and drank heavily even when racing—many were upset that Palmer had parlayed his notoriety into a lucrative contract with Specialized Bicycles. Further, he had arrived at the race in a customized bus rumored to have cost hundreds of thousands of dollars. That represented more money than the best riders, many as good as Palmer, were making annually. Indeed, the private bus sometimes separated him even further from other professional riders, although some clearly enjoyed being invited into Palmer's traveling bus entourage. Today, the best downhillers in the sport tend to be extraordinary athletes and train like professionals. However, it is notable that the aesthetic of the sport now closely approximates that championed by Shaun Palmer.

Shortly after I entered the Expo area where the racers and mechanics were preparing for the race, it became evident that this was among the most masculine sporting cultures I had ever encountered. I kept an eye on the interactions between the mostly men downhillers and their mechanics. I was not watching much television at the time—I have never seen coverage of the eXtreme Games, for example—so I was initially flummoxed when I encountered these downhillers, particularly those associated with the "new wave." I tended to gravitate toward the old school racers—and there were still plenty of these—whose preparation resembled what I had expected to encounter. One of the racers staying with me, notwithstanding his views on the equal prize purse for women, was clearly considered a "pro's pro" and much respected by the established riders. His training and race day preparations were among the most diligent I observed. He was also immensely helpful in providing me with the lay of the land, describing the changing politics and the culture being played out daily in the Expo area.

The attitudes of the racers I encountered varied dramatically, but I did routinely encounter male mountain bikers who had an overtly hostile gender ideology toward women generally. That is, when they spoke about women, which they did routinely, it was as if the latter were disposable objects. This attitude even extended to the women downhillers. Very few of these were afforded much respect. Some male riders openly mocked the women's ability even though, in truth, the best women riders were not too far behind them.

The culture appears not to have changed much in the intervening years. Former downhiller Rob Warner, who was still racing when I covered the Massanutten downhill race (his temperament made him hard to ignore), now covers the UCI downhill events for Red Bull in a segment called "Rob's Dirty Business." This double entendre is indicative of the show's content. For example, during his summary of the UCI Downhill season in 2012, "Rob's World Cup Diary," the broadcast began with Rob backing a car against a Porta-John, trapping someone inside. In reviewing the 2012 season he implied that an injured women rider had been beaten by her manager. He told a male downhiller being worked on by a masseuse to make sure he got a "happy ending" at the end of his massage. He mocked an elderly woman. He was shown watching porn with a male downhiller. When Rob got around to covering the actual results of the races they were usually only the men's finishes. Overall, the entire production has a "dancing bear" quality to it: it tends to focus as much on Rob's "look at me" antics as the actual sport of downhill racing.[15]

Notably, during the Massanutten race there were a few excellent women downhillers. When I observed the few women professionals in this area they were often extraordinarily quiet and withdrawn, although a couple had adopted the mannerisms of the men around them. Ironically, this did not grant them entry into the men's club. In fact, the (supposed) masculinity of the women racers was something the two racers staying with me routinely commented on. They routinely said, in effect, that the women downhillers were more masculine than the men. This was often followed by speculation about their sexual orientation.

In retrospect, it seems that during the 1997 event the hypermasculinized gender ideology I observed in the Expo area was mostly practiced, and championed, by a few of the most vocal racers. Indeed, a relatively small number of racers tended to garner a disproportionate amount of attention, not always associated with how successful they were in the sport. Rob Warner, for example, had a relatively modest racing résumé but demanded attention in the Expo at the time I observed him. In this respect, it is not surprising he is now covering downhill racing for Red Bull.

The riders who prepared quietly dominated the downhill series that year. Two of the most impressive riders I observed, Anne Caroline Chaussen and Nicholas Vouilloz, are now considered the best downhillers in the history of the sport. "Anne Caro," in particular, was the antithesis of Shaun Palmer in many respects. She was in her first season when I saw her, just eighteen years old, but she has since become the most decorated athlete in the sport's history. Remarkably, she also won a gold medal at the 2008 Olympics in the BMX discipline. She still races—and routinely wins—in the Enduro format. But riders such as these two, inclined toward thoughtfulness and diligence, often seemed squeezed out during coverage of the event. Preparation clearly trumped style in terms of who actually made it down the mountain the fastest, but it was Palmer who increasingly dominated the media coverage that year.

Women downhillers were still routinely being covered by the cycling media at this time. Indeed, I thought the few women professionals at the event often seemed like more hard-nosed racers. For example, many of the men racers complained about aspects of the course: as a result, the organizers modified some of the more difficult sections. There was considerable pressure on these racers to perform well in order to maintain their sponsorships, and their sometimes-vocal complaints about the course often seemed to be related to a strategy of hedging against the possibility of a bad performance. In effect, if the riders performed badly they could claim it was not their fault because the course was inferior. But I never observed one woman rider complain about the course. As I watched some men nonchalantly toss and kick rocks out of the course during practice—against the UCI rules but something I routinely observed—the women seemed more inclined to take the course as they found it.

During the race there was an intriguing competition among the top women downhillers, particularly Missy Giove, Anne Caroline Chaussen, and Leigh Donovan. The contrast in these women's riding styles was interesting. Missy Giove, somewhat like Shaun Palmer, was associated with a "ride to the edge" style, which contrasted considerably with the more contained style of Anne Caroline Chaussen. And it was Leigh Donovan who won a tightly contested race. At the time, Giove—who finished third among the women—was among the most-recognizable figures in the sport. Notably, she was also considered the "case in point" by the downhillers who stayed with me concerning the supposed masculinity of the female participants. At the time, it was known by some that she was bisexual. But what struck me about her was that she seemed to be having the time of her life—she really enjoyed racing. The rivalry between Giove and Chaussen over the next few years is considered something of a classic period as it relates to women's downhilling.

Despite the disproportionate number of men racing cross-country and downhill compared to women in the early to late 1990s, this appears to have been one of the best periods in regard to media coverage of women racers, at least those from the United States. At this time a small number of U.S. women riders usually outperformed the men in international competitions. But following the retirement of a few notable women racers, particularly Julie Furtado in the cross-country discipline and Missy Giove in the downhill, press coverage of women professionals appears to have declined dramatically. In fact, most evidence indicates that coverage of women in the downhill discipline is currently less than it was in the 1990s.[16]

Women's Bodies and Early Media Coverage in Triathlon

The sport of triathlon was established at roughly the same time as mountain biking. At that early stage, in the late 1970s and early 1980s, there was a tendency to ignore, or at least neglect, the needs of women triathletes. During the 1980s some small companies noticed that women were seldom considered a part of the cycling community and that large companies offered very little equipment or apparel suitable for women's physiques. They quickly began producing women-specific products. Terry Bicycles is a good example of these pioneering firms.[17] The now-trademarked name of the most famous triathlon event, the Ironman, is indicative of the gender ideology that was prevalent in the early days of triathlon. At that time coverage of the sport centered largely on the "Big Four" of male elite racers—Mark Allen, Dave Scott, Scott Tinley, and Scott Molina—despite the fact that there was a strong field of female professionals.

Early media coverage of triathlon tended to value men's performances more, but comparatively—and certainly over time—magazines associated with triathlon showed women racing far more often than did publications associated with competitive cycling and mountain biking.[18] For example, in the November 2013 issue of *Bicycling* not one woman is primarily featured in any of the full-page advertisements. They do sometimes appear in the background, most prominently in a Speed-Play advertisement in which two women are awarding professional rider Peter Sagan a trophy. Women are even less represented in *Mountain Bike Action*. Depending on what was coded (articles or advertisements), triathlon journals' representations of women can vary, but have always been much more numerous when compared to either *Bicycling* or *Mountain Bike Action*. It appears to be an established practice in triathlon journals to report both men's and women's results for all the races covered. Usually, the articles lead with the men, but the amount of space dedicated to covering professionals of both sexes is now often comparable.

Advertising content in triathlon magazines changed dramatically over time, likely related to the increasing rates of women participating in the sport. For example, in some of the early *Triathlete* issues in the 1980s I routinely encountered an advertisement by an apparel company that positioned two women, scantily dressed in non-racing apparel, hanging onto each arm of a man dressed in racing apparel. The subtext of the advertising was clear: If you are a man and do triathlons you will have attractive women draped over you. Every once in a while, but less often, throughout the nineties there was advertising content that was blatantly sexist, but these ads seemed increasingly anomalous when compared to the others, which tended to show women athletes in action. A more recent example of an advertisement that objectified a woman's body is a KINeSYS Performance Sunscreen print piece that appeared about a decade ago: it shows a naked professional triathlete, Jessi Stensland, with the tagline "I'm not naked, I'm wearing KINeSYS."

There have been other occasions when triathlon magazines have sexualized women triathletes as a means of selling copy. Not surprisingly, the cover model on what *Inside Triathlon* called its first annual Sex Issue was a woman triathlete in a state of undress. (See figure 10.) Desirée Ficker is an excellent Ironman distance triathlete—she has a body that has been trained to cover ground quickly—so it is notable that her cover photo does not show her body "in motion." Still, it was far more common in the volumes of *Inside Triathlon* I reviewed, as compared to cycling and mountain bike magazines, to show pictures of women racing—of portraying them as athletes—as opposed to sexualized representations. This was true for both the advertisements and the articles associated with their sporting accomplishments. More so than the other lifestyle sports I investigated, women really seemed "present" in the sport of triathlon.

Changing White Masculinity in Triathlon—
Men and Women Training Together

While my experience may be unique, I rarely observed any overt prejudice by men against women's participation in triathlon. It has been accepted, from the time the sport was established, that women can race very fast over very long distances, probably because most races included women who finished ahead

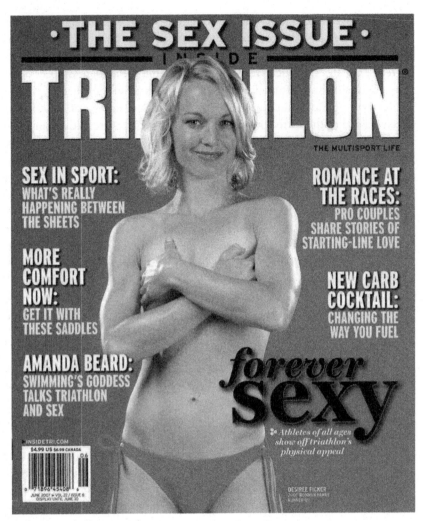

FIGURE 10 Desirée Ficker on the cover of the *Inside Triathlon* "Sex Issue."

of most men. While men initially dominated triathlon competition, women have always been present in the sport. Moreover, their rates of participation appear to have increased dramatically.

When I looked at the race results of a well-known local series in 2013 it was routine that over thirty percent of the participants were women (although this rate tended to drop incrementally as the races became longer and also skewed toward younger athletes). This relatively high comparable rate of participation probably helps to explain the acceptance of women triathletes by men, as has the way the races are staged and timed, with all athletes racing together on the same course. Once the race is over, all of the athletes have access to the times of the entire field; notably, for all but the very fastest men participants, it is a routine experience to find that women have finished well ahead of them.

When I studied past race results I found that a good ballpark estimate for the top woman finisher was that she would be within the top three to six percent of all finishers in a field. This means the top women's finishing time is usually faster than about ninety-five percent of the entire field. In a race with five hundred athletes, for example, the first woman finisher was commonly just inside the top twenty. The excellent men racers I interviewed—those who routinely finish in the top ten percent of the field—were always aware that they routinely finished behind women racers. Indeed, these athletes routinely see women on the race courses, sometimes as these women run and cycle past them.

The fact that everyone races together has likely made men think more about women's performances as racers. Indeed, I often watched men—some of them elite age-group amateurs—grapple with the fact that the top amateur and professional women were faster, sometimes considerably faster, than they were. During a meeting of a collegiate triathlon club I once observed a club officer, a competitive age-group racer, tell the new club members (my paraphrase), "You'll need to get used to the idea that there will be women at these races, and that these women are going to kick your ass." The observation drew laughter from the assembled crowd of mostly men. My impression was that this former wrestler and baseball player was grappling with the fact himself.[19]

This explicit comparison between men and women triathletes appears to be very common. Indeed, many of the men I raced with, very solid athletes who usually finished in the top five percent of the field, often told me that when there was a large competitive field that would draw strong women racers, they wanted to finish ahead of the top women. Another study in Australia encountered this same phenomenon: as researcher Murray Drummond reported, "A common theme running through the interviews of the triathletes and surf lifesavers is the intrinsic desire to defeat every woman in both training and races. . . . the men who gradually moved up the ranks were initially defeated by women, thereby creating a sense of humiliation for them. As a consequence their foremost goal in the beginning was to beat every woman."[20]

While I encountered men who used their rank among the women finishers as motivation, I found their temperaments less hard-edged than the men in Drummond's study. I would describe the most common reaction I encountered by men who were routinely "beaten by a woman" as more akin to chagrin—followed by acceptance—as opposed to humiliation. I observed more than a few good-natured battles between triathlon couples who were sometimes comparable to one another in terms of their race finishes, a not-surprising fact because they were so often training together. I also interviewed one couple where the husband, "Keith," swam directly behind his wife, "Kathy," during their swim practices. He was also a triathlete who indicated to me that he often raced with the goal of finishing ahead of the first female finisher. Kathy, our swim coach, already knew this and thought it was hysterical.

I knew this couple well—I routinely trained with them—but by the time I interviewed them they had disengaged from triathlon following the birth of their daughter. But they were still routinely doing local road races although Keith was training less. As we sat down for the interview, Keith reported that Kathy had beaten him, for the first time, in a local road race just the week previously. He then smiled and shrugged nonchalantly in what I interpreted as a "what are you going to do?" type gesture. My impression was that being the second-fastest athlete in the family had not placed any appreciable strain on the relationship, although I did imagine that Keith might start running more. But he also seemed pleased that his wife was "sticking with it" as he found less time to train.[21] Notably, he is now the third-fastest swimmer in the family: the couple's daughter has developed into one of the top youth swimmers in the region.

Although the group of triathletes I first trained with routinely scheduled bike rides and runs for both men and women, swimming was the most common context in which I observed and trained for triathlon in mixed-gender groups. In the pool, the swimmers sorted themselves according to ability with individuals trying to match the pace of the person in front of them. Among the regular group this meant they were staggered into two to three coed lanes (four to six swimmers to a lane). As both a participant and observer, I never had the feeling that the men in this group were particularly concerned that some of the women present were faster swimmers—although they referenced it on occasion.

At the same time, it may have been somewhat exceptional to find a group where women and men so routinely trained together. When I reentered the sport in the summer of 2000 it was much rarer to observe men and women training together. There were very few women members on the Virginia Tech Triathlon team. When I trained in 2013, I did sometimes swim, in a happenstance way, with a woman at the local YMCA. I do not much like swimming, but those few sessions were the best I had that summer—far more fun and focused then the drudgery I endured when I was swimming on my own.

The fastest women I observed and routinely trained with were former collegiate swimmers who often had more experience in competitive sport than the men triathletes. My overall impression is that, relative to mixed gender training in other sports (which is often nonexistent), mixed-gender training in triathlon has become fairly common. For example, when I play recreational soccer in the local city league our team occasionally has a few women players, but this has been relatively rare as compared to the women I routinely encountered when I trained for triathlon.

Within the context of my own training during this study I sometimes swam with a small Master's swim team and routinely swam behind strong women swimmers. The strongest occasional participant in our group was a woman I will call Laura, a former Division I collegiate swimmer, who joined us one summer when she became interested in triathlon. At this time Laura had recently graduated from college and, to her way of thinking, was no longer in top swimming shape. But whenever she joined our group I knew it would be a difficult workout. In general, while Laura methodically rollicked through our Master's workouts—probably about half the distance of an elite workout—the rest of us in her lane struggled to keep up with her. If I found myself behind her I might try and match her pace—this was made easier because I was swimming in her wake—but by the end of these sessions I was often physically spent. Indeed, among the men in the group there was a ready acknowledgement that whoever swam behind Laura was, more so than usual, going to be pressed to keep up.

At the same time, the mixed-gender training I experienced with this group of athletes may have been exceptional. And notwithstanding the fact that I regarded this as a "welcoming" group—one that eagerly made a place for novice swimmers—I would imagine that for some observers, particularly novices, they were rather imposing. There was the interval clock, which people were focused on, along with hand paddles, kick boards, fins, and other swimming paraphernalia that were nonchalantly passed around, and also the churn of the water as the group rollicked through the workouts. It often looked pretty intense.

One indication that some women may feel uncomfortable training and competing in triathlon with men is the popularity of the women-only Danskin Triathlons. When these races, created to increase women's participation in triathlon, began they were sometimes framed as allowing women to participate in a forum that was less competitive than mixed-gender events. The series also created a program in which new women triathletes are mentored by veteran women triathletes. The women I interviewed—a small sample of generally elite-caliber racers who often trained with men—often reported sometimes participating in "women's only" events and cycling clubs. For instance, my wife used to ride occasionally with a group called GRITS (Girls Riding in the Streets), which sponsored women-only rides. I also interviewed two women who had participated in Danskin races. Both were elite-caliber racers but neither framed her participation as being related to the fact it was a women's-only event. They reported that they raced in the Danskin event because it was well-organized with a field of quality women athletes. Stories related on the company website and one study indicate that many women who train together for a Danskin race, particularly neophyte racers, find the experience remarkably positive and enabling, particularly when they form strong ties with a group of women who routinely train together.[22]

All of the women triathletes and mountain bikers I interviewed were elite-caliber athletes who commonly rode with men. For example, I interviewed a local triathlete who was routinely the only woman who participated in a local bicycle shop's "hard ride." She admitted to me that she did not like riding with the local women's group because they were too slow; still, it was clear that her ideal ride would have been with a group of comparatively fast women riders. More often the elite-caliber athletes I interviewed were actively cultivating and recruiting women into these sports. A few actually sponsored camps for women athletes and women-only training rides. In this respect, these athletes—while they routinely rode and trained with men, perhaps out of necessity—were also active in cultivating women to the sport.

Conclusion: Gender and New Sport

This chapter looked at two "new" sports that have moved in dramatically different directions as related to participation rates for women, even though both were established during the same period and were initially conceived as largely masculine endeavors. On the one hand, women's participation in triathlon is fairly high when compared to participation in other lifestyle sports—and probably other traditional sports too. In general, my interview subjects, both men and women, viewed increasing women's participation in triathlon as a positive goal. Increasingly, women's participation in the sport may be making men rethink traditional ideas associated with sport, particularly that it should be practiced in gender-segregated groups.

Conversely, the gender ideology associated with professional downhill mountain bike racing—at least at the time I observed it—was overtly masculine, sometimes to the point of hostility, by some men towards the participation of women in the sport. Some extreme sports become sites where a hypermasculine ideal is maintained and reinforced by the media coverage associated with these events. Notably, the professional women racers on the downhill circuit ride on the same course as the men and often finish reasonably close to the men's times. Still, women cyclists and mountain bikers are not afforded nearly as much media coverage as women triathletes.

Aspects of popular culture often associate sport that has higher levels of risk with young men. Still, it is notable that there are a few risky sports—downhill skiing might be the most comparable—in which women's participation is routinely covered by the media. The downhill skier Lindsay Vonn, for example, is well-known in the sport. But within the downhill cycling subculture, in a sport that was quickly oriented toward "made-for-television" spectacle, there was an attempt to explicitly design its coverage to appeal to young white men. This reinforced the idea that the sport is a masculine endeavor and likely contributed to, and helped maintain, the wide disparity in participation by men and women.[23]

8
Conclusion

● ● ● ● ● ● ● ● ● ● ● ● ● ● ● ● ● ● ● ●

This text explored the development of lifestyle and adventure sport, particularly mountain biking and triathlon, and why some people find these new sports so compelling—indeed, compelling enough for many to regard them as part of a lifestyle integral to their sense of well-being. Given this enthusiasm it may seem strange to consider whether these sports might sometimes be "constraining" as opposed to "liberating"—whether they limit people's worldviews rather than provide them with greater freedom. In this respect, one question examined was whether lifestyle sport should always be considered "good" for people. There was not an emphatic "yes" or "no" answer: the response often depended on the specific circumstances that different athletes confronted. For many it is possible for these sports to be both "good" and "bad."

Related to the previous was an exploration of how the commodification of new sport—its capture by the market—establishes new "disciplines" associated with their practice. Inevitably, the modern market determines who can play, and also how and why the sport is played. It even provides the "meaning" that many athletes assign to their participation in sport. At the same time, some athletes clearly resent when the market intrudes into their sports. And a few athletes actively create places where they can experience a more authentic sporting experience, places where some of the corrupting influences of the market are cordoned off from the spirit of friendly competition.

It is also important to recognize that not everyone in the United States has the same opportunity to participate in lifestyle sport. These are particularly expensive endeavors and like other, more highbrow American sports, stratified by social class. Practically, these are sports in which people with resources—both time and money—have access to the field of play. While participation rates for women in triathlon have increased dramatically over time, lifestyle sport often remains dominated by a professional class of white men. Of course, the fact that social class offers someone a "ticket" to participate in lifestyle sport is not surprising. Indeed, more traditional sports such as tennis, skiing, and bowling have long been stratified by social class; it would have been remarkable if this was not also true for triathlon and mountain biking. In this respect, lifestyle sport is actually not so different from other sports in the West.

But are there aspects of lifestyle sport that are different from traditional sport? As described in the literature review in chapter 1, much of the early academic literature regarded the former as different in a number of ways. These included the "self-regulated" nature of these sports: the fact that the athletes often practiced them in informal venues without much oversight by governing institutions. The athletes themselves described these sports as different from others, and their commitment to them seemed greater too. At the same time, the lack of structure, at least in some venues, became increasingly rare as these sports developed over time. Some of this change was fashioned by the athletes themselves: they had to show people how to play these sports, for example. Increasingly there were also governing bodies that organized and defined the parameters, so much so that even athletes who remain outside of active competition—people who do not race their mountain bikes, for example—still tend to order and routinize their participation within these sports using forms of discipline established by professionals.

Sometimes, the discipline associated with these sports is so pervasive that it is impossible practice them recreationally, at least in terms of how these athletes train their bodies. For example, in order to be a triathlete one must do more than "swim, bike, and run": one has to enter the market, buy a ticket to race, and then do the swimming, biking, and running at a prescribed place and time with other people. And, of course, athletes have to complete their race in the shortest amount of time possible. The standards of the modern market, particularly "efficiency" and "scientific management" as applied to disciplining the body, are now also the normative standards on which the sport of triathlon is based. In effect, to be a triathlete is to accept one primary standard: that increasing efficiency in terms of how the body is disciplined is the overriding principle of the sport.

All modern sport exists within the market, but I can think of few examples of an activity so completely compatible with market norms as triathlon. Indeed, the sport came of age during a period when market norms in the West were expanding and when an ideology associated with market liberalism—the contentious idea that strong markets increased both freedom and democracy—were increasingly normative too.[1] In this respect, it should not be surprising that triathlon is largely a reflection of a liberal market ideology: a sport founded on the idea that it rewards the individual for hard work and discipline, a sport where "paying to play" is not much questioned by athletes, perhaps because they so often have the necessary resources to play. Most of these athletes are clearly winners within the context of the modern market, so it is not surprising that their sport of choice is structured so similarly to how they work. For many, a sport with an intense focus on both discipline and efficiency may be the only way they can construct meaning during their play. Probably, most do not contemplate whether they might also find satisfaction and meaning—maybe even something like freedom—if they played differently than they worked. Importantly, though, this is work that the athletes usually choose to do, and the degree to which they discipline their bodies is most often a personal decision.

It is also important that many people outside of these sports find these athletes and their devotion to discipline curious. Indeed, to outsiders these sports can appear to be an exhausting and mind-numbing endeavor—the modern equivalent of a Sisyphean task—in which people run or swim or ride in constant circles but are never quite fast enough or fit enough to feel satisfied. But for the athletes, why they do these sports is so self-evident, and so compelling, that they have a hard time understanding why others would not want to join them. Some people have a nagging sense that without these sports they are "missing out on life"—and that buying a mountain bike, or completing a triathlon, will help make that feeling go away. They do these sports because they help "keep them sane." They ride because it allows them some manner of control over their bodies.

Here we encounter perhaps the greatest paradox associated with lifestyle sport: the question of whether these sports are liberating. Are they actually a "challenge to self," perhaps even an "adventure," when, as a practical matter, they ensure that most participants must engage in the exact same modes of discipline, at the same times, in the same venues? Can triathlon be a mode of individual expression when the field of play, and the discipline required, are so tightly prescribed? Whatever the benefits of triathlon for the athletes, and however much satisfaction they experience, one would be hard-pressed to regard it as a sport that reinforces "creativity." Practically everyone plays the sport in the same manner. Indeed, the entire field of play seems designed to reduce athletes to automatons—people who click through their laps, their miles, their intervals, according to identical modes of discipline. The goal of triathlon is not to "escape" calculation and scientific management: it is simply to apply these common workplace goals to the disciplining of the body.

But the discipline associated with lifestyle sport is something that athletes nearly always choose, and this clearly indicates some level of agency, at least within the context of the decision to pursue these sports. Moreover, the athletes commonly feel that participation in lifestyle sport is their most important social activity outside of work. And even though they all train the same way, they nonetheless are emphatic that the appeal of sport is based on the fact that they have some level of "control" over the discipline they use as they fashion themselves into athletes. Obviously, they are not referring to controlling how the sport is practiced, but rather the decision made to discipline and train their bodies. Moreover, all regard this discipline as a positive: it is often a primary reason they regard these sports as superior to others. Their discipline allows them to wrest control of their bodies—and refine them so that they can do extraordinary things.

This aspect of athletes asserting control over their bodies—the idea that running, biking, or swimming makes them stronger and also more attuned with their selves—produces a very strong emotional attachment to these sports. Within the context of the vagaries of modern life, triathlon and mountain biking, likely because of this disciplining of the body, are now considered "adventurous" too. These are places where it is possible to "challenge self," even if the challenge is to cover a set distance—to quite literally run, or swim, or cycle in circles within a certain amount of time. So perhaps what is most notable about these new sports is that this modest sliver of control, the decision to train the body, is what makes the sports so compelling for so many. Given that so many other aspects of modern life in the West are so free of risk and simple human physicality such as lifting and climbing is increasingly rare, these manufactured challenges represent a human response to life's frustrations. In this respect, it should not be surprising that these forms of discipline—even as they grow in popularity and become more routinized—are still considered different from other types of sport by the athletes who practice them.

Appendix

• • • • • • • • • • • • • • • • • • • •

My Experience with
Lifestyle Sport and
Location of the Study

I began this study in the summer of 2000 when I was a Ph.D. student at the Virginia Polytechnic Institute and State University. It had been a while since I raced as a triathlete, but I had been a reasonably competitive amateur athlete in the middle 1980s to early 1990s. In particular, the last couple of years I raced, in amateur events in the Mid-Atlantic region, I often finished among the leaders and occasionally won. I raced often enough and long enough ago that I remembered few details of these races. I do remember that my first triathlon was the Green Mountain "Steel Man" in Vermont, likely in 1986, when I would have been twenty years old. I also remember the last three races I did before I quit in 1992. They included an age-group win at a large Bud Light United States Triathlon Series (USTS) race in Norfolk, Virginia. That race was bookended by two close overall wins—literally by seconds—at the Smith Mountain Lake Triathlon, Virginia, and Outer Banks Triathlon, North Carolina.[1]

I would "guesstimate" that from 1986 to 1992 I did well over fifty triathlons, and maybe as many other offbeat outdoor events related to both running and cycling. The triathlons ranged from "sprint" distance (.75-km swim, 20-km bike, 5-km run) to half-Ironman distance (1.2-mile swim, 56-mile bike, 13.1-mile run) in length. It was also common for me to participate in local running and cycling events, often with very strong regional cyclists, but I was never a United States Cycling Federation (USCF) licensed racer. Later, during this study—in the years 2000–2001 and 2013–2014—I completed another twenty events.

In retrospect, I became a solid triathlete in what might seem like an ad hoc manner. Mostly, I was an enthusiastic road cyclist who went swimming if I did not have enough time to ride my bike or if the weather was bad. This eventually put me in touch with an affable group of regional triathletes with whom I started racing. This group "discipline," which made my training more routine, probably caused much of my improvement in the sport. During this period, as I improved, the owner of a local bicycle shop "floated" me a more state-of-the-art time-trial bike, which bolstered my finishes too. This bike is considered antiquated now, but still high-tech enough that I felt comfortable using it when I reentered the sport to conduct this study.

Mostly, though, I came to prefer a leisurely morning ride around the Shenandoah Valley, with friends or alone, to a weekend of travel and racing. Importantly, the place where I lived at the time, and to which I have since returned, is near a stretch of the Appalachian Mountains that represents an expanse of the largest uninterrupted national forest on the East Coast. Given this vast expanse of wilderness, literally outside my front door, I eventually began to think that an adventure travel company in the region could be successful. Ultimately, among the many reasons I initially quit competing was so I could establish The Pineapple Pedalers, a company that I operated for six years in the middle 1990s. It primarily offered active cycling vacations, both on road bikes and mountain bikes, in the Shenandoah Valley and surrounding mountains. This was never a very profitable enterprise—I often had as many as two other jobs during this period—and I eventually sold some components and shuttered others in 1998. That was also the year I began my Ph.D. program at Virginia Tech.

Reentering the Field of Lifestyle Sport in 2000

After I joined the Touch of Grey Twenty-Four Hour Team (see Introduction) I decided to reenter the sport of triathlon and adventure racing that summer. Much of this motivation was because I had decided to write this text, but I also missed riding my bike with friends. In most respects, I found that adventure sport was not much changed, but one important difference was that the term "lifestyle sport" had become an explicit marketing term used to sell adventure racing. Lifestyle sport, it appeared, was now firmly embedded in the popular culture.

During this period some of my steadiest training partners were fellow members of the Virginia Tech Triathlon Club, a group with which I formally raced during a regional competition against other universities. The "Big Lick Triathlon" at Smith Mountain Lake, Virginia, was designated the regional collegiate championship. A Virginia Tech teammate, Dan Peairs—at that time among the best amateurs in the region—won that race. I finished fourth and the Virginia Tech team finished a very close second to UNC–Chapel Hill. By the time this race was held, and after a summer of racing while conducting this study, I was considered a pretty fast regional triathlete, although not as fast as when I previously raced.

Throughout this period I conducted both formal and informal interviews, some with my Virginia Tech teammates and others with friends with whom I reconnected with while doing this study.[2] I think I was well liked by my teammates, although some club members—some still in their teens—found me curious, mostly because I was more than a decade older than most of the other racers. But I had no problems blending in. Indeed, after a few training rides my status within the club as a veteran racer with considerable racing experience was established. Along the way I met many other long-time cyclists and distance runners in the Blacksburg, Virginia, community, a few of whom remain my friends more than a decade later.

During my reentry into the sport in 2000 I mostly raced at events in North Carolina and Virginia. Unlike the past, I kept track of my race results. Excluding an eXterra adventure race where I flatted twice, I finished somewhere between first and fifteenth place overall in the races I competed in that summer. In the first triathlon that I labored through in the summer of 2000, the Colonial Beach Triathlon (1-km swim, 40-km bike, 10-km run), I finished in about two hours, just fast enough, at age thirty-four, to win the thirty-to-thirty-five age group. Previously, in 1991 and 1992, I had finished third and second overall in the same race with times about ten to twelve minutes faster.[3] The Colonial Beach Triathlon is typical of the sort of race I most often competed in. It was local, within easy driving range, and I could stay with an aunt and uncle who lived in nearby Fairview Beach. The field usually consisted of a few hundred amateur athletes. That summer I had one overall win at a very small adventure race, the inaugural New River Trail Challenge, which began in the small town of Fries, near Galax, in southwest Virginia. This was a thirty-mile bike ride on a cinder "rails-to-trails" path along the New River Trail, followed by a 13.1-mile run on the same trail, and then a twelve-mile canoe paddle down the river.[4]

Reentering the Field in 2013

Following those races in the summer of 2000 I mostly stopped training seriously, even though my friends convinced me to race again on the Touch of Grey team at the twenty-four-hour race in West Virginia and I participated in a few more local races that summer. But following the summer of 2001, I slowly disengaged from sport while I worked at completing my doctoral dissertation. Shortly thereafter, I took a job as an assistant professor of sociology at James Madison University. Not too much after that, two children were added to my immediate family. In short, I experienced the sort of routine life events—work and family, life and death—that often push people from participating in sport. Indeed, when my children were very young I was happy enough if we managed a hike of a couple of miles on a nearby trail, or even managed some time playing in a nearby creek or lake. Practically, I lost contact with many of the people I used to run around with. So, even though I had produced a first draft of this text in the summer of 2001, the project had been shelved for more than a decade before I made contact with more athletes in 2013 and completed a final draft in the summer of 2014.

When I returned to the initial draft of this text I was surprised to realize that more than a decade had passed. Had it really been over ten years since I had ridden my mountain bike? I found the bike in the basement, both tires flat. It had clearly not been used in some time. I decided to pump up the tires and started riding once in a while. But most often when I stumbled across boxes of old racing equipment in my basement, most of it now more than two decades old, I no longer felt much nostalgia. In fact, my time as an athlete seemed like a foreign experience. So when I made the decision to finish this text I decided to "check back in" with lifestyle sport.

Unlike my previous reentry into the field, this time around I had some trepidation concerning whether I was up to racing. I had not been entirely idle: I still occasionally rode my road bike. However, it had been a long time since I trained for a race. I had just turned forty-seven and was also worried because I had broken my leg playing soccer a year previously. That injury had required surgery and made me contemplate embracing the general idea of going slower rather than faster. But ultimately, in May of 2013, after my schedule opened up, I began to run, bike, and swim in earnest. About five weeks later I completed my first sprint distance triathlon in about ten years. This time around my attitude at the prospect of racing was probably more dutiful than enthusiastic. Of course, I did enjoy reconnecting with some old friends I had known previously through sport. And I made new friends who are active in the local triathlon and mountain biking community, a few of whom enthusiastically consented to being interviewed for this project.

That summer, I participated in three triathlons and spent some time at a regional mountain bike race, the Tour de Burg, known for its difficulty. (See chapter 5.) I was nominally a "racer" for two days of this event, but for the most part my goal was to finish each day without hitting the ground. I then volunteered for the last two days. Notably, I felt enough of an affinity with this race—and particularly the people who routinely participate in it—that I decided to do "the Tour" again in the summer of 2014. In fact, this time around I rode all five stages, mostly "just for fun" rather than for this study. These races put me into the orbit of the local triathlon and mountain bike community in Staunton and Harrisonburg, Virginia. They allowed me to reconnect with the lifestyle sport ethos while I completed this text. I also contacted a few old training partners I had previously interviewed in 2000–2001 and caught up with them too.

The races I participated in were chosen largely for convenience. For example, at the Bath County Triathlon on Lake Moomaw, some friends of mine were camping on the lake that weekend. In fact, this group of several families had already established a tradition of taking over a section of the campground during the weekend, and a few had always participated in the triathlon. As I indicated previously, my approach to racing that summer was often more dutiful than enthusiastic, so while I understood the affection these athletes had for the Moomaw race I still joked with them that I thought the weekend would have been perfect—the food was good, the beer was cold, the kids occupied and the weather magnificent—if only it had not been interrupted by the race. More than a few laughed at this observation. Even some racing enthusiasts associated aspects of competition in triathlon with the fact that it required us to rise at dawn and then navigate the racing hubbub associated with getting our timing chips and setting up our gear. It was self-evident that this enterprise was sometimes a lot of work, inconvenience, and money—the race fee exceeded $100—and, for some at least, perhaps debatable as to whether it was more "fun" than what we were already doing.

It turns out that I was still a reasonably competent triathlete.[5] But practically, I was far slower than previously. Indeed, in the few races I did that season I had a tendency to initially evaluate the course through my younger eyes—to imagine what sort of times I might turn in when young and trained up, when racing was second nature. I then dutifully deducted the time associated with my age, the lay-off, and the "tale of the tape" I confronted during my summer workouts. Indeed, one thing I confronted on race days, and almost every day I trained, was a confirmation that my best days—if best is judged by the ability to go fast—were well behind me.

Having not thought about formal competition for more than a decade, I found this unnerving. Indeed, for many years being fast had seemed beside the point when I found some time to ride my bike. But this response should not have surprised me. It is related to one of the central paradoxes explored within this text. In effect, many aspects of lifestyle sport are comparative endeavors in which athletes literally, and almost constantly, measure themselves—miles covered, speed, elevation climbed—against the experience of others. Triathletes in particular aspire to be faster rather than slower; they take it for granted that satisfaction is directly associated with how fast they can move their bodies. So, it was inevitable that I would decline relative to my past sporting competence. Of course, everyone eventually loses this race. I never seriously contemplated I would be faster when I was older and had not trained for many years. Still, it was startling to find when I reentered triathlon that I could quantify my decline in very specific ways. I could quite literally measure it using the time it took me to cover a distance—the minute longer it took me to run a mile, for example.

If my temperament were different, I might have responded by working harder and trying to "claw back" some of the time I had lost. I might have adopted a program of greater discipline. (See chapter 3.) I might have changed my diet or begun taking training supplements. Perhaps I could have adopted some new goals, something to keep sport fresh and challenging. And there was always the ultimate challenge, that of trying to defy the gods (for a little while) and work at getting faster even as my age increased. People often told me this could be done! But as it turned out, soon after that summer of racing ended I returned to what I had mostly done in the past. Today, I try—as best a "modern" person can—to turn off my mental clock when I go for a ride or run. When I find the time to bike—most often during my summer break from teaching—my goal is to find a beautiful place to ride.

Location of the Study: The Shenandoah Valley and Southwest Virginia

Where this study took place is unique. It began in Blacksburg (located in the New River Valley of southwest Virginia) but later focused on athletes who lived in Staunton and Harrisonburg, Virginia (located in the central Shenandoah Valley). Many of the races described take place in the mountainous regions of western Virginia.

My extended family has long lived in the Shenandoah Valley. I spent a good deal of my childhood in other places, most notably in the Middle East, but for most of my adult life I have lived in this region. I became increasingly familiar with the surrounding national forests when I began mountain biking in the middle 1980s as a student at James Madison University. Probably, because of my family's long residence in this area of Virginia my worldview—in some fundamental ways—has been shaped by this place. It certainly has been shaped by the unique cycling culture that I encountered as a JMU student and observed again during this study.

The geography of the Shenandoah Valley is one of a kind. Basically, it is a wide expanse of river bottom and farmland, sometimes as wide as sixty miles across and sometimes as narrow as a few miles, surrounded by the Blue Ridge and Allegheny Mountains. Much of the mountainous area that surrounds the valley is public land: national forests and national parks. Most maps locate the Shenandoah Valley between Roanoke, Virginia (in the south) and Winchester, Virginia (in the north). Winchester is the closest small city in the valley to Washington, D.C., only an hour's drive away.

The entire Shenandoah Valley is about 200 miles in length. In the northern half the Shenandoah River flows north, eventually into the Potomac River near Baltimore, Maryland. At roughly the middle of the valley the watershed changes and the rivers and streams flow mostly southeast into the James River and then into the Tidewater region of the state. There are a few very large manmade lakes in, and around, this area. Many were constructed specifically for outdoor recreation. For example, Lake Moomaw—site of a triathlon I attended—was created by damming the Jackson River. It is in the Jefferson National Forest, a little more than an hour by car from where I currently live. It has no commercial development along the forty-three miles of its mountainous shoreline.

The Shenandoah Valley ends in Roanoke, but the mountains then converge and rise into a higher plateau that was created by the New River. This is where Blacksburg, Virginia—home to Virginia Tech—is located, the area where this study began. The New River is likely the oldest river in the United States and one of the oldest in the world. Much of the New River Valley, in both West Virginia and North Carolina, is home to world-class rock climbing and extraordinary whitewater rafting. Near Fayetteville, West Virginia, a tremendous single-span steel arch bridge, once the longest in the country, crosses the New River Gorge. It has become widely associated with its annual Bridge Day festivities, and particularly for the people who BASE jump, with specialized parachutes, from the bridge into the New River on that day.

Although these areas of Virginia and West Virginia might sometimes look the same, there is actually tremendous variation in terms of geography, animal and plant life in different areas of the Appalachian range. Some coal mining areas—near Wise County for example—have been subjected to extraordinary environmental degradation, most recently related to "mountain top removal" mining practices.[6] More recently, attempts to open up the George Washington National Forest to "fracking" for natural gas introduced another environmental threat.[7] At the same time, some protected areas in the national forest still have stands of old-growth forest—an extraordinarily rare occurrence on the East Coast of the United States.

There are also a few "micro-climates" in the nearby mountains. About thirty miles west of where I currently live, in Highland County, it is cold enough for maple syrup to be produced in meaningful quantities, the furthest point south in the United States that this is possible. Highland County has long billed itself as the "little Switzerland" of Virginia. It is one of many extraordinarily scenic places in the region, but like many other Virginia counties it has been steadily losing population for the past few decades as single-family farming became less prosperous. According to the 2010 census 2,321 people lived in the county: locals have long claimed it is the least-populated county east of the Mississippi River.[8]

So, this study was conducted in areas where there are some extraordinary outdoor amenities, particularly as related to mountain biking. The local road cycling is also remarkable. For example, the Blue Ridge Parkway and Skyline Drive meander along the crest of the Blue Ridge range for over five hundred miles through both Virginia and North Carolina. The road sometimes cuts through sections of the Shenandoah National Park and both the George Washington and Jefferson National Forests. Many of my friends believe, as do I, that the region has some of the finest mountain biking and road cycling in the United States.

Harrisonburg, Virginia, is currently at the center of a cycling revival in the Shenandoah Valley. This is a small university community—I currently teach at James Madison University—with about 50,000 residents and 20,000 students. It has long been home to a small, but very accomplished outdoor sporting community. Increasingly, it is referred to as a "cycling Mecca" in local print magazines, enough so that the community now bills itself as the "The Cycling Capital" of the Shenandoah Valley. (See chapter 5.) Community organizers now frequently sponsor cycling events to attract tourists to the region. After a long period of resistance, community politicians are increasingly embracing policy designed to make the community more pedestrian- and cycling-friendly. Harrisonburg is in the center of the valley, surrounded by rolling hills and some bucolic small farms, with the mountains a reasonable distance from town. But if you point yourself in any direction from the town center you will soon hit a place to ride a mountain bike or take a hike, usually within a fifteen-minute drive. These are often entry points into public lands that one could spend many lifetimes exploring.

The closest mountain range from Harrisonburg, and also the smallest, is the Massanutten. This is a very popular spot for local riders. To get a sense of the scale represented on the map presented below, the drive from Front Royal—a popular entrance for the Shenandoah National Park—to Pulaski, Virginia (at the southern tip of the map in Figure 11) is about 220 miles. The driving distance from Winchester, Virginia, near where the George Washington National Forest begins, to Wise County, where the Jefferson National Forest ends, is 350 miles. Although not formally delineated on the map, the Monongahela National Forest in West Virginia shares a border with much of

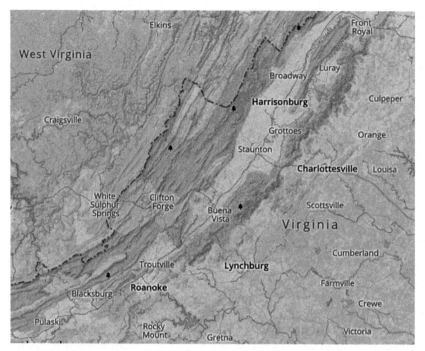

FIGURE 11 Map of the Shenandoah Valley and surrounding national forests and parks. This map was created using the US Geological Survey (USGS) topoView tool.

the Virginia National Forests about thirty to fifty miles directly west of Harrisonburg and Staunton, Virginia. This is another extraordinary area for mountain biking, and is also known for skiing, climbing, and whitewater rafting. Collectively, there are likely close to three thousand miles of trails in the surrounding national forests and parks.

So, the relatively sparsely populated Shenandoah Valley is proximate to an extraordinary range of outdoor amenities, everything from whitewater paddling to world-class climbing and mountain biking. Notably, the local community that routinely spends time in these public spaces is relatively small. When I was introduced to these areas twenty-five years ago by friends in Harrisonburg, we often felt we had much of the national forest "to ourselves." Not surprisingly, some area residents—and I include myself in this group—live here, in part, because there are opportunities to explore reasonably "wild" spaces that relatively few people know about. I have spent some time in many of the areas represented on this map. I have lived as far south as Blacksburg and as far north as Harrisonburg. I have family in the Winchester area, where my mother was born. My father spent his childhood in Waynesboro, a town that borders the Shenandoah National Park and George Washington National Forest. My wife once worked at the Mountain Institute in Franklin, West Virginia, an area close to the Monongahela. Still, after twenty-five years of intermittent exploring, there are many, many side trails, hidden valleys, streams, and rivers in this area that I am entirely unfamiliar with.

This vast area of wilderness has affected the local outdoor sporting subculture in a number of ways. First, this is simply a place that often "builds" people into strong athletes by virtue of its typography. If someone becomes comfortable riding a mountain bike or road bike locally—if they can haul themselves over the steep, rocky ridgelines in the national forest as a matter of routine—most find they can ride comfortably just about anywhere in the world. Indeed, when I first started riding, the small local cycling community used to speculate that it was only a matter of time before a world-class cyclist emerged from or was built in the region. Since then, several notable professional mountain bikers have trained in the region: two of the better-known are Sue Haywood and Jeremiah Bishop. Probably the best young American road rider today, Joe Dombrowski, grew up nearby on the eastern side of the Blue Ridge Mountains. Another international rider, Ben King, lives in Charlottesville, Virginia, and, as his schedule allows, routinely participates in cycling events in the valley.[9]

So the region both attracts and increasingly cultivates extraordinary athletes, many of whom practice their disciplines in relative obscurity. A few studies have found that some lifestyle sport enthusiasts tend to be ambivalent toward formal competition and that is also true of many people in this community.[10] Often, it appears that these are athletes who lost interest in formal competition as they spent an increasing amount of time in the nearby national forest. In short, this is a region where it is not uncommon to encounter people who stopped competing—as climbers, paddlers, runners, or cyclists—or never even started, because they came to believe it interfered too much with the time they spent riding their bicycle, or running, or climbing, or paddling, in the nearby public lands. Why should they travel to compete when there are world-class amenities—and a few serious athletes to spend time with—already in the neighborhood? Even the few local professionals who do travel and make a living in sport often seem to prefer the time they spend off the grid at some local cycling happening to time spent "on the job" when they race.[11] Others, particularly those who might be considered experts but do not aspire to earn a living practicing their sport of choice, have made the calculation that the time they once spent racing was usually far less interesting than the time they spent riding, or running, or climbing in their own "backyard."

At the same time, the region also attracts serious and disciplined regional and national racers. These athletes also appreciate the vast tracts of nearby wilderness and certainly take advantage of the quality of the local cycling, but almost always with the intention of disciplining their bodies so that they can go faster during competition. These two types of regional athletes do not "overlap" too much: their temperaments are so different that even though they use the same equipment they sometimes appear to be practicing very different sports. But there are also local events such as the Tour de Burg where these disparate groups of athletes might find themselves together.

During this study I spent some time with people representative of each of the previous groups. The people who first introduced me to cycling in the region did not approach sport in a manner that most would consider "orthodox." This was despite the fact that a few of these local athletes were among the fastest cyclists and ultra-distance runners in region. Later, through happenstance and during the period this study was begun, I often trained with a far more systematic and disciplined group of triathletes who were primarily focused on formal competition. Importantly, I enjoyed the time I spent with both these groups, but I did often ponder, well before I became a sociologist, as to why these athletes approached the same sports in such different manners. And ultimately, I was among those in the region increasingly ambivalent about many aspects of organized sport and competition. Obviously, this is a reason why I chose to use a critical orientation toward the study of sport. My increasing disenchantment with the discipline and rigors associated with competitive sport is probably not exceptional. In fact, this attitude was clearly shaped by many of the climbers, cyclists, and paddlers who introduced me to the various outdoor sports I have practiced in this region.

So, like others, over time I became more interested in the experience of certain sporting acts (riding a bike in the wilderness, for example) than riding in more formal competitions. That said, to this day when I am with my friends, we sometimes compete with one another in an ad-hoc and informal manner. We try to clear obstacles when we mountain-bike. We try to "drop" each other on difficult climbs. We sometimes sprint back to the parking lot at the end of our rides. And I still routinely encounter many people in this area who are experts at the sports they practice—they would finish well in formal competitions—but are not much interested in formally racing. While these types of communities exist elsewhere, it appears to be a particularly salient feature of the area where this study was conducted.

Notes

Introduction

1   Because Scott is now a public advocate and his identity would have been difficult to obscure, with his consent I am using his real name. A few public advocates, race directors, and professional racers also decided to waive their confidentiality, but most of the people interviewed for this text have been assigned pseudonyms.

2   Belinda Wheaton has most fully developed the academic definitions of lifestyle sport and considered how they might be both similar to and different from traditional sport. For a few examples, see her edited volume *Understanding Lifestyle Sports: Consumption, Identity and Difference* (London: Routledge, 2004). See also Robert E. Rinehart and Synthia Sydnor, eds., *To the Extreme: Alternative Sports, Inside and Out* (Albany: State University of New York Press, 2003).

3   Michel Foucault, *Discipline and Punish: The Birth of the Prison*, trans. Alan Sheridan (1977; repr., New York: Vintage Books, 1995): 135–184.

4   The considerable literature that has applied Foucault's approach to sport is discussed in greater detail in chapters 1–3.

5   See Chapter 1 for a more in-depth discussion. The move from play to sport is not an implicit focus of most studies associated with adventure sport, but the tension is evident in many studies. See JoAnne Kay and Suzanne Laberge, "Oh Say Can You Ski: Imperialistic Construction of Freedom in Warren Miller's *Freeriders*," in *To the Extreme: Alternative Sports, Inside and Out*, eds. Robert E. Rinehart and Synthia Sydnor (Albany: State University of New York Press, 2003): 381–398; Belinda Wheaton, "Selling Out? The Commercialisation and Globalisation of Lifestyle Sports," in *The Global Politics of Sport*, ed. Lincoln Allison (London: Routledge, 2004): 140–161.

6   Many conceptualize resistance by using Michel Foucault, "Technologies of the Self," in *Technologies of the Self: A Seminar with Michel Foucault*, eds. Luther. H. Martin, Huck Gutman, and Patrick H. Hutton (Amherst, MA: University of Massachusetts Press, 1988): 16–49.

7   An early study of adventure sport is Richard Mitchell's *Mountain Experience: The Psychology and Sociology of Adventure* (Chicago: University of Chicago Press, 1983).

A more recent ethnography of sport, in this case boxing, is Loïc Wacquant's, *Body and Soul: Ethnographic Notebooks of An Apprentice-Boxer* (New York: Oxford University Press, 2004).

8   A few would include: Paul Beedie, "Mountain Guiding and Adventure Tourism: Reflections on the Choreography of the Experience," *Leisure Studies* 22 (2003):147–167; Jacquelyn Allen Collinson, "Running the Routes Together: Corunning and Knowledge in Action," *Journal of Contemporary Ethnography* 37 (2008): 38–61; John Hockey, "Injured Distance Runners: A Case of Identity Work as Self-Help," *Sociology of Sport Journal* 21 (2005): 38–58; Lilian M. Jonas, "Making and Facing Danger: Constructing Strong Character on the River," *Symbolic Interaction* 22 (1999): 247–267; Lilian M. Jonas, William P. Stewart, and Kevin W. Larkin, "Encountering Heidi: Audiences for a Wilderness Adventurer Identity," *Journal of Contemporary Ethnography* 32 (2003): 403–431; Jeffrey L. Kidder, "Bike Messengers and the Really Real: Effervescence, Reflexivity, and Postmodern Identity," *Symbolic Interaction* 29 (2006): 349–371; Jason Laurendeau, "He Didn't Go in Doing a Skydive: Sustaining the Illusion of Control in an Edgework Activity," *Sociological Forum* 21 (2006): 31–54.

9   See Leon Anderson, "Analytic Auto-Ethnography," *Journal of Contemporary Ethnography* 35, no. 4 (2006): 373–395.

10 Patricia Adler and Peter Adler, *Membership Roles in Field Research* (Newbury Park, CA: Sage, 1987).

11 Norbert Elias, *The Civilizing Process: Sociogenetic and Psychogenetic Investigations* (Oxford: Blackwell, 2000); Norbert Elias and Eric Dunning, *Quest for Excitement: Sport and Leisure in the Civilising Process* (Oxford, UK: Blackwell, 1986). A recent study of triathlon that uses Elias and Dunning's perspective is Michael Atkinson, "Triathlon, Suffering and Exciting Significance," *Leisure Studies* 27, no. 2 (2008):165–180.

12 The charge of cooption in sociological studies of sport is common. For example, scholars associated with the work of Norbert Elias and Eric Dunning—who used the "figurational" approach and regarded it as a civilizing process—charged that some of their academic contemporaries who were critical of the approach, during studies of soccer hooliganism, had become too close to the hooligans they were ostensibly studying. See Eric Dunning, Patrick Murphy, and Ivan Waddington "Anthropological versus Sociological Approaches to the Study of Soccer Hooliganism: Some Critical Notes," *The Sociological Review* 39 (1991): 459–478. See also Eric Dunning, "The Social Roots of Football Hooliganism: A Reply to the Critics of the 'Leicester School,'" in *Football, Violence and Social Identity*, ed. Richard Guilianotti (New York: Routledge, 2013): 123–52.

13 The few collected editions of extreme and adventure sport tend to have articles written from this perspective. See, for example, Robert E. Rinehart and Synthia Sydnor, eds., *To the Extreme.* Importantly, the editors of that text have also used critical approaches when exploring extreme sport. See Robert E. Rinehart, "'Babes' & Boards: Opportunities in New Millennium Sport?" *Journal of Sport and Social Issues* 29, no. 3 (2005): 232–255 and "Inside of the Outside: Pecking Orders Within Alternative Sport at ESPN's 1995 The eXtreme Games," *Journal of Sport and Social Issues* 22, no. 4 (1998): 398–415. For other essays inclined toward more critical perspectives, see Belinda Wheaton, ed., *Understanding Lifestyle Sport.*

14 Many have asserted that this is common in ethnography. For example, Gary Alan Fine has demonstrated that many ethnographers, even those avowedly adopting a "value-neutral" perspective regarding their objects of study, inevitably, in choosing what to report, make judgments based on the affinity they have with certain people they studied. He describes a number of ways ethnographers orient themselves to the practice of ethnography. The roles they adopt can include: the kindly ethnographer, the friendly ethnographer, the honest ethnographer, the precise ethnographer, the observant ethnographer, the unobtrusive ethnographer, the candid ethnographer, the chaste ethnographer, the fair ethnographer, and the literary ethnographer. See Gary Alan Fine, "Ten Lies of Ethnography: Moral Dilemmas of Field Research," *Journal of Contemporary Ethnography* 22 (1993): 267–294.

15 See Anne Bolin and Jane Granskog, eds. *Athletic Intruders: Ethnographic Research on Women, Culture, and Exercise* (Albany: State University of New York Press, 2003). Granskog's contribution includes: "Just 'Tri' and 'Du' It: The Variable Impact of Female Involvement in the Triathlon/Duathlon Sport Culture," 27–52. See also Michael Messner, *Power at Play: Sports and the Problem of Masculinity* (Boston: Beacon Press, 1992) for a good example of a study that combined the examination of sport—largely written from an insider's perspective—with critical gender theory. More generally, gender theorists have tended to use sport as a useful site of study to think about masculinity and sexuality. See Michael Messner, Jim McKay, and Don Sabo, *Masculinities, Gender Relations, and Sport* (New York: Sage Publications, 2000). See also Jennifer Hargreaves, *Sporting Females: Critical Issues in the History and Sociology of Women's Sports* (New York: Routledge, 1994) and Jayne Caudwell, ed., *Sport, Sexualities and Queer Theory* (New York: Routledge, 2006).

16 For example, Mark Stranger, "The Aesthetics of Risk: A Study of Surfing," *International Review for the Sociology of Sport* 34, no. 3 (1999): 265–276.

17 D. Stanley Eitzen, *Fair and Foul: Beyond the Myths and Paradoxes of Sport* (Lanham, MD: Rowman and Littlefield, 2012).

18 The premise of Stanley Eitzen's *Fair or Foul* is the exploration of the dichotomous approaches to the study of sport that portray them as either all "good" or "bad." Eitzen makes the convincing case that in most respects both perspectives are valid.

19 For example, see Patricia A. Adler and Peter Adler, *Backboards and Blackboards: College Athletics and Role Engulfment* (New York: Columbia University Press, 1991).

20 Michael Messner and Donald Sabo, *Sex, Violence and Power in Sports: Rethinking Masculinity* (Freedom, CA: Crossing Press, 1994).

21 See Eitzen, *Fair and Foul,* and Michael Messner, *Power at Play.*

22 See Messner and Sabo, *Rethinking Masculinity.*

23 I think there are advantages to cultivating "detachment" during a study. For a good exemplar, see Ivan Waddington's "Introduction" in *Sport Health and Drugs: A Critical Perspective* (London: Taylor and Francis, 2000): 1–8. Many prefer the term "detachment" as opposed to claiming to be "value-neutral" when conducting a study.

24 For a good example, see Anthony Giddens, *The Constitution of Society: Outline of the Theory of Structuration* (Cambridge: Polity Press, 1984).

25 See Pierre Bourdieu, *In Other Words* (Stanford, CA: Stanford University Press, 1990). For a nice synthesis of Bourdieu's philosophy that neatly captures his use of

games, see a paper by Craig Calhoun, "Pierre Bourdieu in Context," http://www
.nyu.edu/classes/bkg/objects/calhoun.doc, accessed 3/13/2015.
26   Bourdieu, *In Other Words*, 63.
27   Pierre Bourdieu is among those associated with this endeavor. See *Outline of Theory and Practice*, trans. Richard Nice (Cambridge: Cambridge University Press, 1977). See also Anthony Giddens, *The Constitution of Society*.
28   See Michel Foucault, *Discipline and Punish: The Birth of the Modern Prison* (1977; repr., New York: Vintage, 1995).

Chapter 1 Social Life and Sport

1   The ontology of "play, games, and sport" was a standard in the early sociology of sport literature and was much debated. My investigation of this literature is cursory. For a fuller discussion see Morgan Williams and Klaus Meier, eds., *Philosophic Inquiry in Sport* (Champaign, IL: Human Kinetics Publishers, 1995). See also Stanley Eitzen, *Sociology of North American Sport* (London: McGraw-Hill, 1998).
2   Prominent early sociologists noted that ritual often acts to bind groups together. Emile Durkheim, for example, famously described how religious ritual was powerful not because it effected a real outcome—rain dances probably did not bring rain—but because the ritual bound the group together into a shared consciousness. These acts created community. See Emile Durkheim, *The Elementary Forms of the Religious Life*, trans. Joseph Ward Swain (London: George Allen & Unwin Ltd., 1915). See also Johan Huizinga, *Homo Ludens* (Boston, MA: Beacon Press, 1986).
3   Similar conceptual diagrams are often presented in sociology of sport texts. I adapted this diagram from Stanley Eitzen, *Sociology of North American Sport*. Another text that outlines many of the trends discussed in this chapter is Allen Guttmann, *From Ritual to Record: The Nature of Modern Sports* (New York: Columbia University Press, 2004).
4   See George Herbert Mead, "Play, the Game and the Generalized Other," in *Mind, Self & Society: From the Standpoint of a Social Behaviorist*, ed. Charles W. Morris (1934; repr., Chicago: University of Chicago Press, 1967): 152–164. See also Susan Birell, "Sport as Ritual: Interpretations from Durkheim to Goffman," *Social Forces* 60, no. 2 (1981): 354–376.
5   See for example, Norbert Elias, *The Civilizing Process. Sociogenetic and Psychogenetic Investigations* (Oxford, UK: Blackwell, 2000); Norbert Elias and Eric Dunning, *Quest for Excitement: Sport and Leisure in the Civilising Process* (Oxford, UK: Blackwell, 1986). See also Eric Dunning, *Sport Matters: Sociological Studies of Sport, Violence and Civilization* (New York: Routledge, 1999).
6   See Williams and Meier, eds., *Philosophic Inquiry in Sport*. See also Eitzen, *Sociology of North American Sport*.
7   Elias and Dunning, *Quest for Excitement*.
8   See Gruneau, *Class, Sports, and Social Development* (Champaign, IL: Human Kinetics, 1999).
9   Guttmann, *From Ritual to Record*.
10 Thorstein Veblen, *Theory of the Leisure Class* (1899; repr., New York: Penguin, 1994). See also Richard Gruneau, *Class, Sports, and Social Development*.

11 Thomas C. Wilson, "The Paradox of Social Class and Sports Involvement: The Roles of Cultural and Economic Capital," *International Review for the Sociology of Sport* 37, no. 1 (March 2002): 5–15.

12 One early influential text was Gruneau's *Class, Sports and Social Development*, an important theoretical contribution concerning social class and sport. Michael Messner has worked extensively on issues related to sport and gender norms. See *Power at Play: Sports and the Problem of Masculinity* (Boston, MA: Beacon Press, 1992) for an important early text and *Out of Play: Critical Essays on Gender and Sport* (Albany, NY: State University Press of New York, 2007) for a more recent treatment of gender issues and sport. See also Douglas Hartmann, *Race Culture and the Revolt of the Black Athlete: The 1968 Protests and Their Aftermath* (Chicago: University of Chicago Press, 2004).

13 See David Harvey, *The Condition of Postmodernity* (1990; repr., Oxford, UK: Blackwell, 200).

14 See Fredric Jameson, *Cultural Logic of Late Capitalism*. See also Jean-François Lyotard. *The Postmodern Condition: A Report on Knowledge*, trans. Geoff Bennington and Brian Massumi (1979; repr., Minneapolis: University of Minnesota Press, 1984).

15 For example, see Jean Baudrillard, *The Gulf War Did Not Take Place* (Bloomington: Indiana University Press, 1995).

16 See Jeffrey Montez de Oca, *Discipline and Indulgence* (New Brunswick, NJ: Rutgers University Press, 2013): 32–56.

17 For example, see David L. Andrews, ed., *Michael Jordan, Inc.: Corporate Sport, Media Culture, and Late Modern America* (Albany, NY: State University of New York Press, 1991). Likewise, Edward G. Armstrong, "The Commodified 23, or, Michael Jordan as Text," *Sociology of Sport Journal* 13, no. 4 (1996): 325–343.

18 Stephen Lyng, "Edgework: The Social Psychological Analysis of Voluntary Risk Taking," *American Sociological Review* 95, no. 4 (1990): 851–886.

19 Stephen Lyng, "Edgework," 852–860. See also Stephen Lyng, ed., *Edgework: The Sociology of Risk-Taking* (New York: Routledge, 2005).

20 Anthony Giddens and Ulrich Beck tend to be most associated with developing the concept of a "Risk Society" in which minimizing risk has become an increasingly normative preoccupation of modern life. See Anthony Giddens, "Risk and Responsibility," *Modern Law Review* 62, no. 1 (1999): 1–10, and Ulrich Beck, *Risk Society, Towards a New Modernity* (London: Sage Publications, 1992).

21 See Robert E. Rinehart and Synthia Sydnor, eds., *To the Extreme: Alternative Sports, Inside and Out* (Albany, NY: State University of New York Press, 2003) and Belinda Wheaton, ed., *Understanding Lifestyle Sports: Consumption, Identity and Difference* (New York: Routledge, 2004).

22 See Stephen Lyng, ed., *Edgework.*

23 Lori Holyfield, Lilian M. Jonas, and Anna Zajicek, "Adventure without Risk Is Like Disneyland," in *Edgework: The Sociology of Risk-Taking*, ed. Stephen Lyng (New York: Routledge, 2005): 173–186. See also Lori Holyfield, "Manufacturing Adventure: The Buying and Selling of Emotions," *Journal of Contemporary Ethnography* February 28, no. 1 (1999): 3–32.

24 The most influential work related to sport would be Michel Foucault, *Discipline and Punish: The Birth of the Prison*, trans. Alan Sheridan (1977; repr., New York: Vintage Books, 1995).

25 See David L. Andrews, "Desperately Seeking Michel: Foucault's Genealogy, the Body, and Critical Sport Sociology," *Sociology of Sport Journal* 10 (1993): 148–167;

Natalie Barker-Ruchti and Richard Tinning, "Foucault in Leotards: Corporeal Discipline in Women's Artistic Gymnastics," *Sociology of Sport Journal* 27 (2010): 229–250; William Bridel and Geneviève Rail, "Sport, Sexuality, and the Production of (Resistant) Bodies: De-/Re-Constructing the Meanings of Gay Male Marathon Corporeality," *Sociology of Sport Journal* 26 (2007): 127–144; Laura Frances Chase, "(Un)Disciplined Bodies: A Foucauldian Analysis of Women's Rugby," *Sociology of Sport Journal* 23 (2006): 229–247; Juha Heikkala, "Discipline and Excel: Techniques of the Self and Body and the Logic of Competing," *Sociology of Sport Journal* 10 (1993): 397–412; David P. Johns and Jennifer S. Johns, "Surveillance, Subjectivism and Technologies of Power: Analysis of the Discursive Practice of High-Performance Sport," *International Review for the Sociology of Sport* 35 (2000): 219–234; Pirkko Markula-Denison, "'Tuning into One's Self:' Foucault's Technologies of the Self and Mindful Fitness," *Sociology of Sport Journal* 21 (2004): 302–321; Geneviève Rail and Jean Harvey, "Body at Work: Michel Foucault and the Sociology of Sport," *Sociology of Sport Journal* 12 (1995): 164–179; Holly Thorpe, "Snowboarding Culture, Foucault, Technologies of Self, and the Media: Discourses of Femininity," *Journal of Sport and Social Issues* 32 (2008): 199–229.

26 See Michel Foucault, *The Birth of the Clinic: An Archaeology of Medical Perception* (1963; repr., New York: Vintage Books, 1994). See also Foucault, *Discipline and Punish.* John M. Hoberman has also argued that "science" and "sports medicine" have dramatically changed individual attitudes toward sport. His influential text is *Mortal Engines* (New York: The Free Press, 1992).

27 See Pirkko Markula-Denison and Richard Pringle, *Foucault, Sport and Exercise: Power, Knowledge and Transforming the Self* (New York: Routledge, 2006): 75–76.

28 Michel Foucault, "Technologies of the Self," in *Technologies of the Self: A Seminar with Michel Foucault*, eds. Luther H. Martin, Huck Gutman, & Patrick H. Hutton (Amherst, MA: University of Massachusetts Press, 1988): 16–48. See also Michel Foucault, *Ethics: Subjectivity and Truth: Essential Works of Michel Foucault*, ed. Paul Rabinow, trans. Robert Hurley (New York: The New Press, 1997).

29 For examples of how sport might constitute a resistance to discipline, see Markula-Denison and Pringle, *Foucault, Sport and Exercise*, 137–212. See also Heikkala, "Discipline and Excel," 397–412.

30 Jürgen Habermas is often associated with attempts to reconcile the insights and critical pessimism sometimes associated with the "Frankfurt School" (of which Foucault was not formally a member but is often connected intellectually) with a program of liberation. See "Taking Aim at the Heart of the Present," *Foucault: A Critical Reader*, ed. David Hoy (Oxford: Basil Blackwell, 1986). See also Bent Flyvbjerg, "Habermas and Foucault: Thinkers for Civil Society?" *British Journal of Sociology* 49, no. 2 (1998): 208–233; Fredric Jameson, *Postmodernism, or the Cultural Logic of Late Capitalism* (Durham, NC: Duke University Press, 1991).

31 See Foucault, "Technologies of the Self," 16–48.

32 See also Irene Diamond and Lee Quinby eds. *Feminism and Foucault: Reflections on Resistance* (Boston: Northeastern University Press, 1988). As applied to women triathletes, see Amanda Jones and Cara Carmichael Aitchison, "Triathlon as a Space for Women's Technologies of the Self" in *Sport and Gender Identities: Masculinities, Femininities, and Sexualities*, ed. Cara Carmichael Aitchison (London: Routledge, 2007): 53–73.

33 The exemplary act of appropriation is Susan R. Bordo, "The Body and the Repro-
duction of Femininity: A Feminist Appropriation of Foucault," *Gender Body
Knowledge: Feminist Reconstructions of Being and Knowing*, eds. Allison M. Jagger
and Susan R. Bordo (New Brunswick, NJ: Rutgers University Press, 1989): 13–33.
For a few examples, see Bridel and Rail, "Production of (Resistant) Bodies,"
127–144; Rail and Harvey, "Body at Work," 164–179; Heikkala, "Discipline and
Excel," 397–412. See also Jennifer Hargreaves, *Sporting Females: Critical Issues in the
History and Sociology of Women's Sports* (New York: Routledge, 1994); Jennifer Har-
greaves, "Schooling the Body," in *Sport, Power and Culture*, ed. Jennifer Hargreaves
(Cambridge: Polity Press, 1986): 161–181; Jennifer Hargreaves, "The Body, Sport
and Power Relations," in *Sport, Leisure and Social Relations*, eds. John Horne, David
Jary, & Alan Tomlinson (London: Routledge, 1987): 139–159; Nancy Theberge,
"Sport and Women's Empowerment," *Women's Studies International Forum* 10
(1988): 387–393.

34 Practically, Foucault did not theorize much with respect to market capitalism
and some people even read his later work as an endorsement of neoliberalism.
See Michael C. Behrent, "Liberalism without Humanism: Michel Foucault and
the Free-Market Creed, 1976–1979," *Modern Intellectual History* 6, no. 3 (2009):
539–568. But others explicitly associate market systems as imposing discipline. See
Jameson, *Cultural Logic of Late Capitalism*. See also David Harvey, *The Condition of
Postmodernity* (1990; repr., Oxford, UK: Blackwell, 2000). Harvey explores the idea
that cultural products (particularly art) are now "commodities" (22–24). He also
has a nice review of "modernization" and "alienation" from a neo-Marxist perspective (99–112).

35 Holyfield, Jonas, and Zajicek, "Adventure without Risk Is Like Disneyland,"
173–186.

36 See Robert Crawford, "Healthism and the Medicalization of Everyday life,"
International Journal of Health Services 10, no. 3 (1980): 365–88; Deborah Lupton,
The Imperative of Health: Public Health and the Regulated Body (London: SAGE
Publications, 1995).

37 Petr Skrabanek often uses the Kennedy administration's health programs, particularly the President's Council on Physical Fitness, as an exemplar of how a nation-
state establishes a program of "healthism." See *The Death of Humane Medicine and
the Rise of Coercive Healthism* (Suffolk, UK: The Social Affairs Unit, 1994). For a
specific review of the American program as established after World War II, as well
as a discussion of the American "muscle gap," see Jeffrey Montez de Oca, *Discipline
and Indulgence*, pp. 32–56. Notably, when the PCPF was first created, University of
Oklahoma football coach "Bud" Wilkinson was appointed its director.

38 Skrabanek, *The Death of Humane Medicine*, 15.

39 Ibid, 17.

40 Ibid.

41 Ibid. Associating running with religion is still pervasive in the popular press. For a
typical example, see Sakyong Mipham, *Running with the Mind of Meditation: Les-
sons for Training Body and Mind* (New York: Harmony Publishers, 2013).

42 Nicholas Rose, *Powers of Freedom: Reframing Political Thought* (Cambridge, UK:
Cambridge University Press, 1999): 74–87.

43 This is outlined by Alan Tomlinson, Neil Ravenscroft, Belinda Wheaton, and Paul
Gilchrist in their report, "Lifestyle Sports and National Sport Policy: An Agenda

for Research," *Report to Sport England*, March (2005), http:// www.slideshare.net/ saurabhbca07/lifestyle-sports-and-national-sports-policy.

44 D. Stanley Eitzen, *Fair and Foul: Beyond the Myths and Paradoxes of Sport* (Lanham, MD: Rowman and Littlefield, 2012).

45 See Tomlinson et al., "Lifestyle Sports," 16–26. See also Belinda Wheaton, "Introduction: Mapping the Lifestyle Sport-Scape," in *Understanding Lifestyle Sports: Consumption, Identity and Difference*, ed. Belinda Wheaton (London: Routledge, 2004): 1–28.

46 Tomlinson et al., "Lifestyle Sports," 2.

47 See Alan Tomlinson, *Consumption, Identity and Style* (London: Routledge, 1990).

48 See Belinda Wheaton, "Introduction," 1–28. See also Robert E. Rinehart and Synthia Sydnor, eds., *To the Extreme: Alternative Sports Inside and Out* (Albany, NY: State University of New York Press, 2003).

49 JoAnne Kay and Suzanne Laberge, "Mapping the Field of 'AR': Adventure Racing and Bourdieu's Concept of Field." *Sociology of Sport Journal* 19 (2002): 25–46.

50 Belinda Wheaton, "Introduction," 1–28.

51 Tomlinson et al., "Lifestyle Sports," 16–26.

52 For an example see Robert E. Rinehart, "Pecking Orders within Alternative Sport at ESPN's 1995 'The eXtreme Games,'" *Journal of Sport and Social Issues* 22 (1998): 398–415.

53 During the initial period when I drafted this text my father-in-law—along with a cohort of middle managers at the Benjamin Moore Company—was sent to one of these camps by consultants who had been hired to help reorganize the company. He mostly regarded this experience as evidence that the consultants were incompetent. "They think that strapping a bunch of middle aged, out of shape managers to a zip-line is going to save the company," was roughly how he summarized the experience. Shortly afterward, much of this group was unceremoniously "retired." This cost-saving strategy—essentially firing workers with the longest tenure and highest salaries—was being pursued by many large corporations at this time. Probably even the most stellar performers at "camp" lost their jobs. In the case of my father-in-law, he had worked for the Benjamin Moore company over thirty years—his entire career as an adult.

54 For a good overview of authenticity in a range of adventure sport, see Victoria Robinson's literature review in *Everyday Masculinities and Extreme Sport* (Oxford: Berg Publishers, 2007): 48–50. See also Becky Beal and Lisa Weidman, "Authenticity in the Skateboarding World," in *To the Extreme: Alternative Sports Inside and Out*, eds. Robert E. Rinehart and Synthia Sydnor (Albany, NY: State University of New York Press, 2003): 337–352.

Chapter 2 Looking for Adventure, Looking for Authenticity

1 USA Triathlon (USAT), *The Mind of a Triathlete*, Part 1 (2008): 8. This is a marketing report prepared for the USAT by the Tribe Group. I downloaded the report at the USAT website: http://www.usatriathlon.org/about-multisport/demographics .aspx.

2 I talked with some athletes who expressed the desire to train more, and even a few who were actively trying to rearrange their work (find different jobs) so that they would have more time to train, but none who had actually quit their jobs to train for a race.

Notes to Pages 32–34 • 199

3 In the article the author states that his guiding principle was to routinely ask himself, "What would Lance [Armstrong] do?" when he needed inspiration. Lance Armstrong was a professional cyclist and cancer survivor. In 2013 he admitted to using banned performance-enhancing drugs throughout his career.

4 Jonathan E. Kaplan, "Toughening Up for Hawaii's Ironman," *Washington Post*, March 29, 2000, sec. C4.

5 Interview with "Tom S." on February 9, 2001. Tom was single (with a long-time girl-friend), white, and twenty-seven years old at the time of this interview. Although eight years my junior, he was considered the other "old-hand" in the club.

6 Pictures of the "M-Dot" are easy to find online: just search for "tattoos ironman" and the M-Dots will follow. My impression is that most triathletes like them, but there is an occasional debate about this. For an example, see a post by Trent Ther-oux, "The Girl with the Ironman Tattoo," on the Xtri.com blog. http://www.xtri .com/features/detail/284-itemId.511713583.html.

7 Tough Mudder FAQ, http://toughmudder.com/faq/#jump-post-event-party.

8 As stated previously, many others would not consider a triathlon an "adventure" race.

9 Stephen Lyng, "Edgework: The Social Psychological Analysis of Voluntary Risk Taking," *American Sociological Review* 95, no. 4 (1990): 851–886.

10 Bruce Braun, "On The Raggedy Edge of Risk: Articulations of Race and Nature after Biology," in *Race, Nature, and the Politics of Difference*, eds. Donald S. Moore, Jake Kosek, and Anand Pandian (Durham, NC: Duke University Press, 2003): 175–203.

11 Sarah Jaquette Ray, "Risking Bodies in the Wild: The 'Corporeal Unconscious' of American Adventure Culture," *Journal of Sport & Social Issues* 33, no. 3 (2009): 257–284.

12 See M. Kenneth Brody, "Institutionalized Sport as Quasi-Religion: Preliminary Considerations," *Journal of Sport and Social Issues* 3, no. 2 (1979): 17–27.

13 Mitch Thrower, along with being a triathlete and past "president" of *Triathlete Magazine*, is also a self-professed "author, financier and entrepreneur" who has largely fashioned himself into a self-help guru. My favorite part of Mitch's website is the section where he has compiled a couple of hundred of his own "notable quotes," which he graciously allows people to use "royalty free" so long as he is footnoted as the author. Done! Two Mitch Thrower chestnuts (among the hundreds to choose from) include "Make the time to go find you" and "Only a tenacious few will evade the smudge of history's eventual eraser." See Mitch Thrower, "Mitch's Quotes," http://mitchthrower.com/quotes.html.

14 Mitch Thrower, "Got Adventure?" *Triathlete*, no. 232 (August 2003): 12.

15 Authenticity is a much-used and -debated term in both general sociology and the sociology of sport. See David Grazian, *Blue Chicago: The Search for Authenticity in Urban Blues Clubs* (Chicago: University of Chicago Press, 2005); Richard A. Peterson, *Creating Country Music: Fabricating Authenticity* (Chicago: University of Chicago Press, 1997). See also Gary Alan Fine, "Crafting Authenticity: The Validation of Identity in Self-Taught Art," *Theory and Society* 32 (2003): 153–180. For an application to sport, see Becky Beal and Lisa Weidman, "Authenticity in the Skateboarding World," in *To the Extreme: Alternative Sports Inside and Out*, eds. Robert E. Rinehart and Synthia Sydnor (Albany, NY: State University of New York Press, 2003): 337–352. As related to climbing, see Victoria Robinson's excellent

overview in *Everyday Masculinities and Extreme Sport* (Oxford, UK: Berg Publishers, 2007): 48–50.

16 David Grazian, *Blue Chicago: The Search for Authenticity*, 10–11.

17 See Grazian, *Blue Chicago.*

18 See Gary Alan Fine, "Crafting Authenticity," 153–180.

19 See Ray, "Risking Bodies," 257–284.

20 Informal discussion, notes with no recording, with "Betty" on August 17, 2013.

21 When I listened to post-race narratives people often described an obstacle (a hill, a stream) to one another. Initially, someone would describe how they felt at some difficult section of the race. Then there would be rejoinders by others that they had experienced the same feelings. For example, in my notes after one triathlon where there was two-mile bicycle climb I scribbled that "everyone is discussing the climb" and that "the hill was a killer."

22 Jeff Ferrell, Dragan Milovanovic, and Stephen Lyng, "Edgework, Media Practices, and the Elongation of Meaning: A Theoretical Ethnography of the Bridge Day Event," *Theoretical Criminology* 5, no. 2 (2001): 177–202.

23 See the Tough Mudder "Community" tab—where athletes can join "Mudder Nation"—for an example: http://muddernation.com.

24 Getting an endorphin "fix" or being an endorphin "junkie" was often specifically referenced. It appeared to be part of the popular discourse associated with triathlon at the time. When I did a search for the term I found a considerable number of people (usually personal trainers) who used the same terminology in their businesses. For example, see "EJ" (Endorphin Junkie) Elements at: http://www.ejelements.com.

25 Most studies of leisure time in the United States have showed it declining in recent years for many groups. The effects that social class has on leisure time is debatable. In terms of some long-term trends, leisure has increased for some during the period of modernization. See Kenneth Roberts, *Leisure in Contemporary Society* (Cambridge, MA: CABI, 2006).

26 See Fredric Jameson, *Postmodernism, or the Cultural Logic of Late Capitalism* (Durham, NC: Duke University Press, 1991) and David Harvey, *The Condition of Postmodernity.*

27 Johan Huizinga, *Homo Ludens: A Study of the Play Element in Culture* (Boston: Beacon Press, 1955).

28 Richard Gruneau, *Class, Sports, and Social Development* (Champaign, IL: Human Kinetics, 1999).

29 See Kyle Kusz, "*Fight Club* and the Art/Politics of White Male Victimization and Reflexive Sadomasochism," audiovisual review in *International Review for Sociology of Sport* 37 (2002): 465–470.

30 *Fight Club* was a movie about men. Likewise, most mountain bike racers are men.

31 Similarly, Max Weber famously stated that an "iron cage" of rationalism would produce "specialist without spirit, sensualist without heart;" See Max Weber, *Protestant Ethic and the Spirit of Capitalism* (1930; repr., London: Routledge Press, 1997): 182.

32 See Kyle Kusz, "*Fight Club* and White Male," 465–470.

33 This estimate concerning the average cost of the mountain bikes is an unscientific hunch based on my observations at the race. I actually suspect the average is higher. For instance, people who had subscribed to bicycling magazines, usually serious recreational riders, spent about $2,000 on their most recent

bike purchase at roughly the same period we were racing. See "Buyers Guide," *Bicycling*, April 2003.

34 This may be related to the rather eclectic mountain bike community that has long existed where I lived in Harrisonburg, Virginia. But I noticed the same differences in Blacksburg, Virginia, too. Often, the difference between these communities is exaggerated. Indeed, these cycling communities often overlapped.

35 Thorstein Veblen, *The Theory of the Leisure Class* (1899; repr., New York: Penguin USA, 1994).

36 USA Triathlon, *The Mind of a Triathlete* "Executive Summary," 2. http://www .usatriathlon.org/~/media/e5d25331eee14e8a8f97a562939b42df.ashx.

37 USA Triathlon, *The Mind of a Triathlete* "Report: 2012 USA Triathlon Demographics," 2.

38 *The Mind of a Triathlete*, "What Are the Triathlon Spending Trends?" 1–2.

39 The magazines I investigated do an annual review of new products that are described as "mandatory" for participation in the sport.

40 For an example, see a lively string of posts under the heading "How to spot a Newb Mountain Biker or a Mountain Bike poser," at the *MTBR Review* forum website: http://forums.mtbr.com/general-discussion/how-spot-newb-mountain-biker -poser-788612.htm.

41 In product reviews, a staple of these magazines, it was not particularly hard to read between the lines and realize that a half-hearted endorsement of equipment was actually a recommendation against its purchase.

42 "Buyer's Guide," *Bicycling*, April 2003: 46. The examples I use in this chapter usually refer to this issue of *Bicycling*, and to the July and August, 2003, editions of *Triathlete*. When I looked at *Bicycling*, *Triathlete*, and *Mountain Bike* contents over 11 issues during this year, the same themes occurred in every magazine, so any issue of these publications will likely have plenty of examples of the themes discussed in this chapter. The examples of products reviewed are also a good example of the production of a capitalist "culture" that sells products to a new class of "cultural consumers." See David Harvey. *The Condition of Postmodernity*, 22–24. Indeed, *Bicycling*'s "Style Man" column was a self-conscious, and tongue-in-cheek, representative of a prominent cycling subculture. That the column is tongue-in-cheek is also an example of a subtle subversion of these norms.

43 Most often, having many reviewers comment on the equipment being tested facilitates a "mixed" review of products. Inevitably, different reviewers rate different pieces of equipment as being their favorite, or superior to other pieces being reviewed. Each reviewer offers different reasons why he likes the product. Some magazines appear to take these reviews more seriously than others. I ran across a few "consensus" reviews in *Bicycling* and *Mountain Bike* that stated one piece of equipment outperformed another. Still, most of the reviews in these magazines were mixed, with no consensus emerging concerning quality of the equipment.

44 For example, "Lose 1 Pound a Week—Guaranteed" was featured on the cover of the *Bicycling* "Buyer's Guide," April 2003. Usually there are several articles and advice columns devoted to weight loss or some other aesthetic body improvement.

45 Xterra Series homepage at: http://www.xterraplanet.com/index.html.

46 For example, see John H. Kerr, "Arousal-Seeking in Risk Sport Participants," *Personality and Individual Differences* 12, no. 6 (1991): 613–616. See also Marvin

Zuckerman, "Sensation Seeking and Sports," *Personality and Individual Differences* 4, no. 3 (1983): 285–293.

47 Kathleen J. Tierney, "Toward a Critical Sociology of Risk," *Sociological Forum* 14, no. 2 (1999): 215–242.

48 Edward Albert, "Dealing With Danger: The Normalization of Risk in Cycling," *International Review for the Sociology of Sport* 34, no. 2 (1999): 157–171.

49 Stephen Lyng, ed., *Edgework*. See also Sarah Jaquette Ray, "Risking Bodies in the Wild," 257–284.

50 One study conducted in the 1990s estimated that annually about 900 cyclists in the United States were killed while bike riding, 20,000 were admitted to the hospital, and over a half million received treatment in the emergency room. See Snell Memorial Foundation, "Circumstances and Severity of Bicycle Injuries," *Cycling Science* 8 (1996): 15–23. Report also available at http://www.smf.org/docs/articles/report.

51 One of the Virginia Tech club members I interviewed, a woman, was riding behind the man who was killed. She watched him get hit and stayed with him while an ambulance was summoned. Before I interviewed her I did not know about this experience. After this accident, she found it extremely hard to train and ride her bike.

52 Victoria Robinson, *Everyday Masculinities and Extreme Sport* (Oxford, UK: Berg Publishers 2007): 147–160.

53 The IMBA "trial care crew," Mike and Jan, kept a log of their travels that summer. For a history of their group, see "15 Years of the Subaru/IMBA Trail Care Crew," https://www.imba.com/blog/marty-caivano/15-years-subaruimba-trail-care-crew.

54 Lori Holyfield, "Manufacturing Adventure: The Buying and Selling of Emotions," *Journal of Contemporary Ethnography* 28, no. 1 (1999): 3–32.

55 Ibid.

56 This is, for example, included in the definition of "adventure" in *Webster's New World Dictionary*: http://www.merriam-webster.com/dictionary/adventure.

57 For a good article on how group dynamics affect an adventure travel experience, see Lilian M Jonas, William P. Stewart, and Kevin W. Larkin, "Encountering Heidi Audiences for a Wilderness Adventurer Identity," *Journal of Contemporary Ethnography* 32 (2003): 403–431.

58 The appeal and idea of communing with "wilderness" has a long history. See Roderick Nash, *Wilderness and the American Mind* (New Haven, CT: Yale University Press, 1967) for an early exploration of how "wilderness" was created in the American psyche.

59 Lori Holyfield, "Manufacturing Adventure," 3–32.

60 One of my former students, Katie Mock, has been a whitewater guide for several seasons for a company based out of Fayetteville, West Virginia. We had a few informal discussions about her experiences, for which I am grateful. For the record, while Katie recognized the "manufactured" nature of creating adventure and the "emotional labor" she did, she was adamant that any time "amateurs" were put in a raft, particularly if they were out of shape, obese, or drunk, there was a genuine potential for danger.

61 Jonas, Stewart, and Larkin, "Encountering Heidi," 403–431.

62 Arlie Russell Hochschild, "Emotion Work, Feeling Rules and Social Structure," *American Journal of Sociology* 85, no. 3 (1979): 551–573.

63   George Ritzer, in *The McDonaldization of Society* (Washington D.C.: Sage Publications, 2012) has an account of a failed Mount Everest campaign that Jon Krakauer also wrote about in *Into Thin Air* (New York: Anchor, 1999). Two competing Everest guides thought they had made the climb "routine" enough to take novice climbers to the peak. Instead, a series of mishaps resulted in multiple fatalities among the clients, as well as the deaths of the two primary guides. Ritzer uses the expedition as an example of the "limits" of "McDonaldizing" the adventure travel industry.

Chapter 3 Disciplining Bodies in Lifestyle Sport

1   Allen Guttmann, *From Ritual to Record: The Nature of Modern Sports* (New York: Columbia University Press, 2004) penned the seminal text that described how Weberian rationality led to the bureaucratization of sport. Other scholars have explored how rapidly lifestyle sport was commercialized, with Belinda Wheaton's work sometimes particularly focused on this phenomenon. See Belinda Wheaton, "'Selling Out?': The Commercialisation and Globalization of Lifestyle Sports," in *The Global Politics of Sport*, ed. Lincoln Allison (London: Routledge, 2004). See also Belinda Wheaton, "Introduction: Mapping the Lifestyle Sport-Scape," in *Understanding Lifestyle Sports: Consumption, Identity and Difference*, ed. Belinda Wheaton (London: Routledge, 2004): 1–28.
2   Richard Gruneau, *Class, Sports, and Social Development* (Champaign, IL: Human Kinetics, 1999).
3   John M. Hoberman, *Mortal Engines* (New York: The Free Press, 1992): 20–22.
4   Michel Foucault, *Discipline and Punish: The Birth of the Modern Prison*, trans. Alan Sheridan (1977; repr., New York: Vintage Books, 1995). For example, see David L. Andrews, "Desperately Seeking Michel: Foucault's Genealogy, the Body, and Critical Sport Sociology," *Sociology of Sport Journal* 10 (1993): 148–167; Natalie Barker-Ruchti and Richard Tinning, "Foucault in Leotards: Corporeal Discipline in Women's Artistic Gymnastics," *Sociology of Sport Journal* 27 (2010): 229–250; William Bridel and Geneviève Rail, "Sport, Sexuality, and the Production of (Resistant) Bodies: De-/Re-Constructing the Meanings of Gay Male Marathon Corporeality," *Sociology of Sport Journal* 24 (2007): 127–144; Laura Frances Chase, "(Un) Disciplined Bodies: A Foucauldian Analysis of Women's Rugby," *Sociology of Sport Journal* 23 (2006): 229–247; Juha Heikkala, "Discipline and Excel: Techniques of the Self and Body and the Logic of Competing," *Sociology of Sport Journal* 10 (1993): 397–412; David P. Johns and Jennifer S. Johns, "Surveillance, Subjectivism and Technologies of Power: Analysis of the Discursive Practice of High-Performance Sport," *International Review for the Sociology of Sport* 35 (2000): 219–234; Pirkko Markula-Denison, "'Tuning into One's Self': Foucault's Technologies of the Self and Mindful Fitness," *Sociology of Sport Journal* 21 (2004): 302–321; Geneviève Rail and Jean Harvey, "Body at Work: Michel Foucault and the Sociology of Sport," *Sociology of Sport Journal* 12 (1995): 164–179; Holly Thorpe, "Snowboarding Culture, Foucault, Technologies of Self, and the Media: Discourses of Femininity," *Journal of Sport and Social Issues* 32 (2008): 199–229.
5   Foucault, *Discipline and Punish*, 135–184.
6   See Johns and Johns, "Surveillance, Subjectivism," 219–234, for a specific application of Foucauldian surveillance to elite sport.

7 See David Harvey, *The Condition of Postmodernity* (1999; repr., Oxford, UK: Blackwell Publishers, 2000).

8 Increasing "efficiency" was one aspect of Max Weber's typology associated with bureaucracy and legal-rational organizations. He considered this value a "norm" in rationalized organizations, so I have more generally rendered this the "norm of efficiency." See Max Weber, *Economy and Society* (1921; repr., Totowa, NJ: Bedminster, 1968). Weber described the "iron cage" of rationalism in the final pages (pp. 181–183) of *The Protestant Ethic and the Spirit of Capitalism* (1930; repr., London: Routledge Press, 1997). For the application of Weberian theory to modern sport, see Gutmann, *From Ritual to Record*.

9 At that time bicycle helmets were uncomfortable and clunky, and used far less often—on the road or in the woods—than today.

10 For a good account of this history, see Frank J. Barto, Wende Cragg, and Erik Kosli, *The Birth of Dirt: Origins of Mountain Biking* (New York: Cycling Publishing, 1998).

11 For Foucault's concept of "correct training" and discipline, see *Discipline and Punish*, 170–194. See also Barker-Ruchti and Tinning, "Corporeal Discipline in Gymnastics," 229–250.

12 Standard monthly columns generally include advice on nutrition and training and technical advice on how to maintain equipment.

13 "Buyer's Guide," *Bicycling*, April 2003: 22.

14 Ibid.

15 See the July and August 2003 "Letters to the Editor" sections of *Triathlete*.

16 I interviewed several club members (mostly the officers) for this study. I also raced, somewhat self-consciously (due to my age), with the triathlon team at the East Coast Collegiate Championships.

17 The July 2003 edition of *Triathlete* was the first "swimsuit edition" of the magazine, which drew angry response from some readers.

18 Bob Babbitt, *30 Years of the Ironman Triathlon World Championship* (Meyer & Meyer Publishing, 2008).

19 See Babbitt, *30 Years of Ironman*.

20 For Foucault's concept of "correct training," see *Discipline and Punish*, 135–169.

21 This idea has been increasingly explored by those inclined toward Foucauldian approaches. For example, see Rail and Harvey, "Body at Work," 164–179.

22 Michelle J. Blaydan and Koenraad J. Lindner, "Eating Disorders and Exercise Dependence in Triathletes," *Eating Disorders* 10, no. 1 (2002): 49–60. See also Holly Wethington, Claudia Flowers, Michael Turner, and Rita DiGioacchino, "Eating Attitudes, Body Image, and Nutrient Intake in Female Triathletes," *Women in Sport & Physical Activity Journal*, Fall 2002: 115

23 Sally Edwards established an early small franchise producing books related to triathlon training. Some of her titles include: *Triathlon for Kids, Triathlon for Fun*, and *Triathlon for Women*, all published by Velo Press in Boulder, Colorado. See particularly *Triathlon: A Triple Fitness Sport* (Sacramento: Fleet Feet Press, 1982), one of the first triathlon training books produced. A search on May 1, 2012 of "triathlon training" on Amazon.com yielded 612 electronic and paperback texts, everything from *The Idiot's Guide to Triathlon Training* to *The Triathlete's Training Bible*.

24 "Jonathan," originally from the Netherlands, is a veteran endurance racer who has completed a considerable number of fifty-mile running races. We were occasional

running partners in 2000–2001. He has a Ph.D. in a technical field of food processing and storage that essentially makes him a "food engineer." Currently, he takes care of his two young daughters. I intended, but never managed, to formally interview him for this study. We have remained friends and our families try to meet every year for a camping trip even though we are now living in different communities.

25 For one of the earliest examples, see Edwards, *Triathlon: A Triple Fitness Sport*, which details how she "worked" hard to achieve competence in the sport she enjoyed the least, swimming.

26 This event is described by Steve Harvey, "Only in L.A." *Los Angeles Times*, June 12, 1991 at http://articles.latimes.com/1991-06-12/local/me-370_1_ucla-fans.

27 For Foucault's concept of surveillance, see *Discipline and Punish*, 195–292.

28 See, for example, Joe Friel, *The Triathlete's Training Bible* (Boulder, CO: Velo Press, 2009)

29 Tom Vanderbilt, "How Strava Is Changing the Way We Ride," *Outside Magazine*, January 2013, http://www.outsideonline.com/fitness/biking/How-Strava-Is -Changing-the-Way-We-Ride.html.

30 David Darlington, "The Strava Files," *Bicycling Magazine*, October 3, 2013, http:// www.bicycling.com/news/featured-stories/strava-files.

31 Vanderbilt, "How Strava."

32 Interview with "Ben" and "Brenda," July 14, 2013.

33 Michel Foucault, "Technologies of the Self," in *Technologies of the Self: A Seminar with Michel Foucault*, eds. Luther. H. Martin, Huck Guttmann and Patrick H. Hutton (Amherst, MA: University of Massachusetts Press, 1988): 16–48.

34 For example, see Pirkko Markula-Denison, "The Technologies of the Self: Sport, Feminism, and Foucault," *Sociology of Sport Journal* 20 (2003): 87–107 and Pirkko Markula-Denison, "'Tuning into One's Self': Foucault's Technologies of the Self and Mindful Fitness," *Sociology of Sport Journal* 21 (2004): 190–210. See also Michel Foucault, *Ethics, Subjectivity and Truth* (New York: The New Press, 1997). As applied to triathlon, see Amanda Jones and Cara Carmichael Aitchison, "Triathlon as a Space for Women's Technologies of the Self," in *Sport and Gender Identities: Masculinities, Femininities, and Sexualities*, ed. Cara Carmichael Aitchison (London: Routledge, 2007): 53–73.

35 I do not have space to explore machine/human interactions in sport, but do find it an interesting topic. For a foundational study of cyborgs, see Donna Haraway, *Simians, Cyborgs, and Women: The Reinvention of Nature* (New York: Routledge, 1990).

36 Megan Kelly Cronan and Dave Scott, "Triathlon and Women's Narratives of Bodies and Sport," *Leisure Sciences* 30, no. 1 (2008): 17–34; Jane Granskog, "In Search of the Ultimate," 3–25; Jane Granskog, "Tri-ing Together," 76–91; Jane Granskog, "Just 'Tri' and 'Du,'" 27–52. See also Jones and Aitchison, "Triathlon as a Space for Women's Technologies."

37 Blaydon and Lindner, "Eating Disorders and Exercise Dependence in Triathletes." See also Rita DiGioacchino, Claudia Flowers, Michael Turner, and Holly Wethington, "Eating Attitudes, Body Image, and Nutrient Intake in Female Triathletes," *Women in Sport & Physical Activity Journal* Fall (2002): 115–129.

38 The association between being a female athlete and a greater prevalence towards eating disorders—usually associated with a greater preoccupation with weight control—has been well established. See Dr. Jorunn Sundgot-Borgen, "Eating

Disorders in Female Athletes," *Sports Medicine* 17 (1994): 176–188. With respect to collegiate athletes, see Craig Johnson, Pauline S. Powers, and Randy Dick. "Athletes and Eating Disorders: The National Collegiate Athletic Association Study." *International Journal of Eating Disorders* 26 (1999): 179–188. See also a meta-analysis of studies completed by Vikki Krane, J. Stiles-Shipley, Jennifer Waldron, and Jennifer Michalenok, "Relationships among Body Satisfaction, Social Physique Anxiety, and Eating Behaviors in Female Athletes and Exercisers," *Journal of Sport Behaviour* 24 (2001): 247–264.

39 A study of eating disorders among women triathletes indicates that this might be a common scenario. In effect, the most disordered eating was self-reported among "beginning" triathletes participating at sprint distances. See DiGioacchino, Flowers, Turner, and Wethington, "Eating Attitudes, Body Image, Female Triathletes."

40 Megan Axelsen, "The Power of Leisure: I Was an Anorexic; I'm now a Healthy Triathlete," *Leisure Sciences* 31 (2009): 330–346.

41 Ibid.

42 As relates to triathlon, see Cronin and Scott, "Triathlon and Women's Narratives," 25–28. See also Pirkko H. Markula, "Firm but Shapely, Fit but Sexy, Strong but Thin: The Postmodern Aerobicizing Female Bodies," *Sociology of Sport Journal* 12, no. 4 (1995): 424–453; Leslie Haravon Collins, "Working Out the Contradictions: Feminism and Aerobics," *Journal of Sport and Social Issues* 26, no. 1 (2002): 85–109.

43 Cronin and Scott, "Triathlon and Women's Narratives," 25–28. See also Granskog, "Tri-ing Together," 76–91.

44 I did not interview enough women to have a statistically significant sample size. This may be a trend associated only with the group of athletes I interviewed. But do see DiGioacchino, Flowers, Turner, and Wethington. "Eating Attitudes, Body Image, Female Triathletes."

45 See the September/October 2013 edition of *Inside Triathlon* and its first "body issue." The manner with which triathlete Mirinda Carfrae describes maintaining her femininity in a masculine sport was interesting. First, she describes the masculine nature of the sport—the "drool on the chin," the unflattering representations of the body while racing, the sweat associated with the sport—and then comments that even so, she tries, when she races, to maintain her femininity by having coordinated racing outfits. See *Triathlete*, "Inside Triathlete's Body Shoot," http:// triathlon.competitor.com/2013/10/video/inside-triathlons-body-shoot-mirinda -carfrae_82326. Notably, the women athletes interviewed also make reference to the machinelike qualities of their bodies—strictly related to performance—which are similar to the men's comments.

46 See Susan Bordo, *Unbearable Weight: Feminism, Western Culture, and the Body* (Berkeley, CA: University of California Press, 1993).

47 Markula, "Firm but Shapely," 424–453.

48 See Blaydon and Lindner, "Eating Disorders and Exercise Dependence," 49–60.

49 See Fletcher Linder, "Life as Art, and Seeing the Promise of Big Bodies," *American Ethnologist* 34, no. 3 (2007): 451–472.

50 Interview with "Ben" and "Brenda," July 14, 2013.

51 Interview with "Tom," August 17, 2013.

52 In video interviews associated with the "body issue" of *Inside Triathlon* in 2013, the professional male athletes featured—Craig Alexander and Sebastian Kienle—both

tend to reference their bodies in ways similar to the men I interviewed. In particular, they both use the "machine" and "performance" analogies. See *Triathlete*, "Inside Triathlon's Body Issue" http://triathlon.competitor.com/2013/09/video/inside-triathlons-body-shoot-craig-alexander_82323.

Chapter 4 Types of Lifestyle Athletes and Team Touch of Grey

1 Max Weber's most famous typology is his "authority types," which are traditional, charismatic, and legal-rational. In manufacturing these types Weber had to justify their use. See *From Max Weber: Essays in Sociology*, eds. H. H. Gert and C. Wright Mills (New York: Oxford University Press, 1958).

2 Typologies have been criticized, although Weber actually anticipated many of these when he pioneered their use. The basic argument is that they simplify the social world too much. The utility of constructing typologies is that they help people organize information and can aid them in making meaningful comparisons.

3 A favorite disclaimer regarding the construction of typographies was offered by Manuel Castells, who wrote, "Please accept the usual disclaimer about the inevitable reductionism of this, and all typologies, which I hope will be compensated for by examples that will bring the blood and flesh of actual movements into this somewhat abstract characterization." See *The Power of Identity: The Information Age: Economy, Society, and Identity, Vol. 2* (New York: Wiley-Blackwell, 2003): 72.

4 For an excellent critical study of the "corporeal unconscious" in adventure culture, see Sarah Jaquette Ray, "Risking Bodies in the Wild: The 'Corporeal Unconscious' of American Adventure Culture," *Journal of Sport & Social Issues* 33, no. 3 (2009): 257–284. Ray makes the point that the prospect of bodily damage is a celebrated part of adventure sport, but that the culture normalizes "able-bodiedness" and makes disability "the other." Ray states that "disability is the category of 'otherness' against which both environmentalism and adventure have been shaped and revises environmental thought to include all kinds of bodies" (257). I admire this article, but in observing the way people responded to Scott on a personal level I never saw any social distancing. In fact, he was invariably someone people wanted to talk to, perhaps because he was the rare "other" engaged in adventure sport, but also because he was, I think, someone people sincerely admired.

5 This was before powerful disc brakes had become more affordable. Scott, remarkably, was using powerful hydraulic-caliper brakes. Notably, in our follow-up interview he actually described these as better than the disc brakes now commonly used because they could be more fine-tuned and subtle.

6 His name is Brett Wolfe. See Kristin Dizon, "With One Leg and an Iron Will, Brett Wolfe Sets Himself Apart from Biking Pack," *Seattle Post Intelligencer*, July 25, 2001, http://www.seattlepi.com/lifestyle/article/With-one-leg-and-an-iron-will-Brett-Wolfe-sets-1060803.php.

7 Bill Hughes and Kevin Paterson, "The Social Model of Disability and the Disappearing Body: Towards a Sociology of Impairment," *Disability & Society* 12, no. 3 (1997): 325–340.

8 J. D. Kimple, "The Badass of the Ohio Valley Cyclocross: An Interview with Charles Scott McDonald," *Cyclocross* April 4, 2013, http://www.cxmagazine.com/badass-ohio-valley-cyclocross-interview-charles-scott-mcdonald.

9 Interview with Charles Scott McDonald, August 24, 2013.

10 For example, Stephen Lyng, "Edgework: The Social Psychological Analysis of Voluntary Risk Taking," *American Sociological Review* 95 no. 4 (1990): 851–886, argued that a decline in risk in daily life may be causal with respect to people's decision to engage in risky sport.

Chapter 5 Resistance to Discipline in a Cycling Community

1 Shenandoah Valley Bicycle Coalition, Newsletter Archives: April 1984, http://svbcoalition.org/downloads/newsletters/archives/1984-04-april.pdf?70f7af April 1984 Newsletter.

2 Michel Foucault, "Technologies of the Self," in *Technologies of the Self: A Seminar with Michel Foucault*, eds. Luther H. Martin, Huck Gutmann, and Patrick H. Hutton (Amherst, MA: University of Massachusetts Press, 1988): 16–48.

3 Jeremiah Bishop is probably the best-known local professional. A past Tour de Burg winner, at times he has been considered one of the best all-around professional mountain bikers in the United States. Sue Haywood, a top U.S. women's cross country rider who is now semi-retired, has finished first among the women riders in several Tours.

4 Becky Beal and Lisa Weidman, "Skateboarding: An Alternative to Mainstream Sports," in *Inside Sports*, eds. Jay Coakly and Peter Donnelly (London: Routledge, 1999): 133–140; Becky Beal and Lisa Weidman, "Authenticity in the Skateboarding World," in *To the Extreme: Alternative Sports Inside and Out*, eds. Robert E. Rinehart and Synthia Sydnor (Albany, NY: State University of New York Press, 1994): 337–352; Iain Borden, *Skateboarding, Space and the City: Architecture and the Body* (Oxford, UK: Berg, 2001).

5 Nancy Midol and Gerard Broyer, "Toward an Anthropological Analysis of New Sport Cultures: The Case of Whiz Sports in France," *Society of Sport Journal* 12 (1995): 204–12. See also Tim Dant and Belinda Wheaton, "Windsurfing: An Extreme Form of Material and Embodied Interaction," *Anthropology Today* 23, no. 6 (2007): 8–12; Duncan Humphreys, "Selling out Snowboarding: The Alternative Response to Commercial Co-optation," in Rinehart and Sydnor, *To the Extreme*, 407–428; Belinda Wheaton, "After Sport Culture: Rethinking Sport and Post-Subcultural Theory," *Journal of Sport and Social Issues* 31, no. 3 (2007): 283–307.

6 Victoria Robinson, *Everyday Masculinities and Extreme Sport* (Oxford, UK: Berg Publishers, 2007): 41–59.

7 Mark Stranger, "The Aesthetics of Risk: A Study of Surfing," *International Review for the Sociology of Sport* 34, no. 3 (1999): 265–76.

8 Belinda Wheaton, "'Just Do It': Consumption, Commitment and Identity in the Windsurfing Subculture," *Sociology of Sport Journal* 17, no. 3 (2004): 254–74; Belinda Wheaton, "'Selling Out?': The Commercialisation and Globalization of Lifestyle Sports," in *The Global Politics of Sport*, ed. Lincoln Allison (London: Routledge, 2005): 127–146; Belinda Wheaton and Becky Beal, "'Keeping It Real': Sub-cultural Media and Discourses of Authenticity in Alternative Sport," *International Review for the Sociology of Sport* 38 (2003): 155–176.

9 Mark Stranger, *Surfing Life: Surface, Substructure and the Commodification of the Sublime* (New York: Ashgate, 2011): 187–214.

10 Victoria Robinson, *Everyday Masculinities*: 147–160.

11 See Stranger, *Surfing Life*, and Robinson, *Everyday Masculinities*.

12 See Holly Thorpe, *Snowboarding Bodies in Theory and Practice* (New York: Palgrave Macmillan, 2011).

13 Pirkko Markula-Denison, "'Tuning into One's Self': Foucault's Technologies of the Self and Mindful Fitness," *Sociology of Sport Journal* 21 (2004): 302–321. See also Michael Atkinson, "Entering Scapeland: Yoga, Fell and Post-Sport Physical Cultures." *Sport and Society* 13, no. 7/8 (2010): 1249–1267.

14 Ian Austen, "Lululemon Athletica Combines Ayn Rand and Yoga," *New York Times*, November 27, 2011, http://www.nytimes.com/2011/11/28/business/media/combines-ayn-rand-and-yoga.html?r=0. I have a friend who is a serious practitioner of Ashtanga-yoga. After reading this chapter he informed me that Sonia Tudor, the wife of hedge-fund billionaire Paul Tudor Jones, is funding a series of yoga centers with the blessing of Krishna Pattabhi's family. Sri Krishna Pattabhi Jois, now deceased, is considered an Ashtanga-yoga master. My friend did not think these "country club" sites were sustainable. The Tudors are also financing an Ashtanga program at the University of Virginia connected to the Center for Contemplative Sciences. See Bethany McLean, "Whose Yoga Is It, Anyway?" *Vanity Fair*, April 2013, http://www.vanityfair.com/business/2012/04/krishna-pattanbhi-trophy-wife-ashtanga-yoga.

15 See Michel Foucault, "The Subject and Power," *Critical Inquiry* 8 (Summer 1982): 777–795. See also Michel Foucault, "Technologies of the Self," in *Technologies of the Self: A Seminar with Michel Foucault*, eds. Luther H. Martin, Huck Gutmann, and Patrick H. Hutton (Amherst, MA: University of Massachusetts Press, 1988): 16–49.

16 Foucault, "Technologies of the Self," 18.

17 Rachel Aldred, "'On the Outside': Constructing Cycling Citizenship," *Social & Cultural Geography* 11, no. 1 (2010): 35–52.

18 Zack Furness, *One Less Car: Bicycling and the Politics of Automobility* (Philadelphia: Temple University Press, 2010).

19 See the League of American Bicyclists (formerly the League of American Wheelman), http://www.bikeleague.org.

20 Joe Garofoli, "Critical Mass Turns 10: A Decade of Defiance: Cyclists Celebrate 10 Years of Clogging Streets En Masse," *San Francisco Chronicle*, September 26, 2002, http://www.fgate.com/politics/joegarofoli/article/Critical-Mass-turns-10-A-decade-of-defiance-2767020.php.

21 Stranger, *Surfing Life*, 205.

22 See the Shenandoah Bike Company website, http://www.shenandoahbicycle.com/about/location-pg81.htm.

23 This has happened in other "new" sports. See Becky Beal and Charlene Wilson, "'Chicks Dig Scars': Commercialisation and the Transformations of Skateboarders' Identities," in *Understanding Lifestyle Sports: Consumption, Identity and Difference*, ed. Belinda Wheaton (London: Routledge, 2004): 31–53.

24 Franz Lidz, "Midnight Riders," *Sports Illustrated*, June 18, 2001, http://sportsillustrated.cnn.com/vault/article/magazine/MAG1022790/index.htm.

25 David Grazian, *Blue Chicago: The Search for Authenticity* (Chicago: Chicago University Press, 2003): 10–11.

26 The Tour de Burg Facebook page is at https://www.facebook.com/tourdeburg.

27 Laird Knight was inducted into the Marin Mountain Bike Museum Hall of Fame in 2002 following his success at drawing corporate sponsorship to the 24 Hour races

his company produced. For a self-narrative in terms of how the races he organized "grew"—including how corporate sponsorship became "necessary" to grow the sport—see the account in his own words, "Marin Museum of Bicycling: Laird Knight," http://mmbhof.org/laird-knight.

28 At this writing, the old 24 Hours at Snowshoe race website is still available at Granny Gear Productions, http://www.grannygear.com.

29 Lidz, "Midnight Riders," *Sports Illustrated.*

30 Mike Carpenter interview, August 6, 2013.

31 Thomas Jenkins interview, August 6, 2013.

32 Mike Carpenter interview, August 6, 2013.

33 Lidz, "Midnight Riders."

34 The press release is still available at this writing: "All Good Things Come to an End," http://www.mtntouring.com/htm/snowshoe2000.htm.

35 To see the rides and organization associated with the Shenandoah Mountain Festival, see the Shenandoah Valley Bicycle Coalition website, "Shenandoah Mountain Festival," http://svbcoalition.org/events/annual/shenandoah-mountain-bike -festival/.

36 For an excellent video of the event, see Scott Wooten's "Adventure Seen" production at http://www.shenandoahbicycle.com/about/local-videos-pg68.htm.

37 Personal e-mail correspondence June 28, 2002.

38 Ibid.

39 You can see some footage of the 2013 July 4 stage, shot by Scott Wooten, at his "Adventure Seen" website, http://www.adventureseen.com/#!portfolio/cwvn

40 All the 2013 letters of intention are at Shenandoah Valley Bicycle Coalition: "2013 Letters of Intent," http://svbcoalition.org/events/annual/tour-de-burg/2013-letters -of-intent.

41 Michael Atkinson, "Enduring Bodies in Triathlon," in *Tribal Play: Subcultural Journeys through Sport*, eds. Michael Atkinson and Kevin Young (Bingley, UK: JAI Press, 2008): 295–296.

42 Ibid.

43 This is recreated from memory, not taped and transcribed.

44 Entry in Bryan Lewis' personal cycling blog, http://2feetto2wheels.weebly.com/ blog/tour-de-burg-stage-5.

45 Jennifer Lee, "When 'Slumming' Was the Thing to Do," *New York Times*, July 6, 2006, http://cityroom.blogs.nytimes.com/2009/07/06/when-slumming-was-the -thing-to-do/?_php=true&_type=blogs&_r=0.

46 Mike Carpenter interview, August 6, 2013.

47 Facebook post on the "Tour de Burg" page, https://www.facebook.com/ tourdeburg.

48 This is recreated from memory of the race on July 5, 2013. This exchange was not taped or transcribed.

49 Ibid.

50 "Letters of Intent (2013)."

51 This is reconstructed from memory of events on July 2, 2013. The exchange was not taped or transcribed.

52 Wikipedia summary of *Jackass: The Movie*, http://en.wikipedia.org/wiki/Jackass: TheMovie.

53 Tom Wolfe, *The Electric Kool-Aid Acid Test* (1968; repr., New York: Picador, 2008)

54 This is recreated from memory of events on July 4, 2014.

55 Interview with Thomas Jenkins, August 6, 2013.

56 The town's website describes it as the "cycling capital" of the Shenandoah Valley. See Harrisonburg, Virginia, "Cycling," http://www.visitharrisonburgva.com/things-to -do/outdoor-recreation-sports/cycling.

57 Nan K. Chase, "The Road Less Traveled: Virginia's Route 11 Leads Home for the Holidays, or Just to a Back-Road Jaunt," *Washington Post*, November 19, 1995, p. E01.

58 Harrisonburg Downtown Renaissance, http://www.downtownharrisonburg.org. This organization was previously "Citizens for the Downtown."

59 Graham Averill, "The Harrisonburg Road Trip: Stars, Bikes, and Beer," *Blue Ridge Outdoors*, July 25, 2013. Available at: http://www.blueridgeoutdoors.com/biking/ the-harrisonburg-road-trip-stars-bikes-and-beer/.

60 Interview with Thomas Jenkins, August 6, 2013.

Chapter 6 Why So White?

1 I thank Tiffany Gayle Chenault for making the trip with me, and for this particular insight.

2 Robert Fletcher, "Living on the Edge: The Appeal of Risk Sports for the Profes-sional Middle Class," *Sociology of Sport Journal* 25, no 3 (2008): 310–330; Thomas C. Wilson, "The Paradox of Social Class and Sports Involvement: The Roles of Cultural and Economic Capital," *International Review for the Sociology of Sport* 37, no. 1 (2002): 5–1. See also Pierre Bourdieu, "Sport and Social Class," *Social Science Information* 17, no. 6 (1978): 819–840.

3 For examples, see Patricia Hill Collins and Margaret Andersen, eds., *Race, Class and Gender: An Anthology* (Boston: Cengage Learning, 2013). See also Leslie McCall, "The Complexity of Intersectionality," *Journal of Women in Culture and Society* 30, no. 3 (2005): 1771–1800.

4 Max Fennell long aspired to become the first black professional triathlete. See "About Max Fennel," http://maxfennell.net/about.php. When I first began this chapter I took a look at the now-defunct website "Blacks Do Tri," formerly at http://blacksdotri.wordpress.com. Later, when I returned to this site, just a couple of months before the final draft of this text was due, I discovered that the Black Triathletes Association, http://www.blacktriathlete.org, had been established. This led me to send a modified questionnaire to a few members of this organization. These were mostly the same open-ended questions that I used when I interviewed athletes in person—with a few at the end associated with their experiences as a black triathlete.

5 See Wilson, "The Paradox of Social Class," 5–15, for a discussion of how cultural and economic capital affect participation in elite sport. Scholars in leisure studies have long investigated structural constraints, as well as interpersonal constraints, that limit people from participating in certain leisure activities. Initially, the constraint model focused on interpersonal types of variables that usually neglected how vari-ables such as race and gender could be used as analytic categories that constrained behavior. See, for example, Tom Hinch, Edgar L. Jackson, Simon Hudson, and Gordon Walker, "Leisure Constraint Theory and Sport Tourism," *Sport in Society* 8, no. 2 (2005): 142–163. More recently, both race and gender have been added to the constraint theory model. See Stephen F. Philip, "Race and Leisure Constraint,"

Leisure Sciences: An Interdisciplinary Journal 17, no. 2 (1995): 109–120. See also Susan M. Shaw and Karla A. Henderson, "Gender Analysis and Leisure Constraints: An Uneasy Alliance," in Edgar L. Jackson, ed., *Constraints to Leisure* (State College, PA: Venture Publishing, 2003): 23–34.

6 USA Triathlon (USAT), *The Mind of a Triathlete*, Parts 1–4. See Part 1, "The Executive Summary," and particularly "What Are the Triathlon Spending Trends?" 1–2, http://www.usatriathlon.org/about-multisport/demographics.aspx.

7 *The Mind of a Triathlete*, "Part I: Introduction," 1. The original table is at USA Triathlon, "Demographics," http://www.usatriathlon.org/about-multisport/demographics.aspx. I modified the table by separating out the "blue-" and "gray-" collar workers.

8 *The Mind of a Triathlete*, Parts 1–4.

9 See USA Triathlon, "Demographics."

10 *The Mind of a Triathlete*, "Executive Summary," 3.

11 See Hinch, Jackson, Hudson, and Walker, "Leisure Constraint Theory," 142–163.

12 Donald W. Hastings, Sammy Zahra, and Sherry Cable, "Drowning in Inequalities: Swimming and Social Justice," *Journal of Black Studies* 36, no. 6 (2006): 894–917.

13 See Fletcher, "Living on the Edge," 310–330; Wilson, "The Paradox of Social Class," 5–16. See also Cassandra Y. Johnson, Michael J. Bowker, Donald B. K. English, and Dreamal Worthen, "Wildland Recreation in the Rural South: An Examination of Marginality and Ethnicity Theory," *Journal of Leisure Research* 30 no. 1 (1998): 101–120.

14 Joseph. W. Meeker, William K. Woods, and Wilson Lucas, "Red, White, and Black in the National Parks," *The North American Review* Fall (1973): 3–7. See also H. Ken Cordell, Gary T. Green, and Carter J. Betz, "Recreation and the Environment as Cultural Dimensions in Contemporary American Society," *Leisure Sciences* 24, no. 1 (2002): 13-41.

15 See Carolyn Merchant, "Shades of Darkness: Race and Environmental History," *Environmental History* 8, no. 3 (2003): 380–394. See also Cassandra Y. Johnson, "A Consideration of Collective Memory in African American Attachment to Wildland Recreational Places," *Human Ecology Review* 5, no.1 (1998): 5-15.

16 See Perry L. Carter, "Coloured Places and Pigmented Holidays: Racialized Leisure Travel," *Tourism Geographies* 10, no. 3 (2008): 265–284; Michael D. Woodard, "Class, Regionality, and Leisure among Urban Black Americans: The Post–Civil Rights Era," *Journal of Leisure Research* 20, no. 2 (1988): 87–105; Anne G. Coleman, "The Unbearable Whiteness of Skiing," *Pacific Historical Review* 65, no. 4 (1996): 583–614; Caroline Fusco, "Cultural Landscapes of Purification: Sports Spaces and Discourses of Whiteness," *Sociology of Sport Journal* 22, no. 3 (2005): 283–310.

17 Johnson, "A Consideration of Collective Memory," 5–15. See also Merchant, "Shades of Darkness," 380–394.

18 Derek Christopher Martin, "Apartheid in the Great Outdoors: American Advertising and the Reproduction of a Racialized Outdoor Leisure Identity," *Journal of Leisure Studies* 36, no. 4 (2004): 513–535.

19 Coleman, "The Unbearable Whiteness," 583–614.

20 Ibid.

21 Anthony Kwame Harrison, "Skiing, Everyday Racism, and the Racial Spatiality of Whiteness," *Journal of Sport and Social Issues* 37, no. 4 (2013): 315–339.

22 See Coleman, "Unbearable Whiteness," 583–614.

23 For a recent interview with James Bethea see "Gravel: Interview with James Bethea," *Switchback Magazine: Fuel for the Trail*, Oct.–Nov. (2013): 56–60, http://www.switchbackmagazine-digital.com/switchback/october_november_2013?folio=56#pg63.

24 Some of the blogs are available at Black Triathlete Association, "Member Spotlight," http://www.blacktriathlete.org/member-spotlight.

25 Roderick Nash, *Wilderness and the American Mind* (New Haven, CT: Yale University Press, 1967); Alan W. Ewert, Deborah J. Chavez, and Arthur W. Magill, eds. *Culture, Conflict, and Communication in the Wildland-Urban Interface* (San Francisco: Westview Press, 1993). See also Cassandra Y. Johnson, Patrick M. Horan, and William Pepper, "Race, Rural Residence, and Wildland Visitation: Examining the Influence of Sociocultural Meaning," *Rural Sociology* 62, no 1 (1997): 89–110; Johnson, et al., "Wildland Recreation in the Rural South," 101–120; and Johnson, "A Consideration of Collective Memory," 5–15.

26 Kevin DeLuca and Anne Demo, "Imagining Nature and Erasing Class and Race: Carleton Watkins, John Muir, and the Construction of Wilderness," *Environmental History* 6, no. 4 (2002): 541–560. See also Martin, "Apartheid in the Great Outdoors," 513–545; and Bruce Braun, "On the Raggedy Edge of Risk: Articulations of Race and Nature after Biology," in *Race, Nature, and the Politics of Difference*, eds. Donald S. Moore, Jake Kosek, and Anand Pandian (Durham, NC: Duke University Press, 2003): 175–203.

27 See Nash, *Wilderness and the American Mind.* See also Johnson, Horan, and William, "Race and Wildland Visitation," 89–110.

28 The local representative to the Virginia House of Delegates for Rockingham County and Harrisonburg, Virginia, Tony Wilt, is also a past president of a local bear hunting club. Rockingham County (where Harrisonburg is located) usually has more bears killed than any other Virginia county during annual hunting season. Not surprisingly, Wilt has sponsored a range of hunting laws during his short tenure in the legislature.

29 For information and pictures of the mountain bike park at Snowshoe, see "Snowshoe Bike Park," http://www.snowshoemtn.com/the-mountain/snowshoe-bike-park/bike-index.aspx.

30 To see some ATV-specific trails in West Virginia, including a short "ride" video, see Wild Wonderful West Virginia, "Things To Do: ATV Trails," http://www.wvcommerce.org/travel/thingstodo/outdoorrecreation/atv.aspx.

31 Meeker, Woods, and Lucas, "Red, White, and Black in the National Parks," 3–7. See also Cordell, Green, and Betz, "Recreation and the Environment," 13–41.

Chapter 7 Where Are the Women?

1 I wrote a series of articles for the *Villager*, a monthly publication distributed within the Massanutten Four Seasons Resort. The publication was not online at the time, but it can now be accessed at http://massanuttenvillager-stage.afpbusiness.com.

2 See also Sal Ruibal, "Going Downhill Fast and Sober," *USA TODAY*, November 28, 2005, http://usatoday30.usatoday.com/sports/olympics/torino/2005-11-28-palmer-olympics_x.htm.

3 For an interesting retrospective on Shaun Palmer's athletic career, and his impact on snowboarding, skiing, and mountain biking, see the documentary *Shaun Palmer:*

The Miserable Champion, financed and promoted on Kickstarter, http://www
.kickstarter.com/projects/1665898043/shaun-palmer-the-miserable-champion. See
also Ruibal, "Going Downhill Fast."

4   USA Triathlon Website, "Demographics," http://www.usatriathlon.org/about
-multisport/demographics.aspx.

5   With respect to triathlon, see Jane Granskog, "Tri-ing Together: An Exploratory
Analysis of the Social Networks of Female and Male Triathletes," *Play and Culture*
5, no. 1 (1992): 76–91; Jane Granskog, "Just 'Tri' and 'Du' It: The Variable Impact
of Female Involvement in the Triathlon/Duathlon Sport Culture," in *Athletic
Intruders: Ethnographic Research on Women, Culture, and Exercise*, eds. Anne Bolin
and Jane Granskog (Albany, NY: State University of New York Press, 2003): 27–52.
For examples in other new sports, see Becky Beal, "Alternative Masculinity and its
Effects on Gender Relations in the Subculture of Skateboarding," *Journal of Sport
Behavior* 19, no. 3 (1996): 204–20; Belinda Wheaton and Alan Tomlinson, "The
Changing Gender Order in Sport: The Case of Windsurfing Subcultures," *Journal
of Sport and Social Issues* 22, no. 3 (1998): 252–74.

6   Sean Brayton, "'Black-Lash': Revisiting the 'White Negro,' Through Skateboarding," *Sociology of Sport Journal* 22, no 3 (2005): 356–372.

7   Rebecca Heino, "What Is So Punk about Snowboarding?" *Journal of Sport & Social
Issues* 24, no. 2 (2000): 176–191; Holly Thorpe, *Snowboarding Bodies in Theory and
Practice* (New York: Palgrave Macmillan, 2011).

8   See Robert E. Rinehart, "'Babes & Boards': Opportunities in New Millennium
Sport?" *Journal of Sport and Social Issues* 29, no. 3 (2005): 232–255 and "Inside of
the Outside: Pecking Orders within Alternative Sport at ESPN's 1995 The eXtreme
Games," *Journal of Sport and Social Issues* 22, no. 4 (1998): 398–415.

9   See the Women's Mountain Bike and Tea Society (WOMBAT) website at: http://
www.wombats.org/index.html.

10   Sophie Taysom, "Reading Mountain Bikes through Technoscience and the
Cyborg," *Social Alternatives* 17, no. 4 (1998): 18–26.

11   See Rinehart, "Inside of the Outside," 398–415; and Michael Messner, Michele Dunbar and Darnell Hunt, "The Televised Sports Manhood Formula," *Journal of Sport
and Social Issues* 24, no. 4 (2000): 380–394.

12   Sherry M. Huybers-Withers and Lori A. Livingston, "Mountain Biking Is for Men:
Consumption Practices and Identity Portrayed by a Niche Magazine," *Sport in
Society* 13, no. 7/8 (2010): 1204–1222.

13   Messner, Dunbar, and Hunt, "Manhood Formula," 380.

14   Huybers-Withers and Livingston, "Mountain Biking Is for Men," 1215.

15   "Rob's World Cup Diary: Rob Warner Presents a Review of the 2012 UCI Downhill World Cup Season as Only He Can," http://www.redbull.com/en/bike/
stories/1331589496791/robs-world-cup-diary.

16   Huybers-Withers and Livingston, "Mountain Biking Is for Men," 1204–1222.
Recently, a study that investigated twenty-five years of sports media indicated
the same trend in coverage of all women's sports. See Cheryl Cooky, Michael A.
Messner, and Michela Musto, "It's Dude Time! A Quarter Century of Excluding
Women's Sports in Televised News and Highlight Shows," *Communication and
Sport* 3 (2015): 261–287.

17   Terry Bicycle Company, http://www.terrybicycles.com.

18   Huybers-Withers and Livingston, "Mountain Biking Is for Men," 1215.

19 Observation on September 14, 2000.
20 Murray J. M. Drummond, "Sport and Images of Masculinity: The Meaning of Rela-
    tionships in the Life Course of 'Elite' Male Athletes," *Journal of Men's Studies* 10,
    no. 2 (2002): 134–145.
21 "Keith" and "Kathy" interview, October 21, 2001.
22 Megan Kelly Cronan and Dave Scott, "Triathlon and Women's Narratives of Bodies
    and Sport," *Leisure Sciences* 30, no. 1 (2008): 17–34.
23 This is generally the perspective of Robert E. Rinehart, "Babes and Boards" and
    "Inside the Outside." See also Messner, Dunbar, and Hunt, "Manhood Formula."

Chapter 8 Conclusion

1 Here I am primarily referencing work closely associated with the University of
   Chicago's Department of Economics. See particularly Milton Friedman, *Capitalism
   and Freedom: Fortieth Anniversary Edition* (Chicago: University of Chicago Press,
   2009).

Appendix

1 I likely remember these races because the finishes were so close. To double-check my
   memory I looked for race coverage in the local papers and found a story concerning
   the Outer Banks Triathlon in the online archives of the *Virginia-Pilot*, "Racing into
   the Water During the Outer Banks Triathlon," Sept. 20, 1992, Section: Carolina
   Coast: 38.
2 In 2001 I tape-recorded and transcribed twelve semi-structured interviews, usually
   about an hour in length. Many of these were with Virginia Tech club members. In
   2013 I interviewed six more athletes. Practically, I used these interviews far less then
   I originally intended, probably due to my familiarity with the sport previous to
   making the study. I also conducted informal interviews, usually at race sites, when
   I struck up a conversation with competitors who knew I was interested in their
   participation in sport.
3 I found the race details described in an article in *The Free-Lance Star* archives. Gary
   Rhodes, "Triathlon Winners Maintain Record Setting Pace," *The Free-Lance Star*,
   July 15, 1991, sect. B1. See also Gary Rhodes, "Knight Repeats as Triathlon Champ,"
   The Free-Lance Star, July 13, 1992, sect. B1.
4 Aaron McFarling, "An Enjoyably Rugged Weekend: Triathlete Poulson Fast on
   Rail, Water and Bike," *Roanoke Times*, Oct. 4, 2000.
5 I placed in the top three in my age group in races in Bath County, Virginia, and
   Luray, Virginia (roughly 200 and 600 participants respectively). Overall, I finished
   eighteenth and thirty-fifth, respectively. I almost won bragging rights as the
   top finisher in a tiny local race (fewer than thirty people) sponsored by the
   Staunton YMCA. I was actually passed by my neighbor—who had finished the
   Coeur d'Alene Ironman a couple of weeks previously—during the last mile of
   the race.
6 The practice is more widespread in West Virginia than Virginia. Indeed, Julia Fox
   has argued that West Virginia actually constitutes an environmental "sacrifice zone."
   See "Mountaintop Removal in West Virginia: An Environmental Sacrifice Zone,"
   Organization Environment 12 (1991):163–183.

7   See the Southern Environmental Law Center, "A Treasured Place at Risk," concerning the environmental hazards of "fracking" for natural gas. https://www.southern environment.org/projects/gwfracking.

8   Census figures for Highland County, Virginia, are available at the U.S. Census Bureau, "State and County Quick Facts," http://quickfacts.census.gov/qfd/states/ 51/51091.html.

9   Ben King is briefly interviewed about the riding community in Harrisonburg at the Shenandoah Bicycle Company website, "Harrisonburg: The Bike Capital of Virginia," http://www.shenandoahbicycle.com/about/local-videos-pg68.htm.

10   See the literature review in Belinda Wheaton, "Introduction: Mapping the Lifestyle Sport-Scape," in *Understanding Lifestyle Sports: Consumption, Identity and Difference,* ed. Belinda Wheaton (London: Routledge, 2004): 1–28.

11   Some sponsor crossover events. For example, see the footage of "Jeremiah Bishop's Alpine Loop Gran Fondo," (by Adventure Seen), at http://www.shenandoahbicycle .com/about/local-videos-pg68.html.

Index

218 • Index

marketing: authenticity, 38–42, 117–119; by lifestyle sport magazines, 43–44; resistance to, by athletes, 113–115; to subcultural groups, 115–116; by USA Triathlon, 41–42, 147, 158

market liberalism (free market): and adventure, 17, 20, 25–26, 33–34, 42, 46, 48–51; and alienation, 15–16; and alternative sport, 25–26; and authenticity, 3, 38–42, 117–119, 175; constraining participation in sport, 3–4, 9–10, 15–16, 20–22, 25–29, 38, 51–59, 175–178, 197n34; and discipline, 10, 20, 27, 28, 29, 52, 176–177, 197n34; and healthism, 22; and mountain biking, 118–119; resistance to, in sport, 113–114; responsiveness to subculture practice, 115–116; as a social field, 9–10; and triathletes, 53, 55–56, 59, 176–177

Marx, Karl, 15, 17, 38

masculinity: in mountain biking, 160–165; in triathlon, 167–172. See also hegemonic masculinity

Massanutten Mountain, 132, 134, 186

Massanutten Resort, 159, 161, 164, 213n1

Mauck, Craig "Rearview," 111–112

McDonald, Charles "Scott," 2, 95, 98, 207n4

McGaheysville, VA, 161

McMurdo Base, Antarctica, 107

Mead, George H., 12, 17

Men's Health (magazine), 145

Men's Fitness (magazine), 145

men lifestyle athletes: body discipline of, 178–179; eating disorders, 77; masculinity in mountain biking, 160–165; masculinity in triathlon, 167–172; pursuit of body ideal, 178–179

Messner, Michael, 193n15, 195n12

methodical athletes, 88–90. See also typology: of lifestyle athletes

Mickulas, Peter, x

Mind of a Triathlete, The (report), 41–42, 146–148, 158

Mitchell, Richard, 191n7

Mock, Katie, 202n60

Molina, Scott, 166

Monongahela National Forest, 186, 188

Montgomery Hall Park (Staunton, VA), 149

moralism: and good health, 21–22; of some lifestyle athletes, 22–23, 34

Moss, Julie, 61–62

Mount Everest, failed expedition and adventure travel, 203n63

Mountain Bike (magazine), 42–44, 59, 201nn42–43

Mountain Bike Action (magazine), 158, 162, 167

mountain biking: and 24 Hour racing, 118–123; in adventure travel, 47–48; and authenticity, 117–118; as building community, 137–141; as a commodity, 56–57, 175–178; conformity and routinization of, 58–59, 175–178; and correct training, 57–58; development in Harrisonburg and Shenandoah Valley, 111–112, 137–141, 186–188; evolution from play to sport, 82, 114; as lifestyle sport, 4–5, 27–28, 53–53; media coverage of men and women, 166–167; risk in, 45–46; social class and race/ethnicity of riders, 146, 150–151, 154–155; and the Tour de Burg, 124–137; white masculinity in downhill racing, 159–166; and women's participation, 159

Mountains of Misery (cycling event), 104

mountain top removal, 185, 215n6

mundanity: as motivation to do sport, 17, 51, 95; as part of adventure sport, 44–47

muscle gap, in United States compared to other countries, 20

narcissism, of some lifestyle athletes, 34

national fitness programs, 20–21

National Forest Service, U.S., 139–140

nation-state, and national health standards, 20–22. See healthism

nature. See wilderness areas

new athletes, 90–92. See also typology: of lifestyle athletes

New River, 36, 49, 181, 185

New River Bridge, 36, 185. See also Bridge Day

New River Gorge, 185

New River Trail Challenge, 181

New River Valley (Virginia), 184–185

Nissley, Mark, 111

About the Author

STEPHEN POULSON is associate professor of sociology at James Madison University. His past work has included the study of twentieth century Iranian social movements. He is currently investigating patterns of violence undertaken against civilians during the most recent conflicts in Iraq. He lives in the Shenandoah Valley of Virginia with his wife, Christine, and their son, Benjamin, and daughter, Sidney.

CPSIA information can be obtained
at www.ICGtesting.com
Printed in the USA
LVOW13s2106020317

525958LV00015B/672/P